PRAISE FOR THE REIKI BUSINESS BOOK

I LOVE this book! So many beautiful stories and practical examples of the power of Reiki. Wonderful tools to add to your "Reiki Toolbox." Whether you are developing a Reiki business or wondering how to incorporate Reiki into your profession, this book is filled with inspired ideas to move you forward. I plan on recommending it to all my Reiki students.

Thank you Pam for developing this amazing book!

— JULIE RUSSELL, OC WHOLE FAMILY WELLNESS

This book deep dives into some of the very important aspects of creating your Reiki practice and business. It is relevant to all levels of Reiki business experience and helps the reader develop their Reiki practice according to what they really want. It is a great blend of practical small business advice and personal discovery.

— COLLEEN BENELLI, REIKI LIFESTYLE

This is the book I have been looking for! It is spiritual and practical, scientific yet intuitive.The Reiki Business Book *is needed in the Reiki community: practicality, maturity, real advice, and actionable steps.*

Reiki practitioners who want an authentic, Reiki practice that effectively helps themselves and others should read this book and apply the information in it.

— MUNIQUI MUHAMMAD, HEALING LAND REIKI, JAPAN

Pam's compassion, kindness, and dedication to service shine throughout this book.

She shares her vast knowledge and experience in a down-to-earth, conversational style that is sure to resonate with anyone guided to create their own successful Reiki business. A must-read for Reiki professionals!

— KATHLEEN JOHNSTON, UNIVERSOUL HEART, LLC

The Reiki Business Book *offers a holistic approach taking the reader on a purposeful journey toward creating an authentic Reiki business in resonance with the individual's unique goals and vision.*

Far beyond the usual how-to steps, Pamela Allen-LeBlanc includes a comprehensive set of resources including meditations, exercises, and inspirations to inspire and empower the reader to build their own Reiki business upon a strong foundation for lasting success.

— ANDREA KENNEDY, MAINSTREAM REIKI

THE REIKI BUSINESS BOOK

DISCOVER THE UNIQUE REIKI CAREER THAT LIGHTS YOU UP!

PAM ALLEN-LEBLANC

Edited by
KAREN CAIG

Foreword by
COLLEEN BENELLI

Copyright © 2022 by Pamela Allen-LeBlanc

All rights reserved.

Reiki from the Farm™ Press

Durham Bridge, NB, Canada

No part of this book may be reproduced in any form or by any electronic or mechanical means, including information storage and retrieval systems, without written permission from the author, except for the use of brief quotations in a book review.

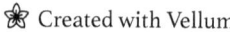 Created with Vellum

*For all Reiki practitioners and teachers
Who want to spread the light of Reiki in the World
Thank you*

CONTENTS

Foreword ix
Introduction xi

1. Define the Practice That Works for You 1
2. The Identity of Your Business 30
3. Releasing the Obstacles to Your Business Success 49
4. Develop Your Practice - Giving Reiki Sessions to Others 78
5. Marketing and Branding 112
6. Business Skills 134
7. Teaching Reiki 160
8. Your Evolution with Reiki - The Path to Enlightenment and Beyond 198
9. Becoming a Reiki Mentor 223
10. Blending Reiki with Other Modalities 245

Acknowledgments 269
About the Author 271

FOREWORD

I remember seeing Pam's article in *Reiki News Magazine* and knew that we would work together someday. I hoped she would join the ICRT Licensed Teacher Training Program. When she was accepted into the LRMT Training Program, I was fortunate to be her mentor. The program provides tremendous personal and professional growth, and I was excited to see her gifts and talents emerge in such a good way.

Pam is very devoted to Reiki and her students and clients and wrote this book to help people move beyond their obstacles and into their dream Reiki practice and business. This book moves the student through the obstacles and reveals the practicalities needed to manifest the dream. I love the way Pam explains the Reiki business topic to consider and then follows through with a Reiki exercise designed to help a person listen and discover their own ideas, questions, answers, solutions, and innovations into manifestation.

This book deep dives into some of the very important aspects of creating your Reiki practice and business. It is relevant to all levels of Reiki business experience and helps the reader develop their Reiki practice according to what they really want. It is a great blend of practical small business advice and personal discovery.

It's so good! It's truly a wealth of information. I love how Reiki works!

Colleen Benelli, ICRT Sr. LRMT
    Co-Director of the ICRT LRMT program
    ICRT Animal Reiki Co-author
    Reiki Lifestyle

INTRODUCTION

I am a reluctant Reiki Master and have been from the beginning. As a scientist and businesswoman with a Type A personality, I am a left-brain thinker. But when I developed serious allergies that allergy specialists could not address, I was ready to try anything. I had rashes on my face and neck, blocked sinuses and eyes that ran constantly. I used to joke that someone must have seen me in public and created the tv series, *The Walking Dead*. I looked so dreadful I felt I must have been the inspiration for the zombies in the show!

So when one of my riding students offered a Reiki session in exchange for her lesson to help, I said yes. During that first session, I didn't hear angels sing, and I wasn't instantly healed. But the symptoms backed off enough to provide a respite for a few days. I had my first full night's sleep in months. But beyond that, I experienced an inner peace in that session that I don't remember ever feeling before. I was hooked.

We traded riding lessons for Reiki sessions for a while. Then I met my first Reiki Master, Ellen, and studied level one and two Reiki. I realized that as an empath, many of my unexplained health conditions were a result of holding onto energies that were not my own. I had a lot of clearing and releasing to do to get rid of those energies, and I did it with the help of Reiki.

One of my businesses includes teaching riding lessons. At one point, Ellen offered to attune my horses to Reiki. I noticed that my horses were taking on stress, tension, overwhelm, and anxiety from their students. It showed up in their body language and mood. So I said yes. They immediately released the stress and tension as reflected in their body language. They became happier, healthier, and more peaceful. My riding lessons became effortless. And I noticed that the horses were sharing Reiki with me and with their students! Lessons became magical and fun.

At that point, this left-brain thinker knew there was something to this Reiki energy. After a few months of regular self Reiki, my allergies completely healed. My horses were happy. My business was going well. Situations in my life smoothed out and became easier. People said I looked younger, healthier, happier. The change was remarkable. And for the first time in my life, I was not trying to get to the finish line with something. I was content to be a level 2 Practitioner for the rest of my life. But Reiki had other ideas!

I enjoyed tremendous success training horses and conducting horse clinics with Reiki. I created a Reiki grid to send energy to many things at once. Several of the horses I worked with had health or emotional issues, so I included them in my Reiki Grid. But on days that I couldn't send Reiki, their humans messaged me because they noticed a difference in the horses. That was a tremendous amount of pressure, as there are always days now and again when you can't get to your Reiki grid. So I asked my Reiki Master if she would attune those horses too. But she said, "No. That is for you to do," and I understood the energy was pushing me forward in my Reiki journey.

Still, I was reluctant to become a Reiki Master, as I thought that implied that I needed to teach people. And I didn't like people.

Let me explain. Early in my career, I worked in the agricultural industry as I completed my MBA in the evenings. I was very successful and loved it. I even became the President of our Scientific Society and became the "outstanding young Agrologist in Canada" for my efforts when the public was endangered.

That led to a promotion where I was required to make business happen for some very high-profile trade missions. Although I was very good at it, I didn't love my job. Most of my effort was spent working around the system to get things done. But it was a tremendous success. Companies landed millions of dollars in contracts, and I received several job offers.

I chose a struggling advanced manufacturer with 30 employees and a lot of potential. In 7 years, we grew the company to be the 3rd fastest growing company in Atlantic Canada. Then we spun off a second company, which was the fastest-growing company Atlantic Canada had ever seen. It was remarkably successful. We became the darling of the press and the government as we illustrated what was possible in our small province. But it all came crashing down when we suddenly and unexpectedly lost a $16 million contract and the company closed. I worked without pay, trying unsuccessfully to turn the decision around. My boss and I felt responsible for the job losses and for the people. It was a very heavy responsibility.

When I finally landed, I realized I no longer had to prove anything to anyone. And that being responsible for people was a thorn in my side. I grieved the loss of the company and vowed that I was done working with that many people.

So I became a business consultant, which was very successful, and I made a LOT of money. At the same time, I was teaching horseback riding lessons, which incurred a LOT of expenses but didn't make much money. So I was able to indulge my passion for horses and pay a lot fewer taxes when I put the two companies together.

I began spending more time with animals than people, which was comfortable for me. I decided I was going to stick with animals, that I no longer wanted to work with people.

I mistakenly believed that becoming a Reiki Master meant I would be obliged to teach and work with people. Teaching people? No thank you! So I asked another Reiki Master if she would teach me level 3 Reiki (Master Healer) and show me how to attune animals to Reiki. I explained that I only wanted to work with animals so I asked if it was possible to attune them at this level. She said, come to class, we will ask the guides and see if that is appropriate.

She didn't need to tell me. I knew during class that I was not supposed to learn to attune animals at this level. She agreed but said I was supposed to go to England to study the Reiki Master-Teacher level with William Rand.

I don't know how she knew that I desperately wanted to take that class. But the economy had crashed. My business clients lost their ability to pay me. And for the horse business, we had just built an $80,000 riding arena. I was broke!

I explained to her that I had no money and asked if she would consider teaching me instead. She said, "Call me in a few weeks if you still feel that way," winked, and sent me on my way.

Two days later, I received an unexpected check that was $10 less than the class fee and accommodations. I took that as a sign that I should go to England and study with William Rand. My husband agreed. I had Airmiles and cashed in savings bonds to pay for the flight and headed to England.

The Reiki Master class with William was deeply healing. After class, I asked him how to attune animals and teach children. I still had no intention of teaching adults. But on the flight home, I had an epiphany that "people are animals, and I love animals; therefore I must love people". I realized that I did love people, deeply in the core of my being. And that Reiki is such a loving, healing, life-affirming energy, that I needed to share it with people. People just like me--people who could benefit from the energy as I had. So although I intended NEVER to teach people, I changed my mind and began teaching them right away.

I was terrified to teach that first class. I don't know anyone who isn't. But it went really well and my confidence grew. And although I was teaching to spread Reiki, an unexpected consequence was that I made money. So our financial issues straightened themselves out. And my Reiki business launched.

It's funny. You would think that with my strong background in business, weaving business principles into this sacred practice would have been easy for me. But, in fact, I had a very difficult time with it. Reiki is so sacred, spiritual, and special. And to me, business practices were not and didn't belong alongside Reiki. I know I'm not the only person who feels this way. It can be difficult to find the right balance between charging money and doing God's work. It took me 10 years for Reiki to help me sort that out.

Then Reiki nudged me to apply to become a Licensed Reiki Master Teacher with the International Center for Reiki Training (ICRT). This program involves a rigorous selection process followed by an additional 1,000+ hours of training. It also involves LOTS of paperwork (which I abhor). There's a financial commitment too.

I had never really considered the program. So I was reluctant to apply. I could not see the benefits of the program for me. But at that point, I had learned to follow my Reiki guidance, even and especially when I do not agree with it. And was that guidance ever right!

I was passionate about sharing Reiki with people. And my mentor, Colleen Benelli pointed out that one of the most effective ways to share Reiki with others is with a successful Reiki business. I had a lovely but small Reiki business and I wasn't really sure I wanted to grow it all that much. Colleen encouraged me to heal my deep distrust of technology and to find a way to bring my knowledge and business skills into my practice. I had worked diligently to keep them separate. Bringing business practices into the sacred realm of my Reiki business didn't feel right to me.

I was still sorting through a lot of this doubt in March of 2020 and was still reluctant to use technology. I had just finished teaching Reiki in London when, due to Covid, borders and airports began closing. Flights were canceled and a feeling of panic and anxiety fell over the world. Navigating through Heathrow airport, I was an oasis of calm amidst the chaos. And my life mission was handed to me.

> As I spoke with my panicked husband, he asked, "Why are you so calm?"

"Reiki" I replied. I had asked my students to send Reiki to me and my flights. They are a powerful group so I had every confidence it would work out and it did. I compared the peaceful calm that I felt with the panic and stress around me. And I had another airport epiphany. "Everyone needs Reiki at times like these!"

Colleen Benelli had said in a meeting that her dream was that every family have a Reiki practitioner in it. I remember thinking that was far-fetched at the time. But looking at the chaos around me. And as an empath, feeling the panic and stress, I knew she was right. But it felt overwhelming.

I asked the Reiki energy, "What am I supposed to do?" And I saw that I was to teach the Teachers and Practitioners so that they could reach more people. Then the wonder and beauty of Reiki would spread. Once again, I was shown that the most effective way to share this healing energy is with a Reiki business.

I saw that I was uniquely positioned to help people bring business principles into their Reiki practices and businesses. As an ICRT Licensed Reiki Master Teacher and with my business background, I was to teach the teachers.

Reiki then nudged me to let go of my fear of technology because I care about people, and could see they needed Reiki. So I sat down in a quiet(ish) section of the airport and navigated my first Facebook Live to share a video meditation. I didn't know if it would work or not. I told people that I wasn't sure they could hear me. And that we would probably be interrupted by a British lady with a lovely accent announcing changes to flights. I didn't anticipate the number of people who would see the video. Thousands of people watched it and reached out to let me know how much it helped them.

Once I got home, the ICRT moved classes online to further help people. They gave us extensive training as to how to teach the classes, bringing me much more in alignment with technology. The online classes were more powerful and effective than I could have imagined. They also allowed more people to receive Reiki without the stress and expense of travel. And they effectively lowered the environmental footprint of our Reiki classes. I was grateful to continue reaching people with Reiki at a time when in-person classes were not possible.

So with my fear of technology behind me, I knew it was time to follow up on the guidance I received in the airport. It was time to help people with their own Reiki businesses.

I have always believed that if you want to learn, teach. I knew that teaching others to integrate business principles would force me to figure it out. I also learned a lot as I created my Reiki business and during the LRMT process. So I knew I could provide a level of support to others. I created an online "Reiki Master Mentor" course and offered it to Reiki Masters who were ready to create or grow a Reiki business.

It was hugely successful and filled immediately--with more students than I thought I could handle. They were from all over the world. As I taught, I listened to Reiki and was inspired to create new ways of working with business principles and practices. And the sacred business practices, exercises, and meditations I am sharing with you here were born.

My students say the course changed their lives, their practices, and their relationship with Reiki. They are more comfortable integrating Reiki into what they already do. They tailored everything to their own gifts and talents. This let them share Reiki with the world in the way that is most comfortable and natural to them. A lot of healing took place. Confidence grew. Unique practices were and continue to develop. And those who already had strong practices have stronger ones now.

We all looked forward to our monthly class, especially me. I learned alongside my students. I went into each session with a rough plan, but as I activated Reiki and listened, what came through was often as surprising and enlightening to me as it was to my students.

Ensconced in the magic of that first class, my voice announced that I would turn the course into a book so that it could reach even more people. My students enthusiastically agreed to share their stories so that you could benefit.

Introduction

Just for today, I am grateful. Grateful to do the work I do every day. Grateful to you for your willingness to share the gift of Reiki with others. Grateful to share this book with you so that you might tailor your Reiki practice and business in a way that inspires and energizes you. Grateful that together, we will spread the gift of Reiki to more beautiful souls so there will be more love, peace, and healing in the world.

I open my eyes every morning with a smile, coming out of my dream state thinking about the exciting thing I get to do on this day. I wish that for you and am excited to help you build the Reiki practice and business that lights you up!

Just for today, I am devoted to my beautiful work. And that is opening YOUR eyes to the possibilities that Reiki can bring to your life. We will be doing lots of healing along the way. Embarking on a venture like this moves us out of our comfort zone and brings energies to the surface to heal. But you are ready. The fact that you are reading this book indicates that you have been called. Thank you for heeding that call. And thank you for allowing me to guide you.

There are many ways to use this book. You can jump around to the sections that interest you, or you can go through it methodically, a chapter at a time. Even if you already have a business and business name, it won't hurt to go through Chapter 1 to see if the business is still in alignment with you. And if the name still works. Or if there are other possibilities and potential you haven't yet considered.

One thing I will recommend is that before you go through each section, you do a short Reiki meditation. As you do, activate Reiki in all of your chakras, so the energy of Reiki will guide your decisions and help you integrate. Reiki can help you bring sacred business practices into your own Reiki business. It can ensure the business is aligned with you and with Reiki, bringing you success on every level.

Another thing I encourage my students to do is to take the parts of my teachings that work for them and discard the rest. So, please, if anything doesn't resonate with you at this time, it doesn't mean it won't resonate with you later. You can disregard it for now. And take in the parts of the teachings that do resonate.

Reiki Blessings to you and yours. I hope you have fun with the process!

Note about the use of a name for Source
I use the word God to indicate Source or Creation energy because I healed my religious trauma with Reiki and took the word back into my vocabulary. It is now the most comfortable word for me. But I invite you to replace that word, whenever you see it in this book or in my speech, with whatever word you prefer to use.

Note about the exercises and meditations
Sometimes there's an unfoldment process that needs to take place with them. You don't always get all the information you need during the meditation itself. Sometimes, the meditation is what sets the intention and gets the ball rolling with the process. Additional insights may start to show up as you walk, work, or watch TV after your subconscious has worked with them for a bit.

So if things are not completely clear at the end of each exercise, be aware that the process has begun. You can revisit the exercises as often as you wish. And you can also feel comfortable allowing your subconscious to work away at it, bringing it all together for you in its own time.

I have recorded all of the meditations in the book for you here.[1]

Note about the expansion of Reiki connection throughout this process

Something else to consider is that when we do self Reiki, the Reiki energy has a specific frequency. When we begin treating others, the Reiki bandwidth that we now access expands. When we teach, it expands again. And there are several other things that you can do to grow your Reiki connection and unlock your unlimited potential with Reiki. I wrote an article about it that you can find here: Allowing Reiki to Guide Your Life[2]

The world needs more Reiki. So it needs more Reiki practitioners and teachers. Whether you decide to teach, conduct sessions, or find another to share Reiki, the world needs you.

∽

Introductory/Meditation: Setting the Intention

Activate your Reiki energy and place your Reiki symbols in the room around you, however you prefer to do this. You may go into Gassho with your hands at your heart. You may draw the symbols in your hands and then spread Reiki around the room or draw the symbols into the room. You may think of the symbols or speak the names. Invite your symbols and your Reiki energy to join you, however you wish. If you work with guides, invite them to join you.

Now invite your Reiki energy to guide and empower you.

Once the energy of Reiki fills the room around you, invite it to flow through you.

Now hold your hands, beaming Reiki to your heart chakra, until it feels full, activating the chakra and asking it to lead.

Then go below your heart chakra to your solar plexus. And beam Reiki into your solar plexus until it feels full.

Now your sacral chakra.

Now your base chakra.

Now the throat chakra.

Now the third eye.

Then the crown of your head.

And return to Gassho.

Now set an intention. Set aside your ego, let go of your agenda and allow Reiki to lead. Say to yourself,

"I am answering the call to spread Reiki and love in the world. Please guide me so that I may do so in a way that works for the highest good of my family, my clients, my students, and myself. I have formed the intention of creating a successful, impactful Reiki business so that I may share both the gift of Reiki and of myself in the world. I invite your assistance and guidance every step of the way. Thank you."

* Holy Fire® and Karuna Reiki® are registered service marks of William Lee Rand

---

1. www.reikifromthefarm.com/reikibusinessbook_meditations
2. https://www.hiddenbrook.ca/wp-content/uploads/2020/09/AllowingReikiToGuide-1.pdf

1

DEFINE THE PRACTICE THAT WORKS FOR YOU

"You are enough. Don't compare yourself to others or think you are not good enough to have a Reiki practice or teach others."
Karen Caig, LRMT

Most people assume that to create a Reiki business, they must conduct Reiki sessions and teach Reiki classes. That is one way to do it. But if you are ready to create a Reiki business, it is important that the business suits you. That it aligns with your lifestyle, your passions, and your interests. That it fires you up. You don't want it to become something that you "have" to do to make a living. And it isn't necessary to have a full-time Reiki business to share the gift of Reiki with others. There are so many ways to spread and share Reiki. In this chapter, we will figure out the best way for you.

MANY PEOPLE also believe that their life purpose needs to be their vocation. But sometimes, our vocation pays the bills to allow us to fulfill our life purpose outside of our daily work. For some, a full-time Reiki practice is the calling. For others, weaving Reiki into what we already do or what we want to do works. There are as many ways to bring Reiki into your vocation as there are vocations. You may be called to create any of these options:

- a full-time, traditional Reiki practice with sessions and classes
- blending Reiki into a vocation you already practice
- or setting up a unique way to blend Reiki into other spiritual modalities
- full time or part-time

Whatever you are called to create, what works best is letting Reiki lead.

Divine Reiki Guidance

If you allow it to, Reiki can guide your life. You will always have free will, but Reiki can provide guidance. And the guidance is always in your best interest. Even when it feels uncomfortable.

IF YOU WOULD LIKE Reiki to take the wheel and steer you in the right direction, I invite you to remember that you may not always WANT to follow the guidance you receive. There may be resistance to it. That's okay. We have exercises in the next chapter that address obstacles and resistance.

MANY TIMES REIKI guided me in a direction that I wasn't even in agreement with. When I heard "become a Licensed Teacher with the ICRT", I said, "I don't really want to do that." Yet, it has been the thing that has made the biggest positive change in my life to date (besides my husband, children, and horses). So I'm happy that I listened. I have learned to listen to Reiki, even and especially when Reiki guides me in a direction that isn't in a direction I intended to take myself.

. . .

So the purpose of the prayer below is to allow Reiki, to take the reins to lead us and guide us. You don't have to do this. But sharing the responsibility of what you are creating with Reiki can be very effective. And it can make a huge difference. You are never alone as you create and grow your business.

Reiki energy can provide guidance, to help you share your gifts, the gift of Reiki, and ensure your ultimate success. We all have unique gifts and talents. It makes sense for us to share Reiki from our areas of strength.

I will still talk about how to do Reiki sessions and teach classes in this book because, at some point, they come up for everyone. So whatever you create now, you may eventually gravitate toward sessions and classes. But your Reiki business may also evolve into something very different. And that's okay too. This book will still guide you along the way to success-- whatever success with Reiki looks like to you.

As we invite Reiki or spiritually guided life force energy to guide our lives, remember, it will never go against our free will. It is always up to us to decide what to do with our guidance. But the Divine guidance of Reiki can assist us in setting up the business that is right for us. Let's get our Reiki guidance working for us. Feel free to change anything in this prayer you need to, to make it work for you.

I realize that a lot of people hold religious trauma and that the word "God" has a charge for some of us. I wasn't comfortable using or hearing the word God for several years. But Holy Fire® Reiki energy healed my Religious trauma, and I decided that God was the word I wanted to use. Use whichever word you prefer to describe the incredible creative life force energy that flows through us all. And if my word gives you a charge, ask the Reiki energy to heal that trauma for you too.

EXERCISE - ACTIVATING REIKI GUIDANCE:
This is a prayer that we can begin our journey with.
Please substitute your word for "God" or "Source"

Close your eyes.
Take some deep breaths, and allow Reiki energy to flow around you and through you.
Dear God, I come to you today with a desire to spread your love to others through the gift of Reiki.
I ask that you bless me with your presence and that you help me better understand my Reiki path.
I am ready to grow in confidence with Reiki.
And I am ready to overcome or release any obstacles that are in the way of my Reiki business so that I can step into my path and into my power, now.
If there are any obstacles to creating a unique and successful Reiki business, I ask that you and Reiki release them now.
I invite your abundance and prosperity.
And ask that my connection with Reiki and with you continue to grow.
I invite you to bring health, wellness, and abundance to me, my clients and my students past, present, and future.
I ask for your help in remaining on my own path to healing.
I ask for your help to continue to learn and grow.
I ask for help with the discipline and self-love needed to nurture myself with Reiki, kindness, and love every day.
I want to continue to grow my connection with you and with Reiki.

I invite the enlightened beings and my guides to assist me. Even and especially when I forget to ask.
I thank them for their assistance and for all that they do.
Please Guide me and heal me throughout this process.
Clear any blockages from my intuition.
Help me understand the Guidance provided and my own way of interpreting it.
And help me develop Discernment.
I am grateful that I live in an abundant society. A society that supports freedom of spiritual and religious expression.
I thank the Reiki practitioners and teachers from every lineage who have come before me. And the descendants who will come after me.
I thank the teachers who have been bringing these ways forward since ancient times.
I am grateful for the gift of Reiki.
And I am grateful to be of a lineage of light-bringers who are creating wellness on the earth today.
Amen. And so it is. Thank you. Namaste.

~

Reiki and Intuition

Reiki works with our intuition in many different ways. Sometimes information comes through our thoughts or ideas. Sometimes we get words or pictures. Sometimes we get feelings. Sometimes we get a knowing feeling. And other times, it works through our imagination. Don't discard the first thoughts that come through. Those are usually the ones your intuition is trying to show you. It's second-guessing that is ego-driven.

And if nothing at all comes through, that's all right. But you may wish to follow up with automatic writing. This often brings information forward.

Follow-up Exercise: When Reiki Guidance Is Not Clear—Automatic Writing

Sometimes when we filter out or don't know how to interpret our intuition. Automatic writing can fill in the gaps.

- As Reiki continues to flow, sit down and write whatever comes to your mind.
- Imagine Reiki flowing through your chakras, your heart, and your mind and into your pen.
- This activates automatic writing, which can be a fantastic source of information.
- Take a few moments and journal each impression.
- Then allow it to keep flowing as you put together your thoughts or ideas around it.
- Reiki will continue flowing through you to assist you.
- Write as many pages as it takes until ideas start to form and gel.

Identify What Is Important

As Reiki provides us with a source of Divine spiritual guidance, we can use it to help create our unique Reiki business. The guidance is very practical and can help us create or grow a business that addresses every facet of our interests. The Divine guidance within Reiki has access to a myriad of possibilities. It can put them together in ways that best suit our needs. So let's see what the best options are for you!

Exercise: Identify What Is Important to You:

- List the parts of your life that are important to you, e.g., romance, home, career, hobbies, passions, or causes.
- Now go into Gassho with your hands together and your thumbs at your heart, as Usui Sensei taught us.
- Activate your Reiki energy and invoke your Reiki symbols.
- Invite your ego to step aside.
- Now go through your list one item at a time, asking Reiki how you can weave Reiki into your current life.
- Spend a few minutes with each of the areas that are important to you.
- Pay attention to any feelings, thoughts, ideas, or knowledge you receive.

∼

Creating a Reiki Business

A Reiki business can allow us to make a living and help people while simultaneously doing something we love. And each and every one of us can do this in the way that works best for us as individuals. That allows the clients and students who resonate with you, your style, personality, and experience to find you.

IF YOU FEEL CALLED to create a Reiki business or to grow an existing business, the first step is to make sure that the business is in alignment with YOU. There's no sense working at a Reiki business that doesn't fit or that causes you stress. You will move out of your comfort zone for sure. Even if you are in alignment. That's how Reiki operates, teaching us to stretch and grow. But we need to make sure you are in alignment with your business and that it is in alignment with you.

SOMETIMES A BUSINESS MODEL that WAS in alignment with us is no more. And it is time to change things.

. . .

ONE OF THE remarkable things about Reiki is that it constantly moves us forward. And it merges with just about every other interest and modality as it does that. So you can create a Reiki business within your existing career if you are guided to. You certainly don't have to quit your job, create a website and strike out on your own to make it with Reiki. You can create a Reiki business that IS all about sessions and classes, but you do not need to. You can also create a Reiki business that is any combination.

WE MAY BE DISILLUSIONED with the career you are in but Reiki may heal that and return us to the passion we felt for it initially, allowing us to weave Reiki into all that you do.

OTHER TIMES, Reiki becomes a stand-alone thing-- and IS the passion we will work within.

AND YET OTHER TIMES, it becomes a part-time endeavor we can do while still doing the work that pays the bills or holding down a second career.

ANY AND ALL of these combinations are available to you.

IN THIS BOOK, we will discover together the unique way YOU can create a Reiki business to support you. One that lights you up--

- whether it is woven into what you already do or want to do
- a stand-alone practice
- a part-time practice

- or something else that combines your many gifts and talents.

AND THEN, you can share your light with the world in whatever way that works best for you.

OUR FIRST TASK is to discover the unique practice that will fire you up. The one that makes you excited to get out of bed every morning.

YOU MIGHT BE a Reiki yoga teacher, a Reiki artist, a Reiki nurse, a Reiki businessperson, or a Reiki lawyer. Your business might be Reiki--and only Reiki. Or Reiki and past life regression. There are so many possibilities.

AND THE INTERESTING thing is that we can put the Divine guidance of Reiki to work for us to create the Reiki business that is right for us and for the people who need our special style of assistance.

IT MIGHT BE in alignment with what you do now. Or it may be the polar opposite. Let's find out!

IMAGINE SHARING the gift of Reiki with others and incorporating that which gives JOY into the mix. It is a beautiful thing. The world needs you to spread the light of Reiki right now. The fact that you are reading this book is evidence of that. And evidence that you are ready to step forward into your life purpose and onto your path.

. . .

So let's start with the goal of starting some sort of Reiki business that is in alignment with you. And let's leave the details to Reiki. Don't worry; we will be doing exercises throughout this book to help you further define what this looks like for you. Right now, we are simply looking for the direction that is in alignment with your life purpose.

If you ever wondered what your life purpose is, there's an identifying emotion that comes along with it, JOY! So when you feel joy, you are in alignment with your purpose and in alignment with Source. Isn't that interesting? Especially when so many of us were taught that we need to work hard and suffer in this lifetime! It's time to release that limiting belief.

Connect with Your Life Purpose

How do you know you are in alignment with your life purpose? The thing you came to earth to accomplish? The Universe has made it very simple for us. It uses the emotion of JOY. So I invite you to begin noticing when you feel joy. That is an indication that you are in alignment with your life purpose.

It's not uncommon for us to become so disconnected from joy that it is no longer a part of our lives. Often, that indicates we are also disconnected from our life path.

There is a common thread throughout our cultural conditioning that we must work hard to accomplish things. No pain, no gain. When has a high school guidance counselor ever asked, "What brings you joy? OK, do that!" I'm sure it happens but rarely. We believe we have to work hard to make a living. We believe life is hard. That is certainly a belief system. But Reiki, if you allow it, can align you with a different belief system. One in which everything flows. It is a much less stressful space to inhabit!

In nature, we are the hardest "working" animal. Most animals do what they need to do to make a living and spend the rest of their time enjoying life. Bees are busy - but then they get to eat honey! So I guess it's worth it.

The opposite of joy is depression. Many people suffer from depression in our society. Could it be because we are not living according to our life purposes?

Joy means our thoughts are in alignment with those of God and with our higher self.

~

EXERCISE - IDENTIFY Your Life Purpose part 1:
So if joy is an indication of being in alignment with God or Source energy, I'd like you to make a list now of the things that give you joy. It could be a long list. Take your time. If you can't think of anything that brings you joy, go back to what gave you joy when you were a child. And if you still draw a blank, imagine what could give you joy. Or ask people you are close to what brings them joy until you find resonance.

Once you have that list together, I'd like you to make two more lists. Make these lists quickly without giving them much thought. So set a timer for 3 minutes--the pressure is on. And please don't read ahead; do each task one at a time.

1. List at least 5 things that you feel passionate about. If there are more than 5 that is okay. (1-3 minutes)
2. Next, list 5 things that you have accomplished in your life that you are proud of. Again, if there are more than 5 that is okay. (1-3 minutes)
3. Finally, without giving it much thought at all, quickly

circle one thing in the top category and one in the bottom that are the most important to you. (30 seconds)

Those 2 things, my friends, are most likely connected to your life purpose.

EXERCISE: **Identify Your Life Purpose Part 2:**

1. See if you can put the two things together to make a sentence to create a direction.
2. Once you have a sentence, think to yourself, what's the one thing that I could do in my life that would mean the most to me in the world? So that by doing it, everything else would be easier or unnecessary?
3. Now think of someone in your life who knows you really well--someone who might be interested in helping you with this exercise. Share this sentence with them and ask them if that sounds like you? And ask them how they would describe your gifts and talents.
4. Now activate your Reiki energy and see if you can incorporate what they have told you into your life purpose and mission statement. You can talk to more than one person, but don't make this too complicated. My husband helped me pull it all together.

My result: Reiki, growth, and helping others showed up for me. My husband pointed out that I love to inspire people to learn and grow so they can become their best selves and that I am a very effective teacher. He said for years he watched people walk into my Reiki classes and very different, glowing beings walk out. So I realized that as much as I love doing Reiki sessions, my life purpose is really around teaching and inspiring others with Reiki. That's what led to this book.

A lot of us live our lives, never knowing what we came here to do. You now have an indication of your life purpose. You can keep reworking the words until they feel comfortable to you. Until they inspire you. Until they roll off your tongue. Until you really connect with them. But you don't have to have this perfect to move on. This statement reveals what you came here to do.

So now, with this in mind, I invite you to notice going forward when you experience the energy of joy. And understand that when you do, you are on the right track.

~

Weaving Reiki into Your Current Occupation

Many times, my students are fed up with their jobs or vocations. Some are burned out. When they learn Reiki, it has such a profound effect on their lives that their first instinct is to quit their job and practice Reiki full time. But it is important to complete the healing process and move forward from that space rather than create a business from the wound.

Many times, you entered your vocation for a reason. You had a passion for some aspect of it. You may have become frustrated, disillusioned, or tired in the course of your career. But the passion is likely still there underneath all that. Reiki can show you a different way to approach and work within the profession you have chosen. Besides, it can show you how to expand so that a Reiki business can effortlessly become part of your life. Or maybe it can even become a part of the vocation or job you already do.

Reiki has shown me that 40 hours per week doing what we are passionate about can be too much. And having to earn a living from our passion can create a layer of stress that is not comfortable or necessary. This stress can strip us of the joy we once derived from our passion.

Even though I have a "full-time" Reiki practice, I don't work at it 40 hours per week every week. Some weeks I work more. But many weeks I work less. I divide my time between Reiki sessions and classes, my horse business, my essential oil business, and writing. I use Reiki in all of them. And I'm passionate about all of them. But weeks, when I have to work 40 hours or more with the horses, get tiring. As do those types of weeks with Reiki, essential oils, or writing. Generally, I work 10-20 hours per week at each, and that feels just right.

Many of my students integrate Reiki into what they already do. For instance, massage therapists weave Reiki into their massages or offer combined sessions. Lawyers offer Reiki sessions to clients to assist them with the legal process. Teachers use Reiki in their classrooms to help their students learn. Hospital administrators use Reiki with staffing, clearing the space, and helping staff and patients with overwhelm. Front line healthcare workers use Reiki to balance themselves and assist their clients. Some of my students use Reiki in part-time businesses. Others volunteer with hospice, animal welfare groups, or other organizations. There are many ways to weave Reiki into whatever you do.

There are as many ways to weave Reiki into your own life and career as you can imagine. So while a Reiki business (part-time or full-time) may be your end goal, take a few moments now to ask Reiki how you can weave Reiki into your current life. And pay attention to what you receive.

Often this question is the first step in getting to know Reiki better. And to spending a larger part of your day in the Reiki energy. Sometimes, a Reiki business spins out of this process. It can be a very comfortable, organic transition instead of a process of great upheaval. So connect with the energy and have some fun! There are ideas for weaving Reiki into your daily life in chapter 8. Take a few minutes to check them out.

Then, if you feel guided, you can create a plan. Or you can turn the planning over to Reiki. Simply invite Reiki to weave itself through your life in the way that is the most aligned with you. In a way that accomplishes your goals.

You can also take each section, one at a time, activate Reiki, and journal on it. Then discuss your findings with a friend. Sometimes the thoughts gel into a plan that way. And if they don't, don't worry. The plan is likely working itself out below the surface. It takes time to create form from the formless. But we have lots more exercises to help. These exercises should begin to get things flowing for us.

I've recorded this as a meditation you can use to assist you if you wish.[1]

How to talk to people about Reiki
Reiki can be really difficult to describe. I mean, how do you explain something that can create miracles? That can touch so many aspects of your life? That changes your life from the moment that you connect with it? Something so spiritual that it's hard to put into words?

Well, it is completely appropriate to discuss Reiki in the language and vocabulary of whatever group you are speaking with. If you are speaking with medical professionals, use medical language. If you are speaking to spiritual people, use spiritual language. And if you are not certain of the background of the audience you are talking to, you can use generic language and feel it out.

One of the most important aspects of communicating, however, is listening. So be sure to listen to the questions being posed to you. Listen to the language being used. Listen to the body language and the energy around the people you are communicating with. And listen for the message under the words.

Usui Sensei was interested in the spiritual aspects of Reiki, stayed focused in that direction, and used that language. When Dr. Hayashi asked him to shift into a more medical focus, Usui Sensei refused. And instead, he encouraged Hayashi to develop those aspects of the energy himself. It was not something he was interested in.

Hayashi did develop the medical aspects of Reiki. And he began to use more medical terminology and knowledge of anatomy to describe Reiki.

Mrs. Takata painted over her sign advertising "Reiki" and called the modality "Short Wave Therapy" for some time after the Pearl Harbor attack when Hawaiians were repulsed by anything Japanese. So you can see that it is completely acceptable to adjust your language to your audience. It's possible to maintain your integrity and choose the aspects of Reiki to talk about as well as the language that will be best understood.

I used to stutter and stammer and be caught completely flat-footed when someone asked me what I do or asked about Reiki. And often, I expected to be judged when I explained what I did.

When I began teaching Reiki in 2011, a lot of people seemed to judge me. Some because they didn't understand Reiki. Others believed Reiki was in contradiction to their religious upbringing. I even felt judged occasionally by Reiki teachers from different lineages. When I mentioned this problem to my teacher, William Rand, he pointed out that if I felt judged, I was also judging. Which was funny because judgment was something that Reiki was working very diligently with me to clear. So I re-doubled my efforts.

I realized that I would begin my explanation with an expectation of being judged. And that if I was doing that, there must be aspects of Reiki that I didn't feel completely comfortable with yet. So I began to look deep within my psyche around my attitudes. Using Reiki. I realized that my religious upbringing had still not reconciled with my new direction. So I began applying Reiki to this issue. Eventually, I found I was no longer "judged" when I spoke about Reiki so my own judgment must have healed.

Once, at a blood donor clinic, I ran into my priest from a previous church. We hadn't seen each other in a while but were friends. He had baptized my three children, and I thought the world of him. He asked what I was doing now? I told him I wasn't sure his Pope was in agreement with what I was doing. He replied, "Oh, don't worry about him, there are lots of things he doesn't agree with." I told him that I did Reiki and taught horseback riding lessons with horses who worked with Reiki energy. He found it fascinating, and we had a lovely visit over cookies and juice.

Some of my students expected to be judged by the members of their church for becoming Reiki practitioners. Most were pleasantly surprised that their parishioners, church leaders, and ministers were open to Reiki. The church members mentioned that they had friends or relatives who practiced Reiki or had received a treatment. One of my students was asked to give a talk in her church about Reiki.

Still, other students felt judged but decided to stand in their truth and look a bit deeper inside to determine whether they were judging themselves or Reiki.

Now, when you mention Reiki, it is not as foreign as it was in 2011. Most people know someone who does Reiki, has received a treatment, or has taken a class. So look within yourself for judgment. It can sound something like the internal voice telling you, "They're going to think you're foolish if you tell them you offer Reiki sessions." or "They're not going to like it when you mention Reiki." Work on it, if it's there. And then you can talk about Reiki without the expectation of being judged.

When I learned to listen without judgment, people were very receptive to hearing about Reiki. I was asked to give Reiki presentations at City Hall, universities, and Health care facilities. I even began speaking about Reiki at large horse conferences and leading Reiki meditations in yoga studios. I couldn't believe how many people were interested in learning more once I got over my own discomfort.

Letting Reiki Lead
I have a trick when I am speaking about Reiki, whether I am speaking to a large group or an individual: I let Reiki lead.

To do this, I apply Reiki to my throat chakra daily and particularly before speaking engagements or classes. As I do, I connect with God/Source, invite Reiki and Source to help me find the words that will resonate with the people or group I am speaking with. And I trust that the language, stories, and descriptions that come through will be the ones that people need to hear. I can't tell you how many times I thought, "Boy, why am I telling that story? It doesn't even answer the question the person asked," only to have someone approach me afterward and tell me how much they needed to hear that story at that moment or how much they related to it. So I have learned to turn the task over to Reiki. And trust what comes through.

But how do we begin a conversation about Reiki? And how do we describe it? I have a few generic descriptions that I call upon such as:

- Reiki is a Japanese form of stress reduction that often promotes healing.
- Reiki is a spiritually guided life force energy that can help people heal -- physically, mentally, spiritually, and emotionally.

- Reiki is a spiritual pathway I decided to take in 2010 that dramatically changed my life.
- Reiki is a healing energy that can never cause harm and tends to help people mentally, physically, spiritually, or emotionally.
- Reiki is a Japanese spiritual technique discovered by Mikao Usui in the 1920s that works effectively alongside traditional health care today.
- Reiki is a Japanese healing energy that is used widely in hospitals and medical establishments throughout the world.
- Reiki is spiritually guided life force energy that can promote healing and connect us with Divine guidance.

Once I use one of my more generic descriptions about Reiki, I use my Reiki listening skills to determine whether the person is really interested or was just being polite. If they were just being polite, the conversation ends there and I haven't stuttered and stammered like a fool. Nor have they had to listen to a long, drawn-out somewhat scattered explanation. But if they are genuinely interested, the conversation continues.

If they are really interested in Reiki, I often ask if they would like a demonstration to feel the energy. That can be one of the best ways to allow them to experience it. I invite them to turn around and ask if I can touch their shoulders. If they say yes, I place my Reiki-activated hands on their shoulders, so they can "sense" the energy themselves. If they are not comfortable with touch, I simply beam Reiki to them.

In groups, I conduct a short meditation with Reiki energy, letting people know that Reiki will not go against their free will. It will only work with them if they want it to, and I ask them to state their intention internally. People are always intrigued once they feel and experience the energy!

Reiki Resources

People often wonder where to find the best resources with the background information we need to speak with different groups. One of my favorite resources is the *Reiki News Magazine*. Subscriptions are available and inexpensive. They come four times per year. And there are all kinds of wonderful articles written by Reiki practitioners, masters, and teachers from every Reiki lineage.

The magazines are full of great ideas and well-written articles. In fact, Licensed Teachers feel so strongly about the benefit of this magazine that we purchase a copy for students who study with us.

The ICRT website has years of articles and information that can be easily searched.[2] Want to learn about Reiki and yoga? It's there. Reiki and medicine, Reiki and religion, Reiki and science--it's all there. And the information has been vetted so that it is evidence-based. So this is usually my first stop.

As a scientist, I often speak about research, facts, and figures with Reiki. So I also turn to the Center for Reiki Research where my friend and fellow scientist Dr. Ann Baldwin works, along with several of her peers.[3] Dr. Baldwin has also written a fantastic book *Reiki in Clinical Practice* if you are looking for more information on the science of Reiki.

There are some fantastic podcasts about Reiki. My own weekly podcast, Reiki from the Farm™ is becoming quite popular at #3 in the top 20 Reiki podcasts. Meanwhile, my peers, Colleen Benelli's Reiki Lifestyle podcast and Karen Harrison's Reiki Call podcast are ranked highly too. And there are other fantastic podcasts out there. Check them out and see which ones resonate with you.

There are some great books about Reiki though not as many as I wish there were. Do a search and see if any look interesting to you.

There are also fantastic Reiki associations that have lots of great information about Reiki. Many of them can connect you with an insurance provider as well. So check them out.

Learning to Listen with Reiki and Reiki Discernment
My mentor, Colleen Benelli, taught me so much about listening! She spent years learning to listen. It turns out that when we don't feel "heard," it is because we have not developed our listening abilities. We are not "hearing" others.

Even sensitive people who receive "too much" information can learn to listen with Reiki. Then, what they receive from their intuition is filtered through the highest frequencies of love. This makes them easier to receive so they are no longer difficult, damaging, or overwhelming.

We learned as we created the ICRT Animal Reiki courses that listening is a critical part of being heard. For our clients and students, one of the most important things we can do is listen to them so that they feel heard. Often, we are busy thinking of what we are going to say next or impatiently finishing someone's story for them-- instead of really listening to what they are saying. Learn to listen underneath the words, so people can feel truly heard.

The next exercise is based on exercises in ICRT Animal Reiki Training. It will open your Reiki listening skills and can be conducted as often as you feel you need until your listening skills are fully developed. You can go through the experience below which have recorded for you.[4]

∼

EXERCISE - DEVELOP REIKI Listening Skills

Close your eyes. Take some deep breaths.

And imagine it's a warm, sunny, bright day and that you are walking down a trail in a beautiful forest filled with great cathedral trees.
As you breathe into yourself, you breathe in the life essence of the forest, and with each step that you take, the energy of the earth flows up through the bottoms of your feet.
Choose a tree that speaks to you. One that stands out to you.
Go over to the tree and sit down, nestled in the roots of the tree with your back up against its trunk.
If you have anything blocking you from listening and "hearing" others, I invite you to surrender it to the earth now.
Sometimes lack of patience makes it difficult to listen. Sometimes it's mind clutter or chatter. Other times, we multitask or lose focus. Occasionally, we assume we know what someone is going to say or how they are going to feel about a situation. Sometimes our prejudices get in the way or we don't agree with what we are hearing. And other times, we are so focused on being heard ourselves that it makes it difficult to listen to others.
We release all of the habits, mindsets, and opinions that prevent us from truly listening to and hearing others now.
Pause.

A beautiful light pierces the canopy above you and shines directly upon you. It contains the lights of focus, clarity, and truth. Allow those lights to absorb into you now, enhancing and improving your ability to listen.
Pause.

Now the Reiki energy activates all of your senses. So that we can listen with all of the parts of ourselves, learning to listen with our body, mind, emotions, and spirit.
We activate our heart, chakras, meridians, and aura, listening with every part of our being.
I invite you to open your listening skills now.
Listen in front of you.
Listen behind you.

Listen above you and listen below you.
Listen to your right.
Listen to your left.
Listen to the quietest sound that you can hear.
And now go inside and listen within you.
Invite the Reiki energy to use these channels, to communicate with you. You are open and you are listening.
Pause.

And now the light of discernment flows through you, helping you to choose your words, your language, the stories to tell, how to relate to a person, group or audience. Allow it to make any adjustments necessary within you to help you develop your own high level of discernment.
Pause.

Now gaze directly into the light, and as you do, the light will begin to guide you. This light is Reiki energy that comes directly from Source. You can decide whether or not to follow the guidance, but for now, the light can show you the next steps in your Reiki journey.

Stay in this space as long as you are guided. When you come back, write about your experience.

∾

Now Set Your Goals

So you know you want to share Reiki with the world. Or at least with your friends, family, and co-workers. What does that look like to you? What are your goals?

Your goals might be to reach a certain number of people with your Reiki, to conduct a certain number of sessions, to teach a class, or any number of things.

Exercise: **Set Your Goals with Reiki**

- Go into the Gassho meditation, activate Reiki, and invite your Reiki symbols to join you.
- Meditate with Reiki to help define your goals.
- Why: Sit with the Reiki energy for some time. Ask yourself why you want to share Reiki with the world. Be honest with yourself. And put together a list. It's okay if money is on the list, but it should not be the main motivator. Really spend some time looking into yourself asking "why" you want to share Reiki with the world. Once you identify your why, you have your main motivating factor. It will keep you fired up even when you hit obstacles or wonder if you can do this. It is even the basis of your marketing. Make a list of the reasons why you want to create a Reiki business in some form to begin sharing Reiki with the world.
- What: Imagine that the Reiki energy is reaching out to others. How does it reach out to them? Is it in a session, a class, or in some other way? Write it down.
- Who: Imagine whom you could reach out to? Make a list. Invite the energy to begin reaching out to others on your behalf. You may find they begin to contact you for treatments, sessions, or even with questions about Reiki before you ever even speak to them about it.
- Where: Imagine you are doing your Reiki work. Where are you doing it? Are you at home? And an office? At your client's home? What surrounds you? Write it down.
- When: With the distance symbol, imagine you are fully in your life purpose, sharing Reiki with the world. When is it? Is it next week? Next month? 3 months from now? 3 years from now?

This exercise can be very powerful. Spend some time with it each day until your goals firm up. Write them down. Then put them into your Reiki grid or hold them in your hands, giving them Reiki each day. You will be amazed at how quickly your goals begin to materialize.

CREATE a Reiki Grid to Help Accomplish your Goals

Once you have set goals, one of the most efficient and effective ways to realize them is to create a Reiki grid. A Reiki grid is a way to use the distance symbol to send Reiki to several things at the same time. You simply write your goals on an index card or a piece of paper. Draw your symbols on it. And hold it in your hands sending Reiki to it daily. You may wish to charge a crystal with Reiki as well and leave it working with your crystal grid. You can be as basic or as elaborate as feels right to you.

If a Reiki grid does not feel right to you, you can use a Reiki box, bowl, board, or vase--whatever you wish. Use the distant symbol because, in 10-15 minutes per day, you can send Reiki to ANYTHING and EVERYTHING you wish. And sending it to your business goals can help you manifest them in the best way possible for you.

I place my favorite crystals on top of my grid and, daily, hold my grid in my hands, activating Reiki for 5-10 minutes. I say the following prayer: "God, please send Reiki, Love, and Light to the situations and souls in my Reiki grid. Please continue to send this for the next 24 hours or until I can charge my grid again." You can add people, events, life goals, etc. But make sure your business goals are there too.

EXERCISE: Create a Reiki Grid

Activate Reiki and create a Reiki grid. It can be as simple or elaborate as you wish. For inspiration or ideas, you can see my article in the Appendix "The Power of a Reiki Grid."[5]

PRO TIP:
Karen Caig, LRMT, Arkansas, USA
Reiki Institute[6]

Many people come to Reiki because they want to help others. But during class, they realize they need to heal themselves, so they work to overcome and release trauma. Then people get that nudge again to share this incredible energy with others. Some of my students consider creating a practitioner-type business, but that's not the only way you can have a Reiki business. You have to find your unique niche: the clients *you* can serve best or the students *only you* can connect to in a special way. Then, you figure out how best to reach those people.

I taught college English for nearly 25 years and knew immediately that I wanted to teach Reiki. But the business aspect eluded me. I think creating a business is an obstacle that a lot of people have. People know that Reiki is about love and healing. But some believe that businesses are only about making money. So those two things just don't go together in many people's minds.

Thankfully, Reiki healed my issues with money, self-worth, business, and more so I can be comfortable being successful in business. I went to networking events, and people helped me. They'd say, "Come here; let me introduce you to a therapist. I bet she will refer clients to you, or let me introduce you to this chiropractor."

I have students that incorporate Reiki with the business they already have. They didn't have to quit what they were doing. I taught a birth doula who now incorporates Reiki into caring for the pregnant mother, the baby, and the entire process. Or estheticians who learned Reiki for themselves then realized they could put it into their facials. I also taught chiropractors, massage therapists, accountants, and business people who incorporate Reiki into what they already do. Other students started a Reiki business on the side. At first, it's not a priority. But often it grows into one.

I even used Reiki as a college English professor. Students needed help and guidance when they couldn't get an essay written. They were stressed about their inability to write, so I used Reiki to help them through. Free mini-sessions in my office didn't pay, so I still needed my teacher's salary. But incorporating Reiki is what got me started.

I started teaching friends so they could do their own sessions. Then a woman with cancer said she wanted to learn Reiki. I wasn't ready to teach, but the woman was insistent, so I started teaching.

Eventually, I quit my job. My friends thought I was crazy. But I was ready to take the leap into a Reiki business. I still had baggage to work through. I'm excited that this book will help people with that.

It will help people get very clear about why they want a Reiki business and what it might look like. They need to ask, "Should I do this? What would it look like? What are my special gifts? How would my Reiki business look different from other people's Reiki business?" You've got to ask the right questions. And that's what chapter one does. It asks the right questions.

And then you move to practical things like where to set it up. What kind of a business should it be? How to attract clients. How to attract students. I will buy this book and recommend it to my students, and I wish it had been available when I started my business.

Recently, Reiki helped me learn about social media. That wasn't part of my plan, but Reiki led me to it. I learned social media because I figured I can't give Reiki to anybody if they can't find me. That's free marketing, attraction marketing. Like you, I believe "if you want to learn, teach." Now I teach classes on using Instagram, Facebook, and other social media to grow your Reiki business.

Reiki helps us find our niche. It helps us understand what we can do, how we can contribute. There is a service aspect to business. The bottom line of creating a successful business is saying, what do people need? And what do I have that can help them fulfill that need?

I don't have an MBA. But as the book shows, if Reiki has helped us heal so much stuff, why wouldn't it help us with our business? Let Reiki lead.

We each focus on different stuff because we're different people. Our journeys have been different, and Reiki helps us draw the people who need us. I get students with self-esteem issues and abundance issues because my story will teach them. My life lessons have been different, so I teach a little bit differently to my students than other teachers may teach. But that's how Reiki spreads.

A lot of my students say, "Oh, I couldn't be a Reiki practitioner," almost like, "Oh, I couldn't be the Pope." I think I felt that way, too, with my teachers. One thing I love about this book is that it helps give students that confidence.

When you take that first step, the entire universe conspires to help you.

Check out our podcast on this chapter.[7]

STUDENT SUCCESS STORY **Amanda McCordic**

I was burnt out with a dysfunctional home life and in my career as a divorce lawyer. I was diagnosed with terminal cancer. Reiki was a huge part of my healing. Afterward, I didn't want to go back to being a lawyer.

MY FIRST INSTINCT was to do Reiki. But every time I thought to close my firm, something pushed me to keep it open. The business continued to grow and I didn't want what happened to me to happen to my staff. This kind of law takes a toll on people.

SO I DECIDED we would practice law differently with Reiki. And the Reiki Mentor Course seemed a logical step in that direction. You said "the trick is to bring Reiki into what you do." so I did!

MY STAFF and I studied Reiki, and we use it on almost everything. Because my office needs me to bill at a lawyer's rate, we hired a full-time Reiki master. Clients who require emotional support begin with the Reiki master, who can offer Reiki, then debrief me in a few minutes. It's more effective and cost-effective and meets people where they are. Lawyers are expensive and poorly equipped to deal with trauma and emotions. So every new client gets one free Reiki session. When our clients are witnesses in trials, we encourage them to schedule a Reiki session to calm themselves.

WHEN MY LIFE WAS CHAOTIC, billing became a secondary priority. COVID was hard on the business, and we needed to make money. So I put together a list of people who owed money that I didn't think would ever pay and sent Reiki to the invoices. People I never expected to hear from again showed up out of the blue with payments.

. . .

We became lawyers because we wanted to help. When we feel very powerless, we do our best and hand the rest to Reiki. I encourage my lawyers to book sessions if they are spinning their wheels, and this generally resolves the situation. Our Reiki master clears the office each morning, releasing the intense emotion that comes through, then invites the energies of productivity and joy. People comment that the whole building has a lightness to it. We are still figuring it out but it is going very well so far.

My life purpose is to spread Reiki. If it helped me with cancer, my husband's suicide, and now my mother's cancer, then it can help many other people. So as it became clear that I wasn't going to die, I asked for Reiki's guidance to be of better service to myself and others. I was shown that business and empowering people is what I am good at. So I understood I was to create a Reiki app called "Dragonfly, A Reiki Marketplace". The app will help talented Reiki practitioners who bring light and love to the world but don't have business experience get themselves out there. It will also help people who need Reiki find a Reiki practitioner. It feels like a Divine calling to help us share the light of Reiki with those who are disconnected, suffering, sad, and struggling. It will be both an online platform, a website, and an app. It will open up Reiki to many people who know about Reiki but don't know how to access services.

Going forward is about trusting my instinct and intuition which are getting stronger. I trust the timing and don't force things. I have lots of projects in the air, but I allow Reiki to prioritize my day. I'm learning patience and trust as things unfold in a way that I would not have expected. I will continue to expand my knowledge and take more Reiki classes. It is a wonderful journey.

---

1. www.reikifromthefarm.com/reikibusinessbook_meditations

2. www.reiki.org
3. https://centerforreikiresearch.com/
4. www.reikifromthefarm.com/reikibusinessbook_meditations
5. https://www.hiddenbrook.ca/wp-content/uploads/2018/11/PowerOfReikiGrid.pdf
6. https://reiki-institute.com/
7. https://www.buzzsprout.com/1364386/10016274

2

THE IDENTITY OF YOUR BUSINESS

"Please don't compare yourself to others. This is YOUR Reiki Journey."
Terry Dulin, LRMT

Create an Identity
Okay, now you know what you came to earth to do in this lifetime. And if you don't know yet, you have a vague idea. And you know a bit more about why and how you want to share Reiki in the world. Now let's get to know your Reiki business by creating an identity for your business. As with most things, we can invite the Reiki energy to assist us in this process.

Basically, a business needs an identity. Once it has an identity, the business has its own energy. And the energy of your business can assist you in understanding how to proceed.

EXERCISE: Create an Elevator Pitch

Let's take the "sentence" you created from the exercise "Identify Your Life Purpose" in the previous chapter. And refine it. Read it through and see if you can simplify it. Move things around. Take your life purpose and make it as succinct as you can. This sentence can become your guiding force. This statement reveals what you came here to do. It gives you your direction.

We are going to work with that sentence until it becomes an elevator pitch. So when someone asks you, "What do you do?" you will have a ready reply.

Go into Gassho, activate Reiki and your symbols. Place your Reiki hands on your sacral chakra to activate your creativity. Then on your third eye to activate your intuition. And finally, on your throat chakra to activate your authentic voice.

Spend as long as you need on each chakra until they feel balanced and empowered. Now ask Reiki to help you create your "pitch" to people in a language they can understand.

You may decide to create different "elevator pitches" for different audiences. It is completely acceptable to talk about Reiki using language appropriate to your audience. Mrs. Takata was living in Hawaii after Pearl Harbor. She painted over the word "Reiki" and called it "short wave therapy" on the sign of her healing business because she felt that Japanese healing arts would not be well received. So we know it is appropriate to speak to each audience in the language they best understand. When I speak with doctors, I use scientific and medical language. When I speak with spiritual or religious people, I use spiritual language to describe Reiki.

Take a moment to ask Reiki to show you who your different audiences are. Then activate Reiki, and work with the sentence you created in Chapter 1 when you identified your life purpose. We will fine-tune it so that it is simple, succinct, and interesting--something that grabs people's attention, and causes them to want more. Something to initiate a conversation about what you do. Something that you may wish to use in your marketing material. And with these "elevator pitches," you can quickly, efficiently, and accurately describe what you do in just a few sentences.

You won't believe how handy this "elevator pitch" is. I used to trip over my tongue trying to explain what I do and what Reiki is. Needless to say, I didn't sound very confident or sure of myself. And people had to be interested and persistent if they wanted to learn more. Just make sure your elevator pitch answers what Reiki can do for your audience. That is what will pique their interest.

IDENTIFY Your Reiki Community and Clients

Who can you think of in your life who could use Reiki? Have you had an opportunity to practice Reiki with friends and family? If not, it's time to get busy. You do not need to charge friends and family. It is important to "practice" sharing Reiki with others. They are your best resource to help with your development.

But once you have practiced enough to feel comfortable with Reiki. It may be time to set up a practice. Time to think about whom to approach to see if they are interested in your Reiki offerings. One of the unique things about Reiki is that the client finds the best practitioner or teacher for them. But we need to get the ball rolling, with our intention. And it helps to determine who your ideal client is. This makes it easier to create marketing material too.

I tell my students, "If someone asks you for a Reiki session or class, you are ready to offer them." If someone asks for an offering we are considering, it is the Universe's signal that we are ready to offer it.

And yet, it doesn't hurt to use standard business practices to help those students and clients find us.

In the beginning, I worked really hard to keep business practices out of my Reiki business. People had to be standing right next to me to find out if I was offering a class. Occasionally, a client would ask for a Reiki session, but I wasn't confident enough and referred them to my teacher. My teacher gently scolded me, saying, "Pam, they asked to receive Reiki from you. That means you are ready." So I worked to heal the division within myself that wanted to keep business principles separate from my Reiki business. And realized I was serving no one by staying small. As I considered how many people I could help if I let people know what I was doing, it was evident I needed to heal this rift As I healed this division within myself, I realized we could adapt standard business practices to merge with Reiki. They became sacred business practices and principles. These not only blended with my spiritual practice but also felt right to me and to my clients and students. More on this in subsequent chapters!

Remember, there is no such thing as competition. Every single one of us could be doing Reiki for ourselves and others 24 hours per day and we would still only touch the surface of what is needed in the world. And each of us brings our own specific gifts and talents into our offerings. No one can work with Reiki in exactly the same way that you do. The clients and students who are meant to find you will find you. And the clients and students who are meant to work with other practitioners or teachers will find them.

～

EXERCISE: **Identify Your Ideal Client**
Activate Reiki and sit in Gassho, thinking about the people in your life who may be open to Reiki. Now make a list of the people who came to mind. Then beam Reiki onto the list and ask yourself

and Reiki who your ideal client is. One name should stand out to you.

Now think about that person. What is it about them that makes them an ideal client? With Reiki activated, set your timer for 7 minutes and begin writing. You have let Reiki and the Universe know that you are open for business. And you have identified the type of client most likely to be drawn to you. Well done! This information is going to come in handy in so many other exercises going forward!

WHAT'S IN A NAME?

Now that you have an idea for a business, it's time to give it a name. And if you already have a name, it may be time to determine whether the name still suits you. It's important that the name speaks to you and identifies what you do for clients, students, and customers. It's best not to make the name too "cute," or it may not be well understood.

You may wish to have your name in the business name, especially if the business will be focused on the different services you offer. Or you may want a more generic name if you plan to have staff and may even step back from the business at some point. You may wish to have the name "Reiki" in the name if your primary offerings will be Reiki-related. But if you expect to combine Reiki with other modalities, again, a more generic name will work best.

To be the most effective, the name and all of your marketing material should be focused on what a potential client can expect to receive from you. You may have already heard a name revealed to you during one of the earlier meditations. Or you may have several ideas. You may already even have a name. But it might no longer be relevant or capable of encompassing where you are going with your business now. Let's see what your name is. It is one of the most important aspects of your business' identity.

The name of my podcast and business, Reiki from the Farm™ was accidental. I had 2 other names in mind for my podcast and couldn't decide which one to use, so I held a poll with my Reiki students. As I was about to send the poll, I thought, "You can't have a poll with only 2 choices," so I pulled "Reiki from the Farm" out of the air and added it to the list.

Reiki from the Farm was hands down the unanimous choice of my students. I didn't even like that name. I didn't know how I could talk about the relevant issues I wanted to discuss pigeonholed with that name. I love animals but did I really want all of my podcasts to be about them? No.

My mentor pointed out that it was the perfect name for me. I do live on a farm with 12 horses, 4 dogs, some of my 3 grown children (it fluctuates), and a husband who has been with me every step of the way. She showed me how living here, doing what I do informs the rest of my life. It brings with it special challenges and opportunities and requires certain gifts and talents. It's who I am and doesn't mean I am any less interested in the other aspects of life or of Reiki. She was right. My students were right. Reiki from the Farm™ is exactly the right name for what I do. Thank you, guys. And thank you, Reiki!

EXERCISE: **Finding or Redefining Your Business Name**
Think about any or all of the following questions.

1. What will your business do for people?
2. What are some of the qualities your business will embody?
3. What are your specific gifts and talents?

4. Where will your business be located?
5. What are some of your favorite things about Reiki?
6. What is your favorite part of your elevator pitch?

Write one down at the top of a clean page.

Now set your timer for 7 minutes and begin a stream-of-consciousness automatic writing experience. Write down anything you can think of to answer each question. Even if it seems nonsensical.

Once the timer dings, you can choose to stop writing or continue. Chances are that at the end of this exercise, you will have a much better understanding of your business. Take what you have written and circle some of the words that stand out to you. They may look "bold" on the page or seem to catch your attention for a moment. You may just really like them or be drawn to them. Can any of them be incorporated into a name? Start doodling with them, noticing if the words change order, reform themselves or if a slightly different variation comes through.

Do this for some of the other questions. Until this exercise feels complete to you.

Now choose 3-4 possible names from what has come through. Then create a poll for the friends and family you identified in the earlier exercise as your "potential client list." Find out what name they like best.

OR

Close your eyes, take a deep breath, activate Reiki and your symbols, and go into Gassho meditation. Invite Reiki and your business to come together and reveal your business name.

OR

Use the distance symbol to step forward into a time when your business is well established. Imagine you are looking at your business cards or website. What name is listed there? Can you see it?

You can do all 3! I know you will find the business name that is just right for you.

~

BRING in Some Focus
Reiki can do so much, and we can do so many things with Reiki, that sometimes, we can spread ourselves too thin. I have a successful Reiki business. But I also have a successful riding-lesson business and a successful essential oil business. I had a Reiki session with an LRMT friend recently about growing my business as I felt stuck and overwhelmed. She said, "You're spreading yourself too thin. Where is your focus?"

I had to really sit down and do some soul searching. I realized that my focus is the Reiki portion of my business-- primarily teaching the teachers. So I needed to let the essential oils and the riding lessons take a backseat, which I can do thanks to my wonderful assistants.

Where is your focus? Is it the Reiki portion of what you are doing? Or is it somewhere else and is Reiki in a supporting role? It's OK if it is. Your focus is probably around the life purpose you identified. But is there an area of focus within your business? Being clear about that can help you stay aligned with your dream. It can bring ideas and inspiration to you. Activate Reiki and give some thought about where your focus is. Then invite Reiki to assist you to bring that focus into your daily life and align it with your priorities.

Setting Priorities

It's okay to have a big to-do list. You may be starting to get a bit nervous now as we are moving into things. Just don't allow yourself to become overwhelmed by the tasks in front of you. Maintain your focus on what is important to you and your business. In her classes, LRMT Laurelle Gaia suggested we create a "Reiki bowl" when our to-do list threatens to spill off the page. You put each task on a piece of paper, place them in a bowl, give the bowl Reiki and allow Reiki to choose your priorities for you. If you ever find yourself overwhelmed in this process, remember that this is available to you.

Be Gentle with Yourself

If I can ask you to do anything, it's to take the pressure off yourself, let go of perfection and feel into the inspiration you are receiving. None of what we do or create has to be perfect. Permit yourself to be messy, let go of perfection and let the ideas flow. Wherever you are in the process, allow it to flow even and especially when it doesn't make sense. You are creating something that hasn't existed before. Giving form to the formless. So take your time going through it. Rome wasn't built in a day.

Good enough is good enough

We're all being asked to step forward now. If we needed to be perfect and have everything in order before we did, we never would.

There's a concept in writing called the "crappy first draft." You have to permit yourself to write a crappy first draft so you don't staunch the flow of ideas. You write from imperfection, then tidy it up later. That's how this book was created. And that's how we can work through the creation of your business.

Meet the Spirit of Your Reiki Business

Colleen Benelli wrote a wonderful article called "Meet the Spirit of Your Reiki Business" several years ago in the *Reiki News Magazine*. It captured my attention. I have coached people to succeed in business and in life for a good portion of my adult life. So I am aware that every business has its own energy and personality. But it never occurred to me to "meet" the spirit of my Reiki business until I read her article.

I had never thought about it that way, and yet it makes so much sense. So we can use Reiki today to introduce you to the spirit of your Reiki business. And then Reiki can help you gain access to the divine intelligence within your business.

As you get to know the spirit of your Reiki business, it becomes your partner and your advocate. It can guide you to reach the goals that you need to manifest your business into the material world. It can also help you create an ongoing relationship with the spiritual and energetic aspects of your business.

We're going to do an exercise that opens a direct line of communication with the spirit of your business. If everything's still a bit vague upon completion, that's all right. Please don't feel that there's any expectation. It's about creating what works for you.

We are bringing form to the formless, and sometimes that takes time. Your purpose or business may not be a full-on business. It might have more to do with volunteering or using Reiki in your daily life or current career or with your family. Whatever it is that you're meant to do, and what's right for you - is where we will focus.

In my class, people were shocked to find that the energy of the business they wanted to create was already there. They were surprised at how strongly they felt toward it. Surprised at how much they accomplished once they made this connection. Surprised at how "formed" the business already was. It was a turning point for quite a few people who then really stepped in and began making serious progress.

Denise hosted an online Reiki share, even though she was moving and didn't want to set up her official business until she was in her new location. Amy realized how Reiki could truly become a part of her existing fabric art business. Steve felt called to create healing meditations for others. While Sheila understood that her true calling was with animals.

I hope you enjoy this exercise as much as we did!

EXERCISE: **Finding Focus**
The next three questions I want you to consider are:

1. Is Reiki your main offering or
2. Is it a Reiki blended offering or
3. Is it another offering with Reiki in the background of what you're creating?

MEDITATION: **Meet the Spirit of Your Reiki Business**
This meditation brings focus and opens the lines of communication. It allows you to co-create with the spirit of your business. It is based on Colleen Benelli's article and meditation "The Spirit of Your Reiki Business."[1]

Make yourself comfortable. Close your eyes, take some deep breaths, and bring your hands into Gassho.
Invite the energies of the power symbol, the mental-emotional symbol, the distance symbol, and any other symbols you have to join you.
If enlightened/illumined beings assist in your work, invite them to join you.
Invite the spirit of your unique Reiki business to join you today, even

if you are unaware of its presence at this time.
Through the bridge of light provided by the distance symbol, connect with your Reiki business.
Imagine crossing the bridge of light and meeting your Reiki business. If you haven't yet heard a name or decided on one, invite your business to let you know what its name is.
Pause.

And now the mental, emotional symbol opens up the field of all possibilities. It becomes a spiritual translator to help you communicate with the spiritual aspects of your business. It helps you receive important information about it.
Pause.

And now the power symbol or master symbol activates the physical nature of your spiritual business, to manifest energy and intentions into form.
Pause.

Place your hands comfortably on your body. Give yourself Reiki and allow the Reiki energy that surrounds you to first heal your beliefs and limitations around this relationship.
Ask your connection with your Reiki business to align with your soul, your spirit, and your life purpose. You are empowered with Reiki to move forward in this relationship and on your soul journey.
Pause.

Release any fears and resistance you have to the existence of your business--and to your ability to work with it or to bring it forward into the world.
Pause.

Invite Reiki to heal all areas where we have resistance to the existence of or the growth of our business.
Invite Reiki to heal any parts of you that may be resistant to the idea

that your Reiki business has a consciousness and can interact with you.
Pause

As you let go of your fears and limitations in developing this relationship, open yourself to living in harmony with Reiki and to working in harmony with the energy within your Reiki business and your daily life.

Ask Reiki to create the priorities that are just right for you and your business. Invite Reiki to imbue you with confidence, alignment, and spiritual purpose, helping you take the actions that will allow your business to become a reality and will allow your business to support you financially.

Invite your mind to stay focused on the day-to-day tasks and practicalities of operating a small business.
Pause.

Now take a moment and listen to your heart to allow it to add intentions.
Pause

Invite your Reiki business to show you how to communicate better with it. Listen with your heart, your mind, your spirit, and your emotions. Listen with your full intention and attention.
Pause.

Invite the Reiki energy to help you align with the physical and spiritual manifestation of your business, bringing in that wonderful alignment and that better understanding. Take a moment now and give the spirit of your business access to you within that space of alignment.
Pause.

Inspiration comes through now, as you open the door for the spiritual energy of your Reiki business to speak to you.

Pause.

Now ask your Reiki business, what are the first steps for you to take?
Pause.

Namaste, Blessings. Amen. And so it is. Thank you.

Take as long as you'd like to return. And simply write those first steps down as you do.

ProTip
Cami Cote, LRMT, Montana, USA
Heart Rhythm Reiki[2]

I am a yoga teacher. A student thought I would enjoy Reiki. Then other people mentioned it. Suddenly, everybody was talking about Reiki. Finally, in an astrology birth chart reading, the astrologer said, "You're a healer and a teacher. What are you doing about that?"

So I studied Reiki one and two in 2012 and masters in 2014. I was happy being a yoga teacher and working in the medical field. But in 2015 I had a life-changing injury and couldn't practice or teach yoga.

Frustrated, I asked the Universe, "What do you want me to do?" And I heard "Reiki." Friends wanted me to teach them. I tried to pass them off to other teachers. Finally, one friend took me by the shoulders and said, "Cami, I want to take Reiki from you." I realized I needed to teach.

Then I was laid off from my job of 15 years. I knew I needed to make my Reiki business successful or go back to work. I spent the previous 10 years creating a life outside the medical field so it felt like Divine timing. I got more serious about my Reiki business, scheduled classes, and got on top of promotion. I offered specials to attract new clients. Now I don't run as many specials, but they helped build my client base.

I included Reiki in my yoga classes. Reiki is complementary to other modalities. I gave hands-on Reiki to students lying in Savasana (the final pose) for approximately 1 minute. The students loved it. They said, "Wow. That one minute of Reiki shifted things for me." So I incorporated 3-5 minutes of Reiki into my restorative yoga classes. I still got amazing feedback.

Later, I got into sound healing. I learned to use singing bowls, tuning forks, gongs, drums, and voice. The singing bowls and gongs were my favorite. So I often incorporate sound therapy into my Reiki sessions. It came in organically and then blended very quickly. I took reflexology training too and incorporated that sometimes.

Some of my students want a broad range of clientele while others have a specific focus. Some work pre- and postnatally, others with hospice or with animals. It's important to decide whether you want to specialize or if you'd like to work with a broad spectrum.

It's a lot of pressure to take a weekend class and decide, "This will be my life and business. This is how I will support myself." It can be a big letdown when people realize that it takes a lot of work to build a business and clientele. It takes 10 years to become an overnight success.

But it really gets me excited to see how people incorporate Reiki into their daily lives. I love watching them decide, "How am I going to live Reiki?"

I have students who are physicians or MDs who work in child psychology. They don't intend to create a Reiki practice but use Reiki on themselves and to clear their space. One physician said it made a huge shift in her work environment.

I also have at least three different lawyers who studied with me. It's an interesting combination. One mediates divorces and other very real-world things that people deal with. She brings Reiki into situations to help people with the massive decisions they need to make. Reiki helps her at the end of the day, too.

One of my best friends creates potions and sprays from essential oils and built an incredible business. Her oils are infused with Reiki. Another student creates and sells Reiki dolls.

I tell my students, "The sky's the limit as far as what you can combine Reiki with. What do you like to do in your daily life? Because you can bring Reiki to every facet of your life."

I loved reading about creating your script: how to talk to people when they ask you about Reiki. It can be challenging to speak as eloquently as we intend. Even now, I sometimes get flustered when people ask. So I created a card about Reiki. It has my contact information, so it's a nice little promotional tool. When someone asks me what Reiki is, I say, here's a card that explains it. I can also look at the card myself if I'm feeling a moment of anxiety or if my mind is blank.

Plug and play different things into your script and add what Reiki means to you. Your script may change over time as you learn more so be open and rewrite it as your understanding of Reiki grows.

Creating a business name is important if you create a stand-alone business. I changed my business name recently. I had to shift to a new website, change over my contacts, and change my business name with the state. I put off so many changes, but I finally did it, and it's been a good thing.

My business name came to me during a Karuna Reiki® class. The name "Heart Rhythm Reiki" came through in the very final ignition. I thought, "Surely that's taken." But as I checked on it, my heart expanded. It wasn't. At the end of class, I said, "I just have to share this name: Heart Rhythm Reiki." Everyone exhaled. It was right. So my business name came through a divine shift guided by Reiki.

As you create your way of sharing Reiki, take the pressure off of yourself. There's no reason to rush or to drive yourself into the ground. Take your time. And enjoy your time as a "new Reiki practitioner". You're only a new practitioner once, and the journey is as important as the destination.

Check out our podcast on this chapter.[3]

∼

STUDENT SUCCESS STORY **Helen Michaels**
The Mentor course helped me by being with other people so committed to Reiki. It was very grounded, practical, and step-by-step. And in the exercises, Reiki really brought in my direction. I wasn't thrilled with the direction at first as I was asked to make a bold move as an artist.

BUT YOUR CLASS INSPIRED ME. I was one of the people asking you to mentor me. You said you weren't ready and in a way that was another way of teaching me. You had to do it in your time and your way and I had to be patient. Then you offered all the pieces in one shot in the course. Watching the other students open up and do their thing with Reiki, gave me courage.

YOUR CLASS HELPED me see that my Reiki business can be art. Reiki affected my art, from the beginning but the fine art world is not open to Reiki or energy. The mentor class brought it all together though and things began to move forward.

I LEARNED a whole new way of painting to express the sort of energy and healing that horses and Reiki do together. It's focused on light with a limited palette. It's very different than how I learned to paint. I only painted one horse in college as it was completely unacceptable and wound up in the trash. So a lot came up for me to be healed with this work.

HORSES SEND energy through the eyes - with Gyoshi-ho. So I painted each horse in the healing herd I work with very specifically so that it would be an eye-to-eye experience. I wanted people to have that intense connection we get out in the pasture working with them.

I CREATED a Reiki art installation of the work which just finished its maiden voyage in public. It was very unusual in a lot of ways. I have not displayed paintings in the fine art world for a long time. In my artist bio, I owned my truth and told people the art was imbued with Reiki. I didn't have anything to sell which is audacious in the art crowd. Some people were really upset that they were not for sale. Normally that would bother me. But thanks to Reiki, it didn't. I will eventually make prints available, but they are not ready yet.

DURING THE EXHIBIT, people said, "This is some of the best work in here." Others said "it's the best thing in the building." But I didn't need them to like it. One woman who enjoyed the art wants to book a Reiki session. I didn't anticipate that. Established artists treated me as a peer. On two separate occasions, women who said they never cry stood there and sobbed. One said she thinks it's what heaven looks like. It was an abundant experience for me in a whole different way and is still a bit of a head rush for me. I don't know where it's all going but I'm happy to be along for the ride.

---

1. http://reikilifestyle.wpengine.com/wp-content/uploads/2014/10/The_Spirit_of_Your_Reiki_Business.pdf
2. http://www.heartrhythmreiki.com/
3. https://www.buzzsprout.com/1364386/10061497

3

RELEASING THE OBSTACLES TO YOUR BUSINESS SUCCESS

"When I started to believe in myself, relax within myself, and release and overcome these obstacles, my life became easier and more aligned with what I truly want."
Tracey Sullivan, LRMT

Obstacles

The main obstacle to getting started is... getting started. When we are ready to start a Reiki business, so many layers come up to be healed that we often believe we are not ready or not worthy to move forward. The truth is, we are putting ourselves out there with Reiki. And we still may not have fully come to terms with it within ourselves. A Reiki business is not only a way to share the gift of Reiki with others, but it is a way to grow our connection with Reiki, Source, and ourselves.

The number of obstacles that will arise is enormous. Here are a few examples.

- Do I know enough to become a Reiki practitioner/teacher?
- What if I fail?
- Who am I to think I can do this?
- Is it right to charge money for Reiki?
- Will anyone want to see me?
- Starting a business is too complicated. I don't have any business skills.
- I'm not sure I'm the right person for this.
- I'm not particularly talented. I don't have gifts or clairvoyance. Should I even try to do this?
- What if people think Reiki is weird? And think I'm weird for doing it?
- What if people make fun of me?
- What if I don't know the answer to a question?
- Can I really make a living doing this? Should I?
- Who am I to be a Reiki Master? Healer? Teacher?

Do you recognize any of these? There are many more. But these are pretty common. Others may come up too. If and when they do, I hope you recognize them for what they are: resistance. Resistance is usually caused by the unhealed or wounded ego. The best way to heal the ego is to go into situations that make you feel vulnerable. As you do, unhealed parts of your ego come up to heal. Simultaneously, old injuries and limiting beliefs come to the surface to release. There is a tremendous amount of growth available to us when we stretch out of our comfort zone and put ourselves out into the world with Reiki.

Sometimes we get in our way with limiting beliefs or reluctance to step into our power. That's certainly been a big part of the journey for me. I remember when my guidance first started coming in. I would resist. I'd receive some guidance, and would say "No, I'm not going to do that." Eventually, I started saying "maybe" to nudges and guidance. And finally, recently, I have learned it's always in my best interest to say yes. Even and especially if I don't know what I'm doing. Or Reiki is pushing me out of my comfort zone.

~

Common obstacles:
1. Money

Now some of you may have difficulty accepting money for Reiki. I certainly did. This reluctance is one of the biggest obstacles to creating a successful Reiki practice or business. But if our purpose is to share the gift of Reiki with the world, a business is a very effective and efficient way to spread this healing energy. Modern business practices are universally understood, offer a venue for energetic exchange, and provide tools that can help spread the gift of Reiki in the world.

Despite how we may feel about it, money is neither good nor bad. It is a form of exchange. Yet so many of us have a charge around money. Some of us may have even taken vows of poverty or servitude in the past that need to be cleared. If you have a charge around money, if your belief system doesn't allow you to charge money for spiritual work, or if thoughts of money stress you out, apply liberal amounts of Reiki to heal these unhealthy, limiting beliefs and practices.

When we charge for our work, it's not that we're charging for the energy, we are charging for our time. And if you aren't compensated for your time, you can't take more Reiki classes or provide healing to as many people. You can't support yourself or your family.

Charging money for Reiki sessions was a huge obstacle for me. It was something I was really uncomfortable with. Once I worked through it so that it was no longer uncomfortable for me, it was no longer uncomfortable for my clients. But while it was still uncomfortable in me, it was uncomfortable for my clients. And that robbed them of the opportunity of receiving Reiki, just as it robbed me of the opportunity of sharing more Reiki.

I was working like crazy to pay for my horses and my courses so I could turn around and give things away. Then, in meditation with my horses, I realized that I could spend more time with them and Reiki, doing what I loved, if I would simply allow myself to be compensated for the work I was doing.

Later, I watched a presentation William Rand gave at a Reiki Retreat. He said, "When you don't charge a person for Reiki, you take a balance of power over them." I was mortified. I never meant to take a balance of power. I never wanted my clients to feel uncomfortable. And I realized, I would not be comfortable receiving a treatment if I were unable to compensate the practitioner. So I made peace with charging money. And you know what? My business flourished. When I didn't charge, people didn't come back. Imagine that?

There is an affirmation from Louise Hay that I repeat and meditate with, as I activate Reiki to help heal this issue. "I charge a fair price for my services, and everyone around me benefits." It has helped several of my students as well. Give it a try.

2. Confidence, Fear, and the Unhealed Ego

A lack of confidence is generally created by fear -- which comes from an unhealed ego. The good news is Reiki can heal our ego, remind us we are vessels or channels for Reiki, and that working with others is not about us. It is about connecting the Reiki energy with the person who has asked to connect with it. Every single one of us is capable of doing that after we are connected to the energy via an attunement. And if fear, lack of confidence, or an unhealed ego is present, it doesn't matter. Reiki flows and works anyway.

A lack of confidence in ourselves, in Reiki, or even in God can hold us back. However, lack of confidence in all of these things can be treated with liberal amounts of Reiki. I can't tell you how nervous I got before giving Reiki sessions until they became comfortable to me. Or how terrified I was to teach until I had some great classes under my belt. And even now, I get incredibly nervous before just about every speaking engagement.

Yet the best way to build confidence is to acknowledge the fear or nerves and invite Reiki to help you move through them. You gain confidence in Reiki by using it repeatedly with clients, friends, and family and receiving feedback from them.

You will gain confidence in God (whatever name you wish to use) as you use Reiki and witness the miracles and lucky "coincidences" that ensue.

And you will gain confidence in yourself with practice and as you expand your understanding and relationship with Reiki.

But what if my Reiki energy doesn't work? Will my session be good enough? What if my intuition doesn't help me? Do it anyway. The energy always works for the highest good of the client, even on the odd occasion it doesn't appear to.

I had a client who wanted me to work on his knee. But I kept being drawn back to his heart. After the session, I asked how his knee felt. It felt no better than before. I acknowledged that Reiki sometimes took time. I said he may improve down the road and advised him that I was continually drawn back to his heart. This made no sense to him, and I could tell he was disappointed with the session.

I saw him downtown three months later. He ran over and said, " Guess what? It didn't make sense at the time when you said you were drawn back to my heart. But I thought about it and realized that I never stopped caring for my ex-girlfriend and despised my job. Something happened in that session that healed my heart, and now

I'm in a new relationship that makes me happy and I have a new job that I love. So I guess the session worked after all even though my knee feels much as it did!"

3. Intuition

You don't have to use your intuition in sessions. Some practitioners offer a lot of "information" and "advice" during Reiki sessions. I avoid that type of practitioner. I prefer to receive Reiki and be allowed to be in my own experience. If I have questions afterward about something I don't understand and they have insight, great. But I don't appreciate unsolicited advice. It is often filtered through the practitioner's reality which is not always in alignment with mine. I prefer sessions where Reiki energy flows. At the end of the session, the practitioner might tell me where they noticed a greater flow, etc. I'll book a psychic reading if I need intuitive advice. In a Reiki session, I want to receive Reiki.

And if your intuition is not fully developed yet - well, that is why Mrs. Takata brought in the hand positions. They always work. I have received powerful treatments from level 1 practitioners who were brand new to Reiki and not at all familiar with their intuition. Let Reiki do the work.

And if the client isn't happy, you can always offer to refund their money. The best way you can learn and grow in confidence is to practice! I guess that's why they call it a Reiki practice.

In the first class he taught, William Rand said he thought he would need to refund everyone's money as he didn't feel anything happening during the attunement. But, he says he is happy he did not speak first. His students were clairvoyant, experienced energy practitioners. They reported incredible experiences. William realized that Reiki responds to our clients' and students' intention to work with it. We are simply a channel. Even if we don't notice a lot happening, as long as we move our ego and personal energy aside, pure Reiki energy flows through us to our clients and students. It's not about us.

4. Time

Going through the steps of creating a Reiki business takes time. Remember the phrase, "It takes 10 years to become an overnight success." So despite our best intentions, it can be difficult to carve out the time to create our business. Particularly if we have young children, a demanding job, or otherwise busy lives.

There are a few things that can help. I tried to break this book down into a way that creates confidence and prevents overwhelm. If you work through one task at a time, even if they are not in order with the book, it will come together. But you also need to commit time to your calendar. I block off time in my calendar to work on my book, my marketing, my podcast, etc. Or they wouldn't happen.

I also use an app called Focus Keeper. It keeps track of time for 25 minutes, with a 5-minute break. I can do anything for 25 minutes. So even if I don't feel like it, I make myself sit down and work on the tasks in front of me for 25 minutes. Typically, once the 25-minute timer chimes, I'm into what I am doing and if time allows, I keep going.

You may also have to look at your calendar and give something up. To create this book for you, I had to give up yoga classes and walk the dogs less than I like. And while I didn't give up self-care, I did a bit less and organized it to occur one day of the week. My husband normally cooks, but I contribute. My contributions had to cease.

I have a friend who says, "If you are saying yes to that, what are you saying no to?" One of my students hired a sitter to carve out time to work on her business. Afterward, her young children told her they were proud of her for following her dream to build a Reiki practice.

Another thing to keep in mind is you don't have to do everything yourself. Are there tasks you can ask for help with? You can hire help, trade services for help, or simply accept a favor. But you don't have to do every step yourself. Be open to assistance and ask Reiki to help you find it.

Finally, if there just isn't time in your life but a Reiki business is calling to you, ask Reiki for help. It can often re-organize things so they work out.

5. Organizational skills

Maybe you feel scattered and unorganized. Or even overwhelmed. This book and Reiki can help. Spend a few moments in Gassho, activating Reiki before you begin to work. Spend some time with your hands on the back of your head to balance the creative and logical sides of the brain as you also activate the "mouth of God" chakra. If you are in the creative process, send Reiki to your sacral chakra. And if you are communicating or marketing, send Reiki to your throat chakra.

If you still feel unorganized, put together a list. And remember, as Laurelle Gaia suggested, you can put the tasks into a bowl or jar, give it Reiki then choose one. This allows Reiki to choose your task for you. Organizing you. It might not be the order you would have chosen. But it typically works. The order often aligns with Divine timing. If you can spend 25-50 minutes per day every day just knocking tasks off your list, you will be amazed by how quickly things come together for you.

Apply Reiki regularly to release organizational blocks and you will be amazed at how organized you become too.

6. Knowledge

Often, there is so much healing that happens during class that we miss a lot of theory and information. We can pick up the information in a well-designed manual if we received one or in books, articles, and podcasts. But one of the most effective ways to increase your knowledge of Reiki is to review a class. Some teachers allow you to repeat a class at a reduced fee if you took the first class at a full fee with them. But, even if they don't, it is often worthwhile to review classes.

You may be guided to another teacher or lineage to review a class. It is well worth paying the full price again. There is probably something that teacher has to offer that you need. And not only will you receive additional healing and knowledge from the class, but you will also gain additional experience should you ever consider teaching.

I have students who review classes with me and say they learn something new every time. Partly because my teaching evolves and also because the group dynamic changes so new conversations happen. Students report that they can retain more information or that they hear it differently so it has a different meaning for them. They also notice the experiences and attunements go deeper. Usui Sensei conducted *reijus* or attunements every time he met with his students. Your connection with Reiki expands with every attunement and class. Your confidence grows, too.

I have taken each Reiki class 3-4 times, from 3-4 different teachers, and I learn something significant and new in every class. My connection with Source expands. And it's not linear. I can get as much from taking a level 1&2 class again–even though I have taught the class hundreds of times–as I can from an advanced class. My frequency and connection expand every time. And each class provides an opportunity for intense, focused healing that my busy lifestyle does not always allow.

7. Self Doubt
My husband once told me before a big speaking event, "I think it's

good that you get nervous before these events. It shows you are humble and that it's important to you." I don't love feeling nervous or the self-doubt that shows up every time I attempt something out of my comfort zone. Yet, I realize this is how we learn and grow. Every time I experience self-doubt, I am growing, learning, and becoming more with Reiki. So I smile now as I remind myself that it's not about me. I invite Reiki to flow through me to calm me. And I can invite it to guide, lead, even conduct the session. So I do.

8. Doubt about Reiki

I can't tell you how many times I asked for "proof" that something was happening in my Reiki sessions. I wasn't as dialed into my intuition at first. So if I thought something was happening, I would ask God for proof. Inevitably, I would receive undeniable and irrevocable proof that something happened. Usually, it was what my fledgling intuition intuited. One day, during a Reiki session, as was my custom, I asked, "If this is working for my client, can you show me proof?" when I heard the clear, deep voice of Source say, "Daughter, I have given you proof 486 times. It is time to have some faith!" I couldn't argue with that. So I stopped asking for proof and decided to trust Reiki.

I believe that if you aren't sure you can trust Reiki, the best antidote is to use it repeatedly and observe the results. It's not long before you begin to trust the "proof" Reiki provides.

9. Social Conditioning

Sometimes, our social conditioning is an obstacle. For example, we believe things have to be "hard" or "difficult" to work. In my social conditioning, hard work led to success. And work was not meant to be enjoyable. If those beliefs are part of your social conditioning, you may need to let them go. It is really rewarding, effortless, and enjoyable to work with Reiki. And it would be a shame if you are blocked by social conditioning or beliefs that prevent this. We experience ease and joy when we are in alignment with our life path and with Source. Suffering need not be part of our experience.

It may also be part of your social conditioning to believe there is a "right way" to practice Reiki or to be a healer. When you think of how many people there are on the planet, you realize that everyone has their own perspective, their own version of reality. Add to that that everything evolves. And you begin to see that there is no "one right way."

And finally, depending on how much experience you have with Reiki, you may have experienced miracles--some of them large, some of them small, all of them astounding. Let go of your expectations and allow Reiki to do what it does. You are bringing form to the formless--creating something new.

Social conditioning causes us to live our lives via the beliefs of others. It is time to let those go so we can decide which beliefs we want to live our lives by.

10. Past Experience and Past-Life Experience

There is never a need to be limited by experiences from our past. Whether they are from past lives or past experiences. Let go of the limiting belief that "this always happens to me" and the expectations that come with that.

Many of us experience extreme resistance when it is time to step into our power. I don't know if you believe in other lifetimes or not, and I struggled with it myself. But I do believe now that we have lived other lifetimes. And I'm pretty sure that in past lifetimes or maybe even in this life, I have abused my power. So that brought incredible resistance to stepping into my power in this lifetime.

And some of us, in this life or other lifetimes, have taken vows that limit us. Some are vows of poverty or service, etc. Even in baptismal services, there can be language you no longer agree with. It can be worthwhile to examine the words you used or that were used on your behalf in spiritual or religious ceremonies. You may still be in alignment with them and if so, that is fine. But if these vows, oaths, or promises are not helpful or aligned with your soul's path, it is time to let them go.

We may also carry injuries or trauma from this lifetime and/or previous lifetimes. Again, it is best to release those so that you can move forward with a clean slate, unencumbered by the burden of them.

11. Inner Critic

Sometimes the most difficult obstacle to overcome is our inner critic. At one point in my Reiki journey, Reiki pointed out how my inner voice treated me. It wasn't kind or pleasant. It was very critical. Many people's inner voices treat them this way.

During my session, the Reiki energy asked the inner critic to come forward. I saw it as a workplace intervention perhaps as a result of my time working in Human Resources. The inner critic was asked to sit down across the desk as Reiki explained that I was making a change in direction. And the way the inner critic was speaking to me would no longer be tolerated.

It made me chuckle and was really poignant for me. At the same time, the energy conducted this intervention most lovingly. It said, "If you would like to be part of the new direction, here's some energy to help you heal, and to help you move forward." Then the light of compassion flowed through the inner critic, allowing it to be kinder and more compassionate.

It was told it would have three chances to get it right. And the enlightened beings who assist me offered to point out when my inner critic fell back into her old ways so I could remind her that it needed to be kind.

My inner critic had been SO critical it was ridiculous. When I wondered if I would EVER talk to another person the way my inner voice talked to me, the answer was NEVER. And the standard that it held me to left no room for error.

My life has become smoother, gentler, and more enjoyable now that the inner critic is kinder. Yours can be too.

12. Clutter

Our outer world always resembles our inner world. With each Reiki class I take, I come home and declutter my home--the same home that I consciously admire before I leave. I return home and wonder where all the clutter came from.

If you are ready to create a Reiki business, look at the space you are working in. Your office space, desk, chair, living room. Wherever you are, ask yourself, "Is it beautiful and uncluttered?" If not, then that external clutter is a sign that perhaps you are not quite ready to embark on this new venture.

You may have a favorite method of decluttering, but if you don't, check out Marie Kondo's KonMari method. When I came home from working with Animal Reiki the first time, I had just discovered Marie Kondo's shows on Netflix. As always, I left home and flew to Portland, Oregon, to work with the energy thinking how lovely my home was. Yet the nudges I received from Reiki caused me to watch every episode while I was away. I purchased her book on the way home, read it, and returned ready to roll. I love how she connects with the energy of a house and asks it to help make the home beautiful as intended. She asks us to look for a "ting" of love and appreciation for each item we keep. And to thank each item we let go, blessing it so that it might make someone else happy. I also loved how my home looked and felt when I finished. It was a long process. I got through my closet in a week. But books took longer. So did kitchen and bathroom things. But eventually, I made it through almost all the areas of my house. It looks amazing. Other upgrades followed naturally. And as I continue to grow in Reiki, the process continues.

Recently, I was striving to make peace within myself between the spiritual practice of Reiki and the material practices of business. I was nudged by Reiki to notice that my office was uncluttered, but my desk and online teaching space was still too cluttered to invite more business. I was guided to declutter my outer world or office/teaching space. This prompted the corresponding internal declutter, which then invited business to flow.

So look around. If any areas of your life need to be decluttered, it's time to make a plan and get to them. Even 25 minutes at a time. It's also not as overwhelming as it seems if you take it in stages.

I did a podcast with Karen Caig on her decluttering journey with KonMari followed by a healing meditation if you need extra help.[1]

13. Shadow Self

Finally, in shadow-self work, we learn that the shadow self is the part of ourselves we are uncomfortable with, so we shove it deep down inside. It takes a lot of effort to keep that part submerged, away from the surface. And we often shove it down so hard and for so long that we become disconnected from it and are not even aware that it is there. All the effort it takes to keep it hidden does not diminish its strength. Instead, it makes it stronger.

How do you know if you have a shadow self? Easy. There is someone or something in your life that drives you crazy! Seriously. If there is someone in your life that gives you a charge, that is because they are reflecting something that exists within you that you don't accept. This can get in the way of moving forward in your Reiki journey and with your Reiki business.

What do you do about it? Well, you think about the person/people/things in your life that drive you crazy--one at a time. You journal about what it is about them that drives you crazy with the understanding that some part of this exists within you. And you do Reiki until it heals completely. You can also check out the podcast I did on the shadow self. It includes a powerful shadow-self meditation.[2]

What I was guided to do whenever obstacles came up is remember that I've got Reiki to help with the obstacles. It doesn't matter if I was aware of the obstacle or not. Reiki was always aware of them and capable of releasing them.

Regardless of what the obstacle is. It may be a real, physical limitation, or a monetary, mental, spiritual, energetic, or emotional limitation. No matter what it is, Reiki can help.

∼

EXERCISE: Part 1: Identify the Obstacles That May Be Holding You Back

Think about your life purpose and your Reiki practice, activate Reiki and invoke your Reiki symbols. Meditate for a few minutes with Reiki. Ask what your obstacles are and pay attention to the images, words, feelings, or understandings you receive.

Then grab a pen and paper and write them down. Don't think about it very much; we're going to use a bit of automatic writing, tapping into our instinct. Write as complete a list as possible. Anything you can think of that could get in your way and make it difficult to accomplish your objectives.

If you think of something later, just add it to the list. But for now, see if you can completely exhaust every block and barrier. If there's a person in your life who might get in your way because they object to what you're doing, you can include them in your list as well.

EXERCISE: **Part 2: Identify the Opportunities**
Give some thought and just write your responses to the following statements as quickly as you can:

1. If there were no limits for me, what are the top three things I would love to achieve with my Reiki business?
2. What opportunities exist for me?
3. What are my strengths?

MEDITATION: **Release Obstacles and Empower Opportunities**
This is a Reiki healing experience specifically designed to help you grow your Reiki connection and move into your life purpose with Reiki. This meditation is based on the Holy Fire® Healing Experience taught in ICRT Usui/Holy Fire® Reiki Master classes.

Begin by bringing your hands into Gassho with the thumbs at the heart as you invite your Reiki energy to flow. We invite the Reiki symbols and the spiritual teachers of your lineage, your guides, the divine earth, the angels and archangels, the enlightened beings, and the divine animal kingdom, all to be with us today. Supporting us in our work and helping us to recognize what that is for us.

Notice the Reiki energy flowing all around you.

Place your hands comfortably on your body now giving yourself

Reiki and making yourself comfortable. Close your eyes and take a few deep breaths.

The light of Reiki is here in the room. Invite it to guide you.

Imagine that it's a beautiful day, warm and sunny and that you're walking down a path in a beautiful forest. As you breathe into yourself, you breathe in the life energy of the forest. And with each step that you take, you feel the energy of the earth flowing up through the bottoms of your feet.

As you walk along, you notice another path going off to the right, and you decide to follow that path. As you follow that path, you come to a clearing in the forest, and in the middle of the clearing is a small hill covered with soft grass and beautiful wildflowers.

As you climb up the hill, feel the grass rubbing against your legs. And when you get to the top of the hill, lie down in the tall grass, feel the grass and the earth beneath your body, and gaze up into the sky.

Gaze up into the sky and see the beautiful white clouds there. As you're gazing up at the clouds, a beautiful beam of light begins to shine down all around you. This is no ordinary light. It is a beautiful beam of Reiki energy that comes directly from the Source of all of that is. The light shines all around you and even flows into you filling you with warmth and feelings of safety and love.

The light now focuses directly on all of the obstacles, blocks, or barriers that you have identified that might be in the way or could get in the way of achieving your life purpose with Reiki. Anything that might prevent you from fully stepping into your power and place in the world. I invite you to focus on those obstacles yourself and simply be willing to let them go. You do not have to do anything to earn this. I simply invite you to be willing to let them go.
Pause.

Now gaze directly into the light, and as you do, the light will begin to guide you. This light is Reiki energy that comes directly from Source. You can decide whether or not to follow the guidance, but for now, the light can show you the next steps in your Reiki journey.

And it can show you what a successful Reiki practice looks like to you. And at the same time can empower the goals that you have set to paper previously, forming an intention. Please don't try to direct the energy. Allow it to direct you and follow the direction you receive.
Pause.

Sometimes we feel overwhelmed. Sometimes we put pressure on ourselves, and sometimes we feel guilty or discouraged because we have not accomplished more sooner. If those feelings exist around your Reiki path or your Reiki journey, invite them to leave. They have no place here.

The Reiki journey is meant to be joyous. It is not meant to add pressure or strain to your life. It is meant to bring about a greater connection with the divine and with ourselves, to enhance the journey. So we purposefully release any guilt or shame or blame or doubt or overwhelm. Any feelings that would get in the way of joyously moving forward at the pace that feels right to us and in the manner that feels right to every one of us.
Pause.

You have everything you need to step into the next phase or the next to take the next step in your Reiki journey. To step into your power and create a successful Reiki practice, whatever that looks like to you.

We invite the Reiki energy to empower our sense of purpose on the path to sharing Reiki with others. You may find yourself filled with energy and enthusiasm. You may find the qualities that you need to move forward on this path. You may find yourself filled with light and love and purpose.

Please continue with your experience as long as you feel guided. Then, when you are ready, take a few deep breaths, bring your awareness to your eyes, slowly open your eyes, and return. Take a few moments to write about your experience

∼

MEDITATION 2: **Advanced Meditation to Release Obstacles and Empower Opportunities**

Because obstacles can be complex and show up in stages, it seems we need a second meditation to release them to move further down the path. You can put this meditation away for now, until you realize obstacles are once more blocking your path and then pull it out.

Begin by bringing your hands into Gassho with the thumbs at the heart as you invite your Reiki energy to flow. We invite the Reiki symbols and the spiritual teachers of your lineage, your guides, the divine earth, the angels and archangels, the enlightened beings, and the divine animal kingdom, all to be with us today. Supporting us in our work and helping us to recognize what that is for us.

Notice the Reiki energy flowing all around you.

Place your hands comfortably on your body now giving yourself Reiki and making yourself really comfortable. Close your eyes and take a few deep breaths.

The light of Reiki is here in the room. Invite it to guide you as we acknowledge our life purpose and step into our power. Stepping into our work, we invite the energy of joy and ease and comfort to flow through us, our path, and our work.

We ask as we move into our direction that guidance occurs at the pace that is the most comfortable for us, whether it be rapid or slow or moves back and forth between the two.

And we ask that Reiki connect us with the highest source of enlightened spiritual energy in the enlightened spiritual realms for the best and highest outcome.

As we become familiar with and comfortable in our divine purpose, we remember that unlike the drudgery of other types of work, when we follow our divine purpose, there is a sense of rightness and ease and comfort and joy.

And there is a sense of divine accomplishment, which is very different from the types of accomplishment that we know. It is a sense that we are exactly where we are meant to be because we are. And it is the understanding that we are working according to Divine timing.

We feel peace and ease in all that we do. Reiki surrounds us and fills the room so that only illumined beings are present in the space and only illumined ideas.

And we come today, with one mind and one heart with a desire to spread God's love to others through the gift of Reiki, in whatever form that shows up to us.

We ask that we be blessed with your presence and your guidance and that you help us to better understand our Reiki path so that we grow in confidence.

And we ask that the next layer of obstacles that would stand in the way of accomplishing our objectives in the months to come be removed so that we can step into our life path to step into our power.

Whatever form the obstacles may take--fear, overwhelm, limitation, worry, acceptance, or any other form that shows up--we invite the light of Reiki to remove them for us now.

We invite abundance and prosperity into our practices. We invite our connection with you and with Reiki to continue to grow. We invite health and wellness into our bodies and those of our clients. We ask the enlightened beings to assist us to remain on our path. We invite assistance with discipline and self-love so that we can continue to grow and heal. Even, and especially, when we forget to ask.

We give thanks, enduring gratitude, for all that you do for us, for the enlightened beings, and we're grateful to live in an abundant society where we are allowed freedom of spiritual and religious expression. And we thank you for the gift of Reiki. We take a moment now to say thank you to every Reiki practitioner on the planet, raising the vibration of the Earth with their light. We are blessed to be of a lineage of light-bringers in the world today. And we say, thank you to the teachers who have come before us and to the teacher that we are becoming. For whether or not you choose to teach Reiki, by simply choosing to live your life with integrity, and in Reiki, you are choosing to become an example to others--a teacher.

I invite you to take a moment and consider whether there may be any obstacles or blocks in front of you preventing you from creating a successful Reiki practice, whatever that looks like to you. And if there are blocks and barriers, I invite you to think for a moment, if those blocks existed in a part of your body, where would they be?

What shape would they have?

What color would they be?

What would the surface texture look like?

Are they heavy or light?

Ask yourself if you're willing to let them go today? Even if you don't believe that it's possible, you don't have to know how to let them go. You don't need to know what needs to happen to let them go. You simply need to be willing. And so if there are any blocks or barriers or obstacles for you today, and you're willing to let them go, I invite you to just breathe them into the Reiki energy that flows in, on your breath.

And it releases those obstacles for you and releases any limiting beliefs. Any fear, any anxiety, any lack of confidence, any worries around worthiness, and it releases the energy of perfectionism, the belief that everything has to be perfect and ready before we can step out into the world. Let Reiki release anything that would get in the way of this beautiful energy, of the friendship that you wish and intend to create with Reiki. Let it release any worries about the expectations of others, any fear that you may not be able to overcome. When we release all of these energies with love into a place where they will be listened to and heard and nurtured, we can heal any blocks or barriers, even if we are unaware of them and even if I have not mentioned what would get in the way of your relationship with the Reiki energy and your relationship with your Reiki business, no matter how far into the future that may be.

We release them now with love.

We'll take a few moments to breathe into that space, releasing any blocks or barriers, any limiting beliefs, anything that might hold you back.

And if the limiting belief is around your intuition, if you're worried, you're not hearing it right, or if you fear that your ego may not be in a place of healing and that it may step in, we release those fears as well. We bring the ego forward to receive healing because the healed ego becomes a beautiful tool for manifesting spiritual realities in the physical plane.

And if we have any issues around abundance or supporting ourselves with spiritual work, if we have any old vows or promises or curses or spells around that may be holding us back from stepping forward into our life purpose, if we have made vows of poverty or suffering or any other vows or promises we may have made in other lifetimes, or this one, we release those too, with love, into the light where they will be cared for on our behalf.

We invite abundance and prosperity into our practices. We invite the understanding that not only is it all right to support ourselves with a spiritual practice, but in doing so, we may help a great number of others.

We invite the lights of health and wellness and abundance for both ourselves and our clients.

And we ask God to assist us as we remain on our path to continue healing, to continue growing, to continue in our development.

We invite the light of self-love, the love that is required to care for ourselves. As we step forward onto the path of assisting others. We are grateful to live in this abundant and free society today, where we have the freedom of spiritual and religious expression. And we say, thank you for the gift of Reiki.

Aho. Namaste. Amen. And so it is.

ProTip
Tracey Sullivan, LRMT, Connecticut, USA
Reiki Integration[3]

I learned Reiki to help others, but Reiki wound up helping me! I was in crisis and felt hopeless in my first Reiki class but hope was restored. It had such a profound effect that I decided to take it as far as I could. In internet searches, William Rand's name continued to show up so I studied the Master class with him in Glens Falls, NY. Later, my intuition led me to apply for the Licensed Teacher Program.

I COMPLETED the program and built my practice, always alongside a full-time job. I incorporated Reiki into my work and other aspects of my life and began to look at my whole life as part of my Reiki practice.

THE MAIN OBSTACLE for me was my fear of what people would think. I was working in a hospital and nobody ever talked about Reiki where I work in nuclear medicine, which is diagnostic radiology. I work with very science-minded people. So I did not tell anybody that I had taken a Reiki class. One of my friends and coworkers suggested that I give Reiki to other coworkers if they had a headache or were upset, and I cringed inside. Now, years later it's just so natural, and I don't have any circumstances where I feel uncomfortable talking about Reiki or offering Reiki. But initially, I did.

EVENTUALLY, more and more people approached me for a Reiki session. So I would go into one of our little injection rooms with my coworkers and give them 10 minutes of Reiki. They had great results from the sessions. It is so hard to describe Reiki to somebody. Especially when you're new to it. So this was something that would take the place of any words that I could use to describe Reiki to this group of people.

. . .

From there, I created many Reiki presentations for diagnostic radiology and different areas of the hospital. I wound up teaching Reiki at the hospital, and I continue to teach there today.

Another obstacle was a knowledge-based thing. For some reason, I felt I needed to know everything about Reiki. Reiki showed me that this is the way that I view myself in my entire life that I don't ever feel like I know enough. I went through a large portion of my life thinking that I wasn't intelligent enough. It was a real eye-opener. And I don't think that I ever would've recognized that about myself without my Reiki practice.

Reiki helped me see those obstacles and heal them. So even though I wasn't a full-time Reiki practitioner, I started to look at everything in my life as part of my Reiki practice because Reiki can affect everything in your life. We are a total being, we don't have little sections of ourselves.

When I was going through the LRMT program, time and organizational skills were huge obstacles for me. You may think that to do what I did, I must be an organized person, but I'm not, and that was a huge obstacle. Lack of time, organization, and procrastination, all seem to be big obstacles for me.

A couple of times, I ran into a problem where people were upset. I learned that when that happens, it's not about the other person. At first, I became upset and thought about giving up. But Reiki made me focus on myself. Because you can be in any situation that exists. And you have the choice of how to react to it: what you will think about it and what you will do about it. So I continue to resolve that obstacle because it continues to be a thing for me.

AT TIMES when I had things to complete for the ICRT, I just put them off and discovered that I have a problem with procrastination. So I began making myself complete tasks right away, whatever the task was. And another thing I did was concentrate on learning how to do things more efficiently. So instead of scanning in one paper at a time, I learned to scan a whole file so I could send all of my paperwork in at once. And I know it might not seem like a big deal, but it became very stressful for me during that time. But Reiki helped me, and it still helps me, to change that and become a more organized person. And it helped me stop procrastinating and get more organized.

AND I BELIEVE I'm not as intelligent as I want to be. The combination of my applications job and Reiki allowed me to look at that. Because if you don't acknowledge something, it comes back. I spent most of my adult life not acknowledging this. But I had deep inner guidance to take a job that, in hindsight, helped me understand that this view of myself is not true. I am so much more than I thought I was.

THE THING that helps me to release all these obstacles is to allow myself to be still throughout the day, no matter where I am. I have a really busy job where I travel and I deal with a lot of different people. But being still each day and in every moment of the day, I'm able to remember who I am. We often look at ourselves through someone else's eyes. But if I spend time each day in some type of meditation, I regain stillness and a comfort level with myself.

OBSTACLES SHOW UP to different people in different ways. I thought I didn't have an obstacle with money but after reading this chapter I realized I charge less than I should for Reiki sessions because of my full-time job. I thought I was helping people, but I am controlling the situation and not giving people an opportunity to contribute to their healing.

I TOOK my first Reiki class 12 years ago and it started a whole stream of activities within me that has become this stillness now. When I started to believe in myself, relax within myself, and release and overcome these obstacles, my life became easier and more aligned with what I truly want.

IT RELATES BEAUTIFULLY to this chapter in your book. Reiki has helped me overcome many obstacles to be able to have a beautiful Reiki practice and be able to work at the same time.

CHECK *out our podcast on this chapter.*[4]

∽

STUDENT SUCCESS STORY SHARON R.
I just saw "mentor" with your course and didn't even pay attention that it was about business. I needed a mentor. I was trying to figure out how to work with this energy. How to become confident enough to teach at the Master level. I was just starting to charge money. I had taught a few people and was charging for teaching. And I realized it was good to have the business piece of it but my main objective was to grow my connection with Reiki. The class was beneficial. The meditations were so guided, they were spot on.

INTEGRATING the meditations from the class was huge for me. You can talk about finding your blocks and releasing them, but by doing it when you can feel and see them, they were no longer abstract. We released blocks that I didn't realize were there. Working with a group made the energy stronger and the group dynamic was great. I made connections with other students and stayed in touch. It's helpful to have connections with like-minded people with different perspectives.

WE LEARNED to trust as we worked on each other. Now I can connect and let Reiki flow without trying to control anything. I'm not second-guessing everything. My Reiki sessions are more effective because I'm letting Reiki just do its thing and am able to trust. I had to work out a lack of trust with Reiki. At some point, religious trauma, and cultural or tribal beliefs can show up. And you have to work through all of that stuff to get to the trust.

I CAN FEEL the lightness and openness of Reiki in my energetic field now. The connection is always on. The field is much more extensive, as I realized I had been restricting it. I embraced your point in expanding my connection and using it everywhere. The growth is continuous. I don't have to be vigilant now.

I DIDN'T HAVE TOO much trouble teaching levels one and two. But once I got to the master level and got into the deeper perspective of it, and you're clearing more profound things, and deeper issues come up, that's where I got stuck and needed help. But your teaching has the ring of truth, and you can feel it from the gut up. I have not taught a master's class yet, but I feel ready to.

THERE ARE times when the connection with Reiki was pretty clean and clear, and then another obstacle would come up. Now it's much more comfortable. I had to let go of a lot of religious trauma, beliefs, and dogmas and reconcile the spiritual piece of Reiki with religion. I now have a much broader perspective both. I have more depth of understanding and have integrated it into my religious beliefs and experiences. It'll continue to develop. I've realized that Reiki has the potential to do anything and heal anything and that there's no way to abuse the power of Reiki.

THE MOST POWERFUL meditation for me was the 12 Heavens Meditation. It helped me find my direction, and my path with Reiki. It helped me understand that you can connect to Reiki internally or externally. You can think of God as an off-planet being or of being inside yourself.

THE 12 HEAVENS Meditation linked those concepts and helped me go internally to find all of those areas within myself. It made it easier for me to do self Reiki once I integrated my Divine and human selves. You realize you have every right to connect to spiritual realms because it's in you from that higher self-perspective. You're working in communion and partnership because the divine is also in you.

WHENEVER THERE'S resistance or obstacles, just keep going and get through to the other side. There's a reason for them. It feels so free and liberating to let them go and to trust.

---

1. https://www.buzzsprout.com/1364386/8240872
2. https://www.buzzsprout.com/1364386/7990018
3. https://www.buzzsprout.com/1364386/10061497
4. https://www.buzzsprout.com/1364386/10061462

4

DEVELOP YOUR PRACTICE - GIVING REIKI SESSIONS TO OTHERS

"I needed to start small and gradually grow into my practice, but I know everyone's not there. So do what you're comfortable doing. And have fun. Everything will fall in place at the right time, but allow Reiki to guide you."
Terry Dulin, LRMT

Starting Out - Friends and Family

Initially, when you are ready to step beyond self Reiki, the best people to practice with are friends and family. You don't need to charge friends and family, so it takes a bit of pressure off of you. This initial period is your practice time. Realize, though, that friends and family may be more critical and less supportive than your actual clients. Or they may be more supportive. But you will practice with people you are comfortable with. So you won't have to take the sessions as seriously as you might with paying clients.

This practice time allows you to develop your style, practice taking session notes, and get comfortable in your space. Check in with your client. Ask how they are doing, if they are comfortable, if they enjoyed the session, what they experienced. This is your opportunity to learn and get comfortable conducting Reiki sessions.

You can make your practice sessions professional so that you can practice before moving on to paying clients. Be sure to let your family and friends know that you are practicing but will have a professional practice in the future. You can even run your rates by them for feedback. Then, they can refer friends to help you and won't expect free sessions forever. Meanwhile, enjoy the feedback and have fun developing your style.

Let's talk about fear for a moment, though, shall we? Most of us feel anxiety or nervousness at the thought of putting ourselves out there with Reiki sessions. We wonder if we will do a good enough job. We worry that we will be judged. That we might not get clients. That we might get too many clients which will eat up our free time. That we will get in over our heads. We worry about so many things that it's a wonder anyone practices Reiki at all.

The funny thing about fear and worry is that we often interpret it as warning us away from something. Or believe it is an indication that something is not part of our path. But, the opposite is true. Fear is an indication that something is important to you. That you are really interested in it. If it were not part of your path, you would feel apathetic.

So let's just include fear, worry, concern, discomfort, and all other forms of fear as an obstacle we need Reiki to clear. We can work on it at the end of the chapter. If you feel twinges of nervousness as you read this chapter, that's good. It means you are interested in Reiki and meant to become a Reiki practitioner!

Reiki Session Myth Busting
You should keep several things in mind when conducting a formal Reiki session.

1. The energy does not come from you; it comes from the source of Reiki and will never cause harm. It also never drains your energy. Simply say a prayer before you begin asking your ego, personality, and personal energy to step aside so that only the pure light of Reiki flows through you and into the client. Then, as long as you are physically comfortable as you conduct the Reiki session, you will not be fatigued after your session or sessions. Instead, you will probably feel invigorated from having had all of that Reiki energy flow through you.
2. You may notice that your clients have a "theme, that several are working on similar issues. When this synchronicity happens, it is often a sign that this issue exists within you in some form. Allow the insights the clients and you receive from the sessions, along with Reiki, to help balance you as you help balance your clients. Be aware that this "coincidence" happens for a reason, and thank Reiki for this gift. We can interpret the issue more clearly when we see it in another.
3. You do not need to provide psychic readings or impressions during a Reiki session. Offering a simple, basic Reiki session without bells and whistles is perfectly acceptable. In fact, as a client, I prefer that. I prefer to work with the energy rather than any individual talents of a practitioner. If I want a psychic reading, I book a reading.
4. I also prefer silent Reiki sessions, with no chatter. I don't mind conversation at the beginning when we are assessing the problem, issue, or goal I am working on. But then, I like to hear soft meditation music and silence so I can relax and focus internally.
5. Bear in mind that many people are sensitive to scents. And while we know that includes incense, essential oils, and scented candles; it may also include scents you are wearing either purposefully or inadvertently. I try using a hand soap with very little odor if I am doing hands-on, in-

person sessions. I am also really conscious of not breathing on a client. During one session I received, the practitioner had recently eaten salami. The scent was on her hands and in her breath. It was a very long 40-minute session surrounded by the smell of salami. After that, I vowed to be really careful with that. I use essential oils in my sessions to sweep the energy or on my hands, which I place on their feet after checking with the client to determine their preference and whether they have any allergies or sensitivities. But otherwise, I am conscious of the scents in my environment and on my hands and body.

6. You ARE ready for the clients who come to you. Reiki works to ensure that the client finds the right practitioner for them. I used to worry that a client's issues were above my pay grade, only to find out that Reiki could handle anything when I asked my ego and personal energy to step aside. Even if it seems insurmountable to me. Over time I learned to trust that Reiki sessions are about the client interacting with Reiki. It had nothing to do with me. That allowed me to gain confidence in the energy. If you do not feel confident or comfortable with the energy or giving sessions to people, do self sessions to work on that. Sessions are about allowing the energy to interact with the client in whatever way the client needs. I am just a vessel for the energy to flow through. So I have learned to put aside my doubts and insecurities and turn the entire process over to Reiki.

7. Sometimes, you may not seem to make progress where the client wants. Reiki is Divinely guided and never causes harm. But sometimes, it directs itself to another, underlying issue. I worked on a client's knee in one session but kept being drawn back to his heart. At the end of the session, I explained that to him–and that it didn't make sense to either of us. After the session, his knee was more or less the same as it was, and we were both

disappointed that the session had not worked the way we had hoped. But I ran into him 3-4 months later. He had a massive grin on his face. He said, "Guess what? I think Reiki knew what it was doing. I hadn't mentioned to you and didn't even admit to myself that I was nursing a broken heart. After the session, I thought about it and decided to let it go. Now, I have met someone, I am in love, and I'm happier than I've ever been in my life. My knee still hurts, but I'm so happy."

Basics of an In-person Reiki Session

1. Before the client arrives, cleanse your energy and activate your Reiki. Then draw the Reiki symbols in and around the room.
2. You may wish to clear your client's energy with the distance symbol before they get to your space. I often clear all of my clients in the morning, before our session.
3. Have your client complete the Reiki Documentation form and sign. If your Reiki association or teacher does not provide a Reiki Documentation form, you can create your own. There is a sample form in the Appendices.
4. Once they have completed the front of the form, you complete the back in discussion with your client to determine what they wish to address, whether they prefer touch or beaming, etc.
5. You will also want to ask if they are sensitive to scents or sage if you plan to use them. Discuss their expectations, and don't make promises on behalf of Reiki or yourself. Reiki sessions always work in the client's best interest, and while miracles sometimes happen, they cannot be guaranteed.
6. Add a prayer that the session serves the highest good of your client. Ask your ego and personal energy to step

aside, allowing only the pure light of Reiki to flow through you to your client (this may be one of the most essential parts of the session).

7. You may wish to play quiet music during the session. I love using *Reiki Chants* with Jonathan Goldman and Laurelle Shanti Gaia. The Usui Reiki symbols are chanted in such a way that the client cannot hear their names. But they add another layer of Reiki energy to the session and amplify the results.

8. Optional: You may wish to begin your session with a meditation. In the Holy Fire® lineage, we can choose from several healing meditations, or you can create your own.

9. You can then begin the hands-on portion of the session for in-person sessions. You may choose to use the hand positions Mrs. Takata created for a thorough session. Or you may choose to use the intuitive style of Reiki with Reiji ho and Chiryo that Usui Sensei taught. If your client prefers that you beam Reiki vs. touch, it works just as well as touch.

10. Some practitioners prefer touch or beaming, but I always invite my client to choose. There is not enough touch in the world. For many clients, this is an integral part of the session. For others, contact is uncomfortable. They may be sensitive, or it may bring up old, deep trauma. So I always ask the client for their preference. If they are unsure, I place my hand on their shoulder with the same pressure I would use in their session, showing them what touch feels like. Then I back off and beam the energy. And they get a better idea of which is most comfortable for them.

11. For distance sessions, you can use a surrogate. Draw the distance symbol over the surrogate and intend that it act as a stand-in for your client. You may make an internal statement such as, "As I give a treatment to this (pillow or stuffed animal), I send the treatment to (the name of your

client)." Then begin as above. I conduct distance sessions in real-time with my clients over the phone. Once we have identified what we are working on, I invite them to relax just as they would in an in-person session and allow the energy to flow. I often use a guided healing meditation. And we give the issues an identity (shape, color, size) so we can check our progress at the end of the session. You can also use Zoom, Skype, FaceTime, or any application that allows video interaction. It is your preference.

12. Allow the energy to flow, enjoying the Reiki you are receiving. When the energy stops flowing and the session seems complete, you can seal your session with Reiki and conduct any other rituals you wish.

13. I usually seal and complete my sessions with love, light, the power symbol, and a prayer. In recent years, I began sealing sessions with the Holy Fire® symbol. Some people gather energy from the earth (below the feet) and sweep it over the body, starting at the feet. Then collect energy from the heavens (above the head) and sweep it over the body, starting at the head. They do this to balance the energy. Some people sweep the energy with essential oils or sage/smudge. Others just use Reiki and go out into the aura, balancing each layer. There are many ways to complete the session. Do some research and decide how you wish to close or seal your sessions. It's a good idea to develop your own style or way of doing Reiki sessions.

14. Once the session is complete, gently bring the client back. Many times they will have gone deeply into the Reiki session. You may have even noticed "Reiki snores." These snores are not usually connected with sleep; instead, they indicate that your client has gone into the "gap," which is a profoundly healing space. In this space, their energy steps aside and allows Reiki to go deeply into the subconscious where the most significant change can

occur. But don't fret. The energy works anyway, even if your client didn't go into a deeply relaxing state.
15. Once your client is back, allow them to lead the follow-up. Some practitioners wonder if they should share the impressions and information they get. Other Reiki practitioners worry that they don't get additional information. I try not to lead my client. I prefer to let them lead. So I ask them to let me know how they feel and what they noticed. The session is about them, not about me. So I like them to share. If they have questions about what I saw after they are done sharing, I am happy to share my impressions.
16. Once a session is complete, I ask the client to think about the identity we gave the issue. I ask them to check their bodies for the shape they identified initially. Then I ask what percentage of the energy remains and tell me the first number they think of between 0 and 100. This tells us whether we have more work to do or if the issue has been completely removed for the client.
17. I typically record the meditations with voice memos and send them to my clients. The recording is imbued with Reiki energy so that they get additional sessions each time they listen to them.
18. If the percentage of the issue that remains is above 50%, I suggest that we book another session as soon as we are able. If it is lower, often listening to the Reiki meditation recording is sufficient to complete the release. I invite them to see how they make out with it and if they feel another session is required for this issue or another, to let me know.

In-person Reiki Sessions

In-person Reiki sessions are the kind that we were all the most familiar with before the pandemic. A client comes to your home or office, and you fill in the paperwork together, identify an area the client wishes to work on, and then lead them in a Reiki healing meditation or begin doing a hands-on Reiki session. I tend to use both during in-person sessions. Certainly, when Holy Fire® Reiki brought us powerful healing meditations, the "hands-on" portion of my sessions became abbreviated. But clients appreciated both.

There are a few things to keep in mind when you do the hands-on portion. If the client doesn't appreciate touch, simply beam Reiki to them. If you are using touch, remember not to be so light that it tickles and feels uncomfortable (think of a fly landing on you and how uncomfortable that is). It's also not a massage, so you don't want to be manipulating muscle or skin. The touch should be confident but gentle. The hands lay on the client over their clothes. The client should feel your touch, but it should feel comfortable. Think of a mother feeling the forehead of a sick child. And go ahead and practice on yourself and friends and family until it is well established. Try different variations asking your clients which is most comfortable.

If you have not learned Reiki meditations as part of your training, you can go ahead and begin the hands-on portion of the session immediately. There are several styles of hands-on sessions. You can use the Japanese style, which relies on intuition paired with Reiki to show where the hands need to be placed. It goes without saying, but always keep the hand positions appropriate. Avoid the women's breasts and genitalia and men's genitalia. You can also use Mrs. Takata's hand positions. In one Reiki class, my teacher said, "I don't know anyone who uses all of the hand positions." I laughed. I was reviewing the class and had been practicing and teaching for years at that point, and said, "I do." It's something I did from the beginning. I drew all of the symbols I had into my hands before each session. And I used all of the hand positions. My type-A personality didn't want to take a chance on getting anything wrong!

I don't flip the client over partway through the session, though, as is suggested in my manual. I find they get so relaxed on the table that I don't like to break that relaxation by asking them to flip onto their stomach. So I keep my client lying comfortably on my table with a buckwheat pillow and bolster under their head and legs. I can comfortably slide my hands under their shoulders and lower back if I need to. Or I can ask the distance symbol to work on the back body even as my hands are on the front body. So I do that instead. I have a student who combines Reiki with reflexology and craniosacral therapy. She does the whole treatment while the client lies on their front. It is an incredibly relaxing experience. I received this session from her as we practiced in class. She wanted to see what I thought. It is one of the few times I both drooled and snored during a session. So it is OK to find your own rhythm and style.

So many people are sensitive to scent these days that I advise you to consider carefully whether you wish to use essential oils or sage. Avoid using scented candles and scented dryer sheets. You can cleanse and clear the space and aura just as effectively with Reiki, so that may be a better option for sensitive clients. I use essential oils to complete the session if my client wishes. I usually rub them on my hands and sweep the aura or hold the feet with whatever healing blend I am guided to use on that day. Sometimes I use Juniper berry to cleanse the heart chakra before beginning a session. But I always check with the client before the session to ensure it is appropriate. I create essential oil healing blends, and many of my clients find me through the blends and use them. So they love it when I use them. But always check.

One of the most important things to do when setting up your Reiki space is to ensure your comfort. Sessions are generally 45 minutes to an hour. Doing Reiki does not drain your energy, but being uncomfortably positioned can take a toll on your body. I used to stand during sessions, thinking that I had better earn it if a client paid money. Thankfully, Reiki helped me let go of this limiting belief, and I decided to be comfortable as I conducted Reiki sessions.

This was helpful–particularly as I began doing more and more of them. So get a lovely rolling stool. I have a "saddle" seat stool from a massage equipment provider. It is really comfortable. And if I decide to treat a client in a sitting position instead of lying down, I use it. It has no back so that they can sit on it, and it is easier to do the hand positions. And I have a wider massage table so that no matter the size of the client, they can be comfortable with their arms at their sides. Set up your massage table so it is the right height for you to work with when you are seated if you prefer a stool, as I do. Or standing if you prefer that. Just ensure that you are comfortable for the duration of the session.

And remember, at the end of a session, even if the client doesn't notice a significant improvement in their condition, Reiki always works for their highest good.

Distance Reiki Sessions

Distance Reiki sessions used to be challenging to wrap our heads around. And for our clients to wrap theirs around too. But since the Covid pandemic, people are much more open to them, particularly if you learned Reiki in an online format. We practice distance Reiki exclusively during online classes, so it becomes very natural.

My first distance session occurred when a client emailed me after reading my article in the *Reiki News Magazine*. Her intuition had guided her to Reiki and me. I was terrified. I spoke with her by phone. She was also nervous about receiving her first Reiki session. She wondered if Reiki went against her religious beliefs. I encouraged her to seek out a practitioner in her local region to receive an in-person Reiki session. But she said her intuition told her that I was the Reiki practitioner she was to work with. I had never learned how to do a distance session in my Reiki classes at that point. But I read about the teddy bear treatment in my ICRT Reiki manual, *Reiki the Healing Touch*. We set up a time for the session and began the session on the phone. Then, we agreed to hang up as I completed the session. I would email her my findings since it was getting late in the evening, and I felt she would likely drift off to sleep as I completed the session.

I used a teddy bear as a surrogate and could not move from the mouth and jaw for a considerable length of time. I also noticed that I needed to stay on one ankle for 5-10 minutes. Afterward, when I emailed her what I noticed during the session, she confirmed that her mouth had been on fire and was a bit disconcerting for her. And although she had not mentioned it to me, her ankle had been bothering her for some time. I learned from that to stay connected, even if just by phone with my client for the session duration. And I learned that distance sessions truly do work.

Later that same week, when a client who lived on an island could not get her dying cat for his third (and most critical) session due to weather, I told her not to worry. I had just learned the teddy bear treatment and could treat him at a distance. I also told her she didn't have to pay me if she didn't want to as I was still uncertain about distance sessions. She lived on an island and could not get off. The drive to get here was over 3 hours for her. She was willing to try anything at that point and agreed to a distance session.

We conducted the session over the phone, and as I worked and told her what I noticed, she told me what the cat was doing. He responded to the session with very obvious body language. That gave us both confidence. Do you know that cat went out of liver failure after the session and is still alive today, nine years later? His veterinarians were astounded!

Something funny happened with my first distance client, though. I never heard back from her, so I told myself that I had failed her and failed Reiki. However, I was eternally grateful to her for introducing me to distance Reiki sessions, which have become a significant part of my practice. She reached out to me two years later, though, and said that she understood that I didn't want to work with her, but would I consider doing just one more session as it's the only relief she had ever received from her condition? I was gobsmacked. I assured her that I was happy to work with her, but I thought perhaps she had been disappointed in the session. She said that she had the impression that I did not want to work with her when I tried to send her to another Reiki practitioner in her region. I'm happy to say that we work together regularly now and have become dear friends. And I learned not to make up stories if I don't hear back from a client.

There are several ways to conduct a distance session. I do sessions by phone. But for clients in countries where I don't have a phone plan, we use Facebook messenger, FaceTime, or Zoom. Skype and other connection software work as well. I prefer to work without the camera as I find it distracting and am a bit shy to be filmed while listening to Reiki and conducting a meditation. But I think real-time face-to-face distance sessions are the way of the future. I record each session and send the recordings to my clients at no additional charge. Each time they listen to the recording, they get additional sessions and seem to appreciate the recordings. Some clients don't get around to listening again, while others listen daily. It is up to them how they use it.

Session Space
People often feel they have to "set up" space in their homes or rent an office to do Reiki sessions. The fact is there are many options.

If you decide to set up a Reiki space, it must be a comfortable, uncluttered place with a relaxing feel. Some people choose only to work with family, friends, and close associates and are comfortable setting up a Reiki space in their homes. My own Reiki space is set up that way, even though I work with a variety of clients. It is a converted porch with lots of windows where people can view the horses if they choose to use that part of the pasture. People can come in by the front door if they choose rather than coming through the main house. I also tend to do sessions while my family is away, which is quieter. It works for me. And if a client doesn't show up or cancels at the last minute, I can simply shift to other work or get supper going. I enjoy my home space though now I primarily do distance work. It means I have to have commercial insurance on my house, but I have that anyway for my horse business.

You may not feel comfortable having people in your home or may not want to deal with the insurance. Or perhaps you simply want the more professional look and feel of seeing clients in an office setting. Indeed, you can rent office space. But if you wind up working simply to pay for the space, or if this puts pressure on you to see clients just to pay for the space, it defeats the purpose.

Consider a shared space at first. You can get together with other practitioners to rent a space. Or find a massage therapist willing to share a space. Massage therapy is physically demanding, so many massage therapists can only work a certain number of hours per week. Find out when their room is available and if they would be willing to take on a partner to help with the rent. The area is often set up just as you need for Reiki sessions. And the vibe or feel is usually appropriate as well. You may find as a bonus that you wind up with referrals from the partnership.

Yet another option is to become a "traveling" Reiki practitioner. You pack up your table and supplies and go to your client's space for sessions. I did this with terminally or extremely ill clients or friends in the past, and it is appreciated. So that is an option.

Finally, you may prefer to conduct your distance Reiki sessions. But I still recommend having a beautiful, peaceful space set aside which feels sanctified to work from. If you conduct sessions via video, spend some time on your background. It should look calm, tidy, and serene. And ensure that your sound is good. You may need to wear earphones or use an external microphone. Clients have to strain to hear me when I connect via my computer without an external microphone. So keep that in mind.

Planning Sessions/Calendar

I used to see clients whenever it was convenient to them. I would miss my daughter's volleyball games and work a lot of evenings and weekends. This was not convenient for my family or me. Then Reiki showed me that this was inefficient and unnecessary. I saw that I needed to ask my clients to work around my calendar. I encourage you to do the same. I looked at my calendar and realized it worked best for me to conduct sessions Thursday afternoons and Friday mornings. I use a paper calendar to help organize my brain. I need to see my entire week in front of me. I was guided to mark the session times that worked best for me, boxing that time out for Reiki clients. Then when clients call asking for 9:30 Friday morning, I could say no, but I have a 10 am spot-free.

Initially, when I explained my new session times to clients who wanted an evening appointment, some said it wouldn't work for them and went away frustrated. I was tempted to capitulate and go back to my old way of doing things, but Reiki had me hold firm. I apologized and let them know that this worked best for my family and was how I would manage now. I offered to help them find a Reiki practitioner who worked evenings. Many reached out a short time later saying, "You'll never guess– my schedule has changed, and I can make it work now!" or, "I thought about it, and I realized that Friday morning works just fine for me." I don't think I lost any clients in the end. But even if I had, having a schedule that worked for my family and me was worth it. In the end, not only did I get busier, but people enjoyed the predictability.

Initially, when people contacted me, there was a lot of back and forth before we found a time that worked. And often, by then, I simply sacrificed something on my end. Now, people ask for my next available session; I give them the options, they get back to me, and it's done. They also appreciate the sessions and don't seem to take them for granted.

I have recently moved to an automated booking system, and I love it! I can't say enough about it. I use Square appointments and have Reiki students who set up online calendars with Wix when they created their website. My online calendar streamlined payment and reminders and saves me a LOT of time now that I see 10-12 clients per week.

I don't have a cancellation policy. You can have. But I usually find that I have someone else who desperately needs an appointment when someone cancels. Or I am running short on time for something I need to do. I notice a lot of movement in my online schedule, and I understand that people's schedules change. Most of my clients reschedule rather than cancel. If it becomes a problem, or if I had to go to an office for sessions, I would put in a cancellation policy. And it is easy to do that with these systems.

You can start out with online booking. Some of my students did. But don't feel you have to. I've been seeing clients for years and only moved my schedule online recently. My practice is busy so booking clients and sending reminders took too much time. The system allows me to be more efficient.

One of the things I do is send Reiki to my calendar. I ask Reiki to help the people who need my Reiki sessions find me and a session that works for them. By leaving it with Reiki, whenever I get an opening, someone is on the waiting list or has an emergency and fills the spot. So I turn the calendar over to Reiki and ask Reiki to fill it with the people who need the sessions the most. Once I began doing that, the people who showed up were aligned with me. And Reiki manages my calendar much better than I can!

Pricing Your Offerings

Once you decide to offer sessions, many people get stuck on what to charge. Typically, you charge the same as a massage therapist in your region. And although a lot of Reiki people struggle to accept money for this sacred work, the fact remains that a business transaction is comfortable for most people and allows for a fair energy exchange. I was really uncomfortable receiving money for Reiki sessions initially and used to give my sessions away. I found it odd that clients didn't return as I was happy to do sessions whenever my schedule allowed. I learned from them and loved spending time in the energy.

I listened to a presentation by William Rand one day where he said that when you don't accept some form of payment for Reiki sessions, you take a balance of power over people. I was horrified. I had never intended to do that. He said instead, think of a fair price you'd like to charge and the number of clients you wish to work with each week, then send Reiki to this goal. And if you are uncomfortable accepting money, ask Reiki to heal that for you because there are people who need us and need us to heal so they can work with us and be comfortable about it. He said everyone has a spirit guide or guides even if they are unaware of them. And that if Reiki helped us solve a particular issue or problem that their person also has, the guides will nudge them toward us. Our spirit guides are always on the lookout for people who can help us. So we need to heal and create a business we are comfortable with so that we can help others.

I immediately sat down and worked on healing my issues to receive money. I thought 2-4 clients per week would be perfect. It would fit into my schedule well. The additional income would be welcome. And it wouldn't interfere with my other businesses. I spent a few hours in that self-healing session. And when I stood up to check emails and phone messages, would you believe three people were looking for Reiki sessions that week? And one person looking for a session the following week? After six months of conducting 8 Reiki sessions in total, with no repeat customers. Unreal.

From that day forward, I always had four clients per week until I shifted, got more organized, and realized I could see more clients weekly. Then I sent Reiki to that, and those sessions filled too.

Although money is often the exchange for sessions, you will still do lots of free work. I offer a free online monthly Reiki share and created a podcast that includes a healing meditation every week. And I regularly send Reiki to world events, students, clients, and friends outside of sessions.

Barter is on the table as well. I still barter with my massage therapist, my reflexologist, and a few others. I also never ask for payment from my family. Just make sure when you barter that it is for something you need. For instance, if you charge $75 for a session, a jar of pickles is not a great barter. Especially if you don't like them or have no use for them. However, I once bartered a Reiki session for two homemade graham cracker crust pies. And I still think I got the better end of that bargain. So just make sure if you barter that you are bartering for something helpful to you.

Do some research to see what other Reiki practitioners in your region charge. You won't want to charge the most, especially if you are just starting out. But you don't want to charge the least either. Choose the middle ground. And if that makes you feel too uncomfortable or puts too much pressure on you starting out, run a special. Set your price, but let potential clients know that you are offering the first session at 1/2 price. Or you can offer sessions 1/2 price to the first ten clients who book, and 3/4 price to the next 10. Do this until you build your confidence and work your way into the price in the middle that you settled on. This incremental increase takes the pressure off of you so you can establish yourself. And it gives your new clients a bargain, particularly if Reiki is new to them. Along the way, you become comfortable with your fee.

I believe that clients get out of a session what they put in. And there will always be financially strained clients. And while I generally work to help these clients, if I give them free sessions, it seems to waste time for both of us. They never get out of the trap of a poverty mindset. And I am not compensated for my time. I could have given a session to someone else who would benefit more in that time. I have also noticed that the poverty mindset is relative. Some people do pretty well financially but are trapped in a scarcity mentality. They request free assistance then spend funds freely elsewhere. And others are not financially flush but never blink an eye at my fee or ask for a favor. One of those clients told me, "Look, I don't drink, I don't smoke, and this therapy helps me SO much, so I don't mind paying for it. It's my treat to myself." She clearly values herself and receives tremendous benefits from her sessions. So now, when someone asks for something for free or a lower fee due to their financial circumstances, I don't offer them as I once did. I have learned that they won't get as much from the session without an exchange. I ask them what they have in mind? Often, they say they only need a small amount of help, which I can easily accommodate. If they don't have anything in mind, I let them know I accept payments. I noticed this helps them release their scarcity mindset. And that mindset probably holds them back in several areas of their lives.

Insurance

Although there are Reiki practitioners who practice without insurance, Reiki practitioner insurance is relatively inexpensive and is great to have. Many organizations offer insurance through their membership. So check with your Reiki organization to see if they do. And if not, go ahead and search insurance providers in your location. There will probably be several. If you can't find any, look for insurers who insure massage therapists, naturopaths, and such. They often also insure Reiki practitioners.

Potential Clients

So you are ready to create your Reiki practice. How are you going to let people know? With an email? A phone call? A Facebook or Instagram post? A video invitation? No matter what method you use to spread the word, word-of-mouth is always your best advertisement. Seriously. The secret is simply to get started.

ONE OF THE best ways to start is with some lists.
Exercise: Make a Reiki List
Place your hands in Gassho. Activate your Reiki energy. And ask Reiki to guide you in answering the following questions.

What are some things I need to do before I can begin to offer sessions?
For example:

- Do I need a website or Facebook page, or other marketing? Do I need cards or pamphlets or brochures?
- Do I need to purchase a massage table or chairs and set up my space? Do I need to find a space? Or purchase software or hardware for distance sessions?
- Who in my sphere of friends might be interested in receiving a Reiki session?
- Should I set up a newsletter? Or send an email or just put the word out that I am doing Reiki sessions?
- Do I need insurance? Do I have a client intake form?
- Looking at my calendar, what works best for me? How many sessions per week would work? What would I charge?
- What are some of the other things I need to do in order to get set up comfortably?

Now, before you get stressed out about the size of this list, write every task on a piece of paper and place it into a beautiful bowl or vase. Place your Reiki symbols on and around the bowl or vase. Give the bowl or vase Reiki and ask the Reiki energy to organize your priorities for you. Now choose one task. That is the task for the day. Just work through them one at a time until they are complete.

Self Care & Reiki Sessions

Now that you are a Reiki practitioner, it's essential that you look after yourself. When we fill our cup, we can be our best for our clients. It is possible to burn out–even doing something as beautiful as Reiki. So pace yourself. But also make a list of the things that fill you up, have a look at your calendar, and book your self-care sessions. I'm serious! I do more self-care than almost anyone I know. It makes me a much more effective Reiki practitioner. In addition to daily self Reiki, I book a Reiki session each month with my mentor. It keeps me stable and balanced. It helps me learn more about Reiki as I can also ask questions or advice. And it keeps me moving forward with Reiki. A session from someone else will always have a slightly different perspective than a self-session. So find someone you want to learn from and book a regular session with them.

Several of my students do the same thing. They have a standing monthly appointment with me rather than wait until they get into a crisis. It seems to keep them more vital in their practices, energetically and personally. And it is an opportunity for us to touch base if they have questions about Reiki. Or need advice. Questions inevitably arise in any Reiki practice.

I also book yoga, massage, surface floats, acupuncture, reflexology, hair appointments, and such. When I put together a new calendar, I book my vacations, Reiki classes, and Reiki session times for the year. Then I contact all of my self-care providers and lock in my appointments for the year. They work more conveniently with my schedule that way. And I know that I will make time for them. If you don't already do this, I highly suggest it. I can't emphasize the value of self-care enough as you create your Reiki business.

Reiki Shares

Whether you are a Reiki Master or a Reiki practitioner, you can host Reiki shares. These are usually free events where people can get together and share Reiki. If you rent a space, you may want to ask for a small fee or donation. Reiki shares provide an opportunity for all of us to be in community with other Reiki practitioners. It is important to spend time with your "tribe."

If you are a new Reiki practitioner, it can be a great way to get started. Invite friends, family, co-workers, and acquaintances to a Reiki share. The people who attend your Reiki share don't have to have Reiki. You can simply show them the hand positions and ask them to intend the frequency of love to flow through to the person on the table as you make it to each person at some point with your Reiki hands.

You can do a small talk at the beginning, explain the hand positions and let people get started. You may also wish to lead people in a Reiki meditation. Then circulate, grounding their feet with Reiki toward the conclusion. Or you can just offer the meditation; that way, it really doesn't matter if the participants have Reiki training.

Once you begin teaching, this is a beautiful opportunity for your students to be in community, learn, and grow. Being in community with this energy allows people to expand and grow and feel comfortable with their gifts and their being. It will enable everyone to stay in touch as well. I used to offer in-person Reiki shares four times per year in my home on a Saturday near Solstices and Equinoxes. When the weather and insects allow, we go outside and have even had the horses join us on occasion. Afterward, I offered tea and coffee, and people brought treats to share. It was a lovely time, but it took up much of the day as people lingered and visited. A few people asked me to hold them more often. But I simply didn't have the time. So I suggested that they consider hosting one and inviting our group, and I would do my best to attend.

As my teaching expanded, so did the number of people who showed up for my Reiki shares, and sometimes my small home could barely accommodate them. I knew if I continued, I would need to begin renting a space to hold in-person Reiki shares.

Now, my Reiki shares have moved online. Initially, I moved them there because of the pandemic, but I plan to keep them online. Because they are online, my students from all over the world can attend. I always felt bad that my students in Australia, the UK, and the US were left out of the shares. So I would record the meditation and share it with them in our private Facebook group. Now, I hold the shares at 7:30 in the evening, which seems to accommodate all of the time zones. I still record them, but they often become my podcast that week. So even when students miss the share, they still benefit from the discussion and healing meditation.

Although my students and clients attend, people I haven't yet met also show up. Some participate because their teachers don't offer Reiki shares. Others check me out before deciding whether they want to take a class. And still, others attend based on interest in the topic I will be covering. I am always delighted to see them for whatever reason they are there.

Many of my regulars put it in their calendars and never miss a share. I always lead people in a talk and a meditation, so everyone gets a free treatment in a way. If there is time, I also use breakout rooms so people can get to know each other and share Reiki. Other times, we beam to each other at the end. Still, other times, people have gone so deep into the healing meditation that we all wish each other well and depart. These groups have led to some lifelong friendships. Some people tell me they meet regularly with their "partner" to share Reiki and offer a sounding board for each other even months later.

If you don't already offer a regular Reiki share, consider it. Just make sure that you schedule and offer it in a format that feels comfortable to you.

Reiki Talks
One of the best ways to get the word out about what you do is offering Reiki talks. Initially, mine were set up by word of mouth. I have spoken in university classes, horse events, hospitals, nursing homes, City Hall, healthcare trade shows and events, aesthetician training courses, drumming circles, etc.

One of my students felt conflicted about mentioning her Reiki training in her church. She worried people would judge it as inappropriate or incompatible with their religious teachings. But one day, she mentioned it. Her minister said, "Oh, I have a niece who does Reiki. I'd love to learn more about it. Would you give a talk about it to our group?" She readily agreed and wound up teaching a class to some parishioners.

I sometimes offer a PowerPoint presentation with my talk. I also talk about and demonstrate Reiki with a meditation or offer hands-on mini-sessions. It depends on the size of the group, availability of technology, and time for questions and answers. I always try to follow the talk with an opportunity to experience Reiki. I seldom do a Reiki talk without booking sessions or having people register for classes afterward. I'm not always comfortable with public speaking. But once I plan my talk to fit the time frame allotted, I Reiki my throat chakra and turn the presentation over to Reiki. I ask Reiki to help me with the discernment to find the right words. I also ask it to flow throughout the talk to anyone who wants it.

Before showing up for the talk, I use the distance symbol and clear the space, imbuing it with the Reiki symbols. I ask that the people who attend get what they need from the talk and that if the Reiki energy needs to reach anyone, it does so. I always leave these talks glowing and have met the most interesting people. Think for a moment of a few places you might offer to give a Reiki talk. And simply let the Reiki energy know that you are ready. It may reach out to you! Or you can contact the organization. It's just one more way to be a force for good in the world as you share the gift of Reiki with others.

Recording Sessions

Initially shy to record myself, I noticed my mentor recorded parts of her classes and sent them to us. She encouraged me to do the same. I didn't like the sound of my voice and was really self-conscious about it. But I realized it was not about me. I also have discovered that the sound of my voice changes when Reiki flows through it, and I like it quite well now. Then as I got busier and couldn't always fit clients in readily for subsequent sessions, I realized that if I recorded sessions for them, using the distance symbol to intend that they get an additional treatment each time they listen, then they can usually work through even a significant issue with just one paid session. My clients enjoy it too.

If I record on my phone, I use headphones to improve the sound. Or I record on my computer, holding it close to me. My microphone picks up background sound, so once, when I used it to give my client a better quality recording, she could hear the backhoe that was installing our solar panels, and it had the opposite effect. I usually record using voice memos and send the recording to my clients immediately when the session is complete. I don't record our conversation before the session. I just record the meditation/treatment.

Sometimes the sessions highlight an issue I need to work on for myself. I will notice a theme with a few clients. For instance, several may be working through grief, anxiety, or insecurity. Whenever that happens, I look at myself and realize that their session is helping me heal something I need to heal. Sometimes it's apparent right away. Other times, it comes with reflection. You will also notice that your connection with Reiki will grow as you begin offering these sessions.

You are ready to begin offering Reiki sessions now. I wish you well! May blessings flow to you and your clients as you all contribute to raising the frequency on the planet.
Namaste.

MEDITATION: **Releasing Blocks or Barriers around Reiki Sessions**
Take a few moments to think about what is blocking you or getting in your way. What is preventing you from doing Reiki sessions and becoming a Reiki practitioner? Make a list. You can work with this list as one. Or you can work on each one individually. Ask if the energy causing this block exists in your body; where would it be? What shape would it have? What color would it be? Then proceed into the meditation.

> Close your eyes and take some deep breaths. Place your hands in Gassho and activate your Reiki symbols.
> Notice the Reiki energy flowing around you, flowing into your body on your breath.

> Invite the Reiki energy to release any of the blocks or barriers you might have that interfere with that next step onto your path.

> It is normal to have blocks and barriers. So please don't judge yourself. If things come up, in fact, in getting through the blocks and barriers, recognizing them, and letting them go, that is the process of learning and growing–strengthening the soul.

> As we begin to develop the discernment to recognize our blocks and

barriers and let them go, we move more steadily towards enlightenment.

We may be aware of the blocks. It might be difficult to talk about Reiki; we may be still working through our faith and belief in Reiki, God, and ourselves or our abilities. Understand that that is all part of the process.

And we welcome the process as this incubation, this moving forward. Sometimes moving forward can be uncomfortable. We're blessed to have Reiki to assist us with that.

There may be blocks or barriers within us that we're unaware of or belief systems that no longer serve us.

Anytime we've ever told ourselves that we were not enough. That inner voice can sometimes be quite critical. We ask that voice to come to the surface now to be healed in the light of compassion so that our inner voice might become kinder and might better support us as we move forward in our work.

We welcome the beauty, we welcome the growth, and we are ready to step forward, whatever that looks like for us.

Ready to step into the comfort of our authentic self. We are becoming a force for good in the world.

We ask Reiki to help us move through that into a place of ease within ourselves. We ask for the discernment to know how to use our voice, when to use it, and what language to use in different situations. And we ask to become receptive. Sometimes our receptivity can be blocked or can be ineffective. We open ourselves to receive now as the light of our authentic self steps forward and is revealed.

We invite any obstacles to our true potential to release. Now we remember that ripple effect that comes with every breath, every step, every move. And every smile, and we bless people just with our being and Reiki.

Aho. And Namaste.

ProTip
Terry Dulin, LRMT, Indiana, USA
Midwest Center for Reiki Advancement[1]

I LOVE EVERYTHING, Reiki, but I just loved how wonderfully the chapter read. I love how you walk practitioners through practical things they can do to build their sessions and confidence. And release fear. There's always fear that we have to get over to do anything growth-oriented in our lives. With many things, we can have anxiety from time to time, but it's essential to take that first step into growth. I give myself Reiki in any situation where I'm fearful.

This chapter is like "Reiki sessions made simple." So there were topics I didn't even think about because I've been practicing for 12 years, and it's become second nature to me. But you went step by step.

My best advice is to be open to everything. I have practiced and done all different types of sessions. Distance. In-person. Traveling to a client. Animal Reiki. Everything that you shared.

I also love how you send Reiki to your clients to clear them before they get to you. I used to do that also. I would send Reiki to allow them to be in a more relaxed state before coming into a session.

I am enamored with William Rand. When I first took training

with him in 2010, I expected a grand Reiki center. When I drove up, he was teaching in his house. And I thought, "This man is so laid back. He's not in ego. He does Reiki right out of his house." Even in Hana, Hawaii, he teaches from his home. So I thought to myself, William Rand teaches classes out of his house, and I can do the same. And then, I found out that most Reiki practitioners do Reiki out of their homes. When I first started, I didn't realize that. So start small if you want. And then build up to where you want.

It was a tremendous relief that I didn't have to build this great big Reiki center to create a business. I could look at the space I have and work with that. Then allow Reiki to help me grow to what I want to become. I'm still a work in progress. I'm still getting where I want to be. It is a process. As we work with Reiki, we grow and change; that's part of life.

When I first started, I tried to be very accommodating. But as you progress with your business, it's not always possible because of other obligations. I work full-time in a nine-to-five job. Then I teach on weekends, so my weekends are generally booked with Reiki classes. So I have to monitor and modify my schedule and have specific times for sessions.

I also have two dogs. One is a therapy dog, and the other is a therapy dog in progress. He's involved in training and testing. So there are priorities and sacrifices. When we are Reiki practitioners doing sessions, it's, ultimately, what we want to do. And how comfortable we are growing our business.

I know I'm not the right practitioner for every client. That's just the truth of the matter. I try to accommodate clients, but I have no problem referring clients to other Reiki masters if it does not work. I generally refer clients to my students to help build their practices. And then, depending on the situation, I also direct them to my fellow Licensed Reiki Master Teachers.

My background is slightly different, so doing Reiki sessions was different for me. My mom is a professional psychic. I learned Reiki in 2002 to help my mom with her healing work. So I've always been exposed to sessions. I had a different perspective because they were not my clients. They came to my mother for a healing session, and I was her assistant. It took some of the pressure off of me. Mom would call and say, "Hey, Terry can you come over? I have a client that wants a Reiki session. Can you help?" I'd say, "Absolutely." I'd reschedule whatever I was doing to help my mom.

An idea for new practitioners is to join a Reiki Share to get experience with Reiki sessions. You can practice with your family and friends, but attending a Reiki share gives you additional practice. It can also help alleviate some of the anticipation or fear around providing sessions. If you can find one in your area, try and get there.

Some people do not hesitate to accept money or barter even at the beginning because they believe that what they're offering is valuable. I wanted to start slow. My prices are very accommodating. I'm in Northwest Indiana, not an expensive center, where people need to charge more for Reiki. And I work, so there is another source of income coming into my household. So my goal is to make sure that I'm affordable for the people who need me. If you have higher expenses and office overhead, charging more is just being responsible for your business and practice.

Many people see and hear things as they do sessions. I'm not one of them. So when somebody comes to me, they get a Reiki session. I'm not psychic. If clients want a psychic reading, I respectfully say, "Please talk to my mom; she's a professional psychic. Tell her, Terry sent me, to get the family and friends discount."

In an actual Reiki session, you, the practitioner, allow energy to flow through you to your client. Reiki comes from a higher level of consciousness, so it knows what clients need. Additional information can be a perk or a bonus, but it is not necessary, and not everyone appreciates it. So even if I notice something, I generally keep it to myself. Reiki is such a beautiful gift in and of itself that while you can offer other things with the session, you don't need to.

Follow your intuition and Reiki guidance about what you want to offer and how to set up your business. Then be clear about your offerings. Some people start slow and build their practice step by step; others hit the ground running. There is no one right way. Wherever you are with it is the perfect place for you to be.

I needed to start small and gradually grow into my practice, but I know everyone's not there. So do what you're comfortable doing. And have fun. Everything will fall in place at the right time, but allow Reiki to guide you.

Reiki can be very formal, and we need to treat it respectfully. But Reiki is also very light, loving, and inviting. So have fun with the process. And give yourself Reiki self-care. I also strongly encourage you to receive Reiki sessions from others.

We know that Reiki comes from a higher level of consciousness; it spans all time and space. So it works on the past, the present, and the future. We don't know where Reiki will flow. But it has Divine Consciousness, so it goes where it's needed.

I always intend Reiki's energy to flow to the root cause of whatever is ailing my client. If it's meant to go to childhood trauma, it goes to childhood trauma. If it is a karmic issue stemming from a past life, I ask that the Reiki go to the past life to heal that. Once that issue is healed, it will then heal everything going forward.

So when I talk to my students and new practitioners, I tell them to follow their intuition and the guidance of Reiki. It won't steer them wrong.

Check out our podcast on this chapter.[2]

STUDENT SUCCESS STORY **Cara Douglas**
I loved being with a group of people with whom we could share our thoughts, ideas, and plans for our businesses and know that they were going to be respected and held sacred. After the Mentoring class, Animal Reiki became my focus.

I'VE ALWAYS DONE distance Reiki with photos. The new thing was the in-person sessions. I was inspired to do what I love during the Reiki Mentoring class. I love being in barns with horses. My friends do, too. I'm not comfortable doing sessions in my home. I'd rather be in a barn. I love being with the horses, the aroma of a barn, the hay, the feed, the horses themselves. It all allows me to tune in to myself very well. And then I feel like I have a much more gentle and focused energy for my client and their horse.

I'M a very hands-on Reiki person and it has to include the caregiver for me. As I work on horses, their caregivers are right there so Reiki spills over to them. I decided to set a Reiki table up in the barn to make it more of a two-way thing that focuses on the person and includes the horse. I not only found the confidence to begin doing Reiki sessions for animals, but I began doing combined sessions with the animal caregivers.

AFTER THE MENTORING CLASSES, I had a client whose horse was highly attached to her. We tried working on him to calm down and become more balanced. But when we began working on them both, it was more effective. Now I can work with them from a distance, and she contacts me to say she feels it.

I HAD another client who was injured in a fall from her horse. I wanted to help with Reiki, but she was an hour from my house. I knew that wasn't going to happen. So I shoved my table in my little car and schlepped it there. It helped with her injury. So this reinforced that I could do Reiki this way. It helped both of them.

FOR THE SESSIONS, the horse is comfortable in his stall. I set up the table in front of the stall, close to the horse but not close enough that he could reach over and physically interfere with the session. It's even evolved beyond me having to take my table there. Sometimes we just sit in the barn setting and run Reiki. Because we're comfortable, it's effortless to allow that energy to flow and be shared. So this was an excellent option. I get as much from the session as my client. It's truly humbling.

WHEN I DO my morning prayers, I recite the Reiki symbols, invite them into my physical body, and ask that I walk and do everything in Reiki and love. The mentoring course made me realize how essential Reiki was to me. I'm grateful for the pandemic because it's allowed me to be in contact with people from around the world with Reiki–all with totally different cultural backgrounds. I could see how Reiki affects their lives with their spiritual beliefs. That's been pretty eye-opening.

THE COURSE MADE me focus on how I present myself as a Reiki practitioner and an Animal Reiki practitioner. I'm still working on the wording for my website, but reading other people's websites helped me focus on what I want to include. The mentoring course made me say yes to Reiki. I like teaching Reiki. But where is my true focus? My true focus seems to be this horse-and-human combined work. It's almost become an obsession.

I NOW CAN BE flexible in how to do a session. To trust Reiki to do what it needs to do. I am becoming more competent. A Reiki practitioner friend and I are even planning to offer Reiki shares at the barn. I think part of it is walking your walk and talking your talk. And I thank Reiki for helping me to do that.

---

1. https://www.buzzsprout.com/1364386/8240872
2. https://www.buzzsprout.com/1364386/10150679

5

MARKETING AND BRANDING

"Marketing is planting seeds. It is not an immediate reward; it is cumulative where people can be watching for some time before they take that first step."

Jules Davis, LRMT

Once you have the intention to share Reiki and the space and equipment sorted out, you are ready to start, right? There are still a few details to wrap up as you will probably need to do a bit of marketing. Many people believe marketing is complicated, expensive, and overwhelming. And it can be. But it doesn't have to be.

Marketing is my background and training. Yet I've always been a guerrilla marketer. I don't like to spend much money marketing, and I look for the biggest bang for my buck when I do. So I suggest that you spend very little money on marketing. But it will take some time.

Most of your clients will come to you through word of mouth. They'll come through friends of friends, Reiki talks, trade shows, or networking. That said, there are a few basics that you should put in place. You need to create a website. It doesn't have to be complicated or expensive. But it establishes the credibility of your business.

You will want a business card. Basic is best. It should include your business name, your name, your credentials, website address, and email address or phone number.

You will also need a list of potential customers and their email addresses to get started, along with the ability to continue building the list.

You may wish to delve into social media. But if that intimidates you, don't worry about it now; leave it for later.

If you have issues with technology, speaking to others about Reiki, social media, or marketing, use Reiki to heal them.

- Technology will become your best friend. Believe me. It is one of the most effective tools for reaching others.
- Speaking to others about Reiki becomes enjoyable once you get familiar with it. And it moves into the realm of magic when it helps you help others with the gift of Reiki.
- Social media can be a fun way to engage your clients and potential clients with Reiki. Or to connect to them and send them Reiki.
- Marketing can be a lot of fun as it helps you reach new audiences and engage with them.

So let go of the overwhelm. Let's not pressure ourselves; just do it one step at a time. It can be fun. And you get a wonderful sense of accomplishment as you move through each step or phase. Particularly the ones that intimidated you.

You can do this. I know you can. But let's enjoy the process.

Think of all these as tools. Tools can be used well or not. Let's use them well.

I used to have difficulties with all these tools, but once I healed my issues, I learned how they could blend beautifully with my business. We can use Reiki in our marketing efforts. And as we bring Reiki into all of them, it raises their vibration and the planet's vibration.

As I embraced technology, my life got easier. So I make it a goal to learn one new thing each week. That prevents me from getting overwhelmed. I take my time. I watch tutorials and videos on YouTube to learn about new tools or technology. My husband insists that if there's anything you don't know how to do, there are videos explaining it on YouTube. That must be why YouTube has become one of the most popular search engines on the planet.

When I speak about Reiki, engaging people with the possibilities, I am rewarded by their interest and excitement. When people take a Reiki class or session, they reconnect with Source. It's beautiful. I have to pinch myself sometimes, as I can't believe that I can do this as my livelihood. My Reiki business, clients, and students bring so much joy to my life. As I spread Reiki, people heal. They reconnect with joy, beauty, and their life purpose and become empowered. This has an impact on the vibration of the planet. It is such an honor to be in a position to share this gift with others.

And whether they choose to work with me or not, I love planting the seeds of Reiki wherever I am. Sometimes I don't get to see those seeds sprout, but other times I do. Or I learn about it later if they decide to work with another practitioner. It's always a beautiful process. I trust that Reiki will guide people where they need to go.

Every person finds the Reiki practitioner or master who is right for them. So when a seed I planted brings someone to another practitioner or teacher, I am delighted for them and the practitioner or teacher. It doesn't bother me in the least. I am happy that they followed up. And I know they had something to learn from that practitioner or teacher.

It sometimes works in the other direction as well. Someone else plants a seed, but the student or client finds me. There is no such thing as competition with Reiki. So go ahead and engage people with no agenda around the outcome. Beautiful things are awaiting you and the person you engage with. I always learn something and often form a lovely alliance or friendship.

Social media can be an effective way to spread the love of Reiki. I hear people talk about the toxicity of social media or say it's draining. But I believe you bring in what you put out. It can be overwhelming if you have a plan or work on it constantly. And if you share strong opinions, expect to receive strong opinions back. I recommend that you keep strong opinions to yourself. So as not to alienate people. And to use Reiki to soften your views.

But social media can help people have a better day if done well. It can help us connect. We can infuse our social media feeds with light, love, and Reiki. Then see what happens. I am grateful for all of these tools. Particularly social media. It allows us to reach so many people at one time, effortlessly, and in a way that doesn't interrupt or disturb their day. If you feel it is a drain or eludes or frustrates you, use Reiki to heal that–so you can see it for the excellent tool it is to your business.

∽

EXERCISE: **Create a SWOT Analysis**
The marketer's best friend is a SWOT analysis. It's a simple way

to get a handle on your strengths and weaknesses, opportunities and threats. Most of your marketing messages are based on your strengths and opportunities. And an awareness of your weaknesses and threats give you something to work on. Let's create a SWOT analysis for your business. You might also ask a friend to help you with this, as we often sell ourselves short and have difficulty realizing our strengths and weaknesses. The SWOT analysis diagram can be found here.

SWOT Analysis

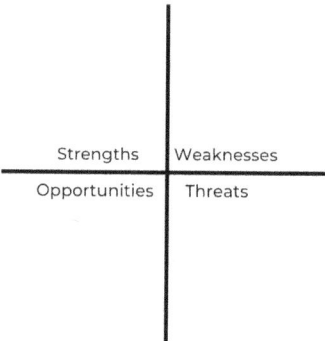

Once you know your opportunities and strengths, you can play these up in your marketing efforts.

List of Potential Clients

The next thing you might want to put together is a list of potential clients. If it's not an extensive list, that's OK. You can get started with as little as 10-15 people. Now look at the list and decide how you will reach out to them. Will you send a group message? A personal message? Will you wait until you see them and talk to them in person? Will you call them? Or will you create an event such as a Reiki share and invite them? Please don't get discouraged if people say no. Reiki is not for everyone. If you only have 1 or 2 people who say yes out of a group of 10-15, that's a great start. People are busy and may have trouble fitting it into their schedules. You can get started with a handful of clients.

You only need a few people to take you up on your offer. You may already have a list of the family and friends you have practiced with. And some of those who have been enjoying your practice sessions will probably be happy to shift to paying clients. Not all of them will, but some will. Some may already be asking you to provide formal sessions. You can let them know your calendar is ready and you are booking clients.

Take the approach with pricing that I suggested in the chapter on sessions. You may even want to offer limited-time specials for the first few people who sign up. This encourages people to sign up more quickly. You can provide current clients a discount on their next session or a small gift for each new client they send your way. Then allow things to grow organically.

You may want to use your list of potential clients to create a newsletter or a regular email. An email list allows you to grow and provides you with a way to spread the word about your offerings with minimal effort. You can also place the list in your Reiki grid and send Reiki to grow the list or convert some to clients. But you can also use this list to do some marketing and planning.

One thing to remember about this list is that you own it. Social media platforms can change so that campaigns that worked in the past no longer do. Then you need to figure out a new way to get in front of your audience. But with an email list, you can consistently connect with your people. So this list is invaluable.

Your Ideal Client

From your list of potential clients, choose just one of them. One person to be your ideal client. You may already work with them and really click in sessions. Or they may be someone you admire. Perhaps they insisted on paying for a session before you thought you were ready. Maybe they are very open to Reiki and appreciative of you. Maybe your sessions with them are magical. Perhaps they are a person you understand or "get." Maybe they make you feel competent and confident in what you are doing. For whatever reason you want, choose one. If there are several and you find it difficult to determine, ask Reiki to help you. Or choose one that represents the others. This is your "ideal" client. And they are going to come in handy as you create your marketing content.

The first thing we can do is send Reiki to attract more clients like that. And you will keep this person in mind, directing your marketing efforts to them specifically. Instead of tailoring your message to the generic "everyone," which is vague and ineffective, you will create your message with them in mind. And it will resonate with your target audience.

Draft an Email or Social Media Message

If creating a newsletter seems daunting, that's OK. Activate your Reiki and put together a simple email or social media post letting people know that you are opening a Reiki practice. Some of your friends will reach out to support you - and will be amazed by the effects of the session. Others will talk to their friends in need. And so on. A shampoo commercial once said, "and they told two friends, and they told two friends... and so on and so on" Each time, they said that the screen added the "two friends" that each person told. It multiplied exponentially. Before you knew it, the screen was filled with people. That's kind of how Reiki works.

Here are a few points you may wish to include in your message:

- That you are opening a Reiki practice or teaching a class.
- What Reiki is and what a Reiki session or class consists of.
- A personal story–such as how Reiki helped you or why you chose to share it with others.
- Your offer (price, length of time for the session or class, location, etc.)
- And that if they are not in a position to book a session or take the class, that's OK. But ask if they would do you a personal favor and share your offer with others?
- Don't use pressure tactics or guilt people into taking you up on your offer. That never works. And is contrary to the nature of Reiki.

Then imbue your message with Reiki to brighten someone's day no matter how it is received.

Your message doesn't have to be serious. If you are a naturally funny person, infuse some humor into it. If you are artistic, allow it to express your creative flair. Reiki Practitioners and Masters rarely "find" their client or student. Their student or client finds them. An email or social media post can help them do that because people need to know about us and what we are doing. So this announcement is a start.

First Offering - Reiki Share, Session, Class

Your first offering is going to make you nervous. Whether it is a Reiki share, a talk, a session, or a class, remember that nervous energy is a sign that this is important to you. So give yourself Reiki, ask it to fill you with confidence, and make that leap. I've found it's best to leap before you are ready. It's making the leap that makes you ready.

If I had waited to hold a class until I was ready, I might not be teaching yet, 11 years later. I don't think we ever really feel ready.

Instead, look at your calendar, pick a date and let people know. That will encourage you to get started and stop procrastinating.

My daughter contacted me as she was completing her yoga teacher training. She said she had just taught her first class and couldn't believe how much she loved to teach. But she said, "I know I'm not ready to teach yet; I will come home and work on myself until I am ready." I said, "Then you will never be ready. Teach before you are ready. That's what helps you 'get' ready."

She thought about it and agreed. Then she got very excited about the possibility of teaching yoga. She applied for and got a job teaching at a ski resort in Austria, allowing her to do meaningful work that she enjoys and ski in her time off. She will follow up by realizing her dream to travel around Europe. Realizing one dream often leads to realizing another. She can't believe how much she loves to teach and gets compliments from students daily.

Once you have chosen the date of your offerings, use the distance symbol to send Reiki ahead to your share, talk, session, or class. Then send Reiki to the people who will attend, even if you don't know who they are yet. Reiki knows, and the distance symbol acts as a homing device. You can even ask Reiki to help the right mix of people attend. And to support the right type of client, find you—the kind of client you enjoy working with or gel with. You can ask it to help people get to your offering effortlessly. Ask Reiki to assist them with any shifting that takes place for them. The possibilities are endless.

For my in-person classes and sessions, people almost always got lost on their way to my home. Even when I sent explicit directions, they lost them or didn't follow them. Eventually, I realized that the flustered state they arrived in helped bring their issues to the surface to heal.

When I first started teaching, one of my Reiki Masters shared that she never knew who would show up for class, especially the level 1&2 classes. I asked her why she thought that was. She felt it had to do with the shifting process that occurs when a student registers for the class. In this process, the discomfort that students feel as they release the energies that hold them back sometimes frightens them. Then sometimes, they decide the class is not in their best interest, change their minds, and choose not to attend it. I noticed the same thing when I began teaching.

Then I discovered that I could place the intention into my Reiki grid to bring together the right mix of students for each class. This made them a Divinely ordered, cohesive group. And I also sent Reiki to my future students to make it easier for them to get through the shifting process and get to class. When I did that, nearly all my clients made it to sessions, and most showed up for class. It became infrequent that they did not get there. And the groups that came together were always a match!

Create a Website
Once you have your space ready (or the online software you need) and a list of potential clients, your website is the next most important thing. I taught for over two years while my website said "under construction" in 2011–and I am a marketer. I have students who have done the same thing. But today, a website is the tool people will use the most to find you, learn about you, learn about Reiki, and decide about classes or sessions.

To many of us, creating a website seems daunting. It is a huge undertaking. As I write this, mine is in the process of a major overhaul that I have put off to finish this book. I will get to it once the book is complete. But it needn't be daunting. Take it one step at a time.

The first thing to do is decide on a name for your business. If you haven't done this already, check out the section "What's in a Name?" in Chapter 2.

Once you have a name, try and get a website domain name that matches. There is nothing wrong with the name "Reiki by Steve" or whatever else you feel is appropriate. And only use the name "Reiki" in your title if that is your primary offering. If you think you may branch out into combined sessions with another modality, stick to something more generic such as "Holistic Healing with Steve."

Don't worry if you can't get .com. There are many other extensions available. There is .org, .net, and even (my personal favorite) .love. .com is the most popular extension for businesses in North America. But in Canada, we use .ca. Germany uses .de. Australia uses .au. So don't get hung up if you can't get .com. If .com is important to you, you may change your business name slightly to accommodate it. Getting your domain name registered is one of the important first steps, and there are several services you can use to reserve domain names. You may even wish to reserve a few extensions. They are not very expensive, and they may be a good investment so that people always get directed to you no matter what they type in.

Try not to be too clever with your business name, though, or people won't be able to figure it out or find you. Simple is best. Once you have settled on a name, search for a domain name to see if the website domain is available. You will want to have something somewhat unique to you to avoid confusion. And if you plan to do quite a lot with your business, you can even trademark its name until you are ready to register it.

If you have no idea what to call your business but want to get started on a website, go ahead and see if your name's domain name is available. For example, mine would be www.pamallenleblanc.com. Once you have paid the fee to assign your domain name, you are ready to roll. If you don't know how to register a domain name with a service like GoDaddy, look through your list of friends or Reiki clients and ask if they can help you. You can even check to see if one of them would be interested in helping you set up your website in exchange for Reiki. Or you can hire help if creating a website is not in your wheel well.

I used to host all of my offerings under the "Hidden Brook Farm" business name and the domains www.hiddenbrook.com and www.hiddenbrook.ca. That included my Reiki business, my horse business, and my line of essential oils. Now that Reiki is my main focus, I am re-branding and aligning my business name with my podcast, "Reiki from the Farm™." My website will still have a small section dedicated to my horse and essential oil businesses, which will continue to be offered under Hidden Brook Farm. But my website domain will change to www.reikifromthefarm.com.

Get Professional Photos (Or Really Good Amateur Ones)
The key to a great website is great photos. It is worthwhile to have someone take professional pictures of you. You can use stock photos on your website. But you will also want a recent photo of you on your main page. As you are getting photos done, you can ask your photographer to take some other images at the same time. Maybe you want a shot of your Reiki room, your classroom, or you can stage a Reiki session. But the main thing is to have a good recent photo of yourself on the website. People can tell a lot, energetically, from an image. I've had people tell me they took a class or booked a session based on my photo. They just "knew" I was the right teacher or practitioner for them.

I am fortunate that my husband is a fantastic photographer, so I book photoshoots with him when I return from the hairdresser and look my best. But before he picked up that hobby, I had Reiki students who were happy to swap Reiki sessions and classes for photoshoots. They also gave me the rights to the photos. It's essential not to use pictures or content that you do not own the right to.

Sometimes, it is easier to use a "website builder," which gives you access to stock photos. Still, you will want to personalize some of the images.

Creating a website can be pretty simple if time-consuming. You can make the site yourself with one of the website-building tools available. Some of my students used wix.com. But there are other website tools like squarespace.com, web.com, WordPress, and more. Do some research, and find the best match for you.

If you know this is not something you want to do yourself, check with friends on your "potential client list" to see if they can help you. They might consider exchanging website services for Reiki sessions which is a win-win. Or you can hire someone to build your site. Ask friends and family for recommendations. Ensure your developer knows you are not looking for a complicated site. And get a firm financial estimate and timeline before beginning.

For most Reiki practitioners, we need to include:

- Information about Reiki
- Our background with Reiki
- Our offering (include details such as what to expect in a Reiki session, the length of the session, whether you offer online or in-person sessions, etc.).
- Include a link to help them book with you. It might be your email address, phone number, or a link to an online scheduling app with a calendar so clients can book online.
- If you offer classes, include information about the cost, the time required, the pre-requisites, and the courses. You may also wish to include a calendar.

- If it is possible to allow clients to register and pay for your class online, it is helpful, but it is not necessary at this stage. Just include registration and payment details on your site.
- Finally, include your contact information and how people can reach you. People seem to prefer clean, simple websites where they can click a link for more details. Then they are not overwhelmed with information.
- Write your copy. It needs to be in your voice to allow people to get to know you better. Don't copy from other people's websites. You can use other people's websites for inspiration. But all writing should be done by you and should be in your voice. Even if you hire a web developer, you need to do this step yourself.
- It's a good idea to hire an editor to edit your website content. I am a pretty good writer, but I can't believe how many small mistakes I make. You want to make sure your website content is well written. Glaring grammatical errors or spelling mistakes will make you appear less professional. English teachers make great editors. My editor used to teach college English, and I love working with her! She makes my work so much better. So get someone to proof and correct your work before it goes online!

Create a Brand

This may seem like overkill. But it doesn't hurt to begin thinking about your brand early on. What makes you stand out? What is the focus of your Reiki business? One of the things I noticed about my own Reiki practice is that we take a very light-hearted approach with Reiki. We enjoy working with each other and have a lot of fun. That is evident whenever we get together for Reiki shares. We may be quiet as we treat each other, but the laughter that can be heard when we are not in sessions is infectious. The angels and enlightened beings we work with seem to enjoy our approach. So my brand must show our friendly but respectful relationship with the Reiki energy.

You may want to create a logo. There are several services like VistaPrint that can do this for you. Or you may wish to play around with Canva, PicMonkey, or a similar marketing application to create your own.

Another thing you should think about is what color palette and fonts you like best. Once you decide the look and feel you are going for, you can remain consistent with all of your content. Then all of your marketing materials will have a consistent look and use a similar color palette. You can choose a color palette that appeals to you on Pinterest.

People will begin to recognize you with a uniform look with all of your material. It also looks professional. This is called "branding." Not many people worry about branding when they start, but it simplifies things later on if you do. It also saves you time and effort in the future and gives you a professional image from the beginning.

EXERCISE: Create Your First Marketing Plan

Take a few moments now, place your hands in Gassho, activate your Reiki energy, bring in your symbols and breathe. Ask yourself the following questions and move into automatic writing with the responses.

1. Imagine you have a website, business card, and pamphlet for your Reiki business. What does it all look like? Feel like?
2. What colors do you like the best?
3. What are some of your unique gifts and talents with

Reiki? Which of these would you like your business to be known for?
4. Is creating a logo for your business something you want to tackle yourself? Or is it something you'd prefer to outsource?
5. Is creating a website something you want to attempt yourself? Or is there someone you know who could help you or build it for you? What form of payment would they require?

Is It Time for a Newsletter?

A newsletter isn't necessary but can be fun. And it can help you reach your audience efficiently.

There are several newsletter providers, but my personal favorite is Mail Chimp. It's free until you have a pretty significant number of followers, at which point, it should not be difficult to pay for it. I've used the free version for years and am only now moving to a place where I may need a paid version. It's also straightforward and more accessible than other newsletter providers I have used. You can choose a design, upload your logo and any photos you wish to use and just start typing. There are pre-set fonts for headlines, subtitles, etc. Or you can use the fonts and colors you have chosen for your brand.

I put out a weekly newsletter, and it's a lot of work being that consistent. Every Sunday morning, I spend a few hours posting my podcast and creating my newsletter. It has become my Sunday morning ritual.

For several years though, I sent out a monthly email when I could get around to it. There were lots of months I missed too! Then I graduated to a proper newsletter and kept to the same schedule, putting it out monthly. I only switched to weekly recently. The main reason I switched to weekly was to let people know about our podcast each week. And in fact, some of my original subscribers unsubscribed, probably because that was too much contact for them. But it's where my business is now, so it works for my subscribers and me. When I looked at the unsubscribed people, they were not utilizing my services anyway. So don't be downhearted when someone unsubscribes. Once I did feel dejected when a trusted and loved student unsubscribed. SEVERAL MONTHS LATER, when I saw her in a class, she said she had mistakenly signed up several times and received multiple copies of the newsletter. So she unsubscribed from one of her email addresses!

If you would like to create a newsletter, one per month or even every two months is just fine starting out. You may never shift from that. And that's all right. If it weren't for the podcast, I might still be working from that schedule.

But when you get a chance, if this interests you, do a bit of research about newsletter providers, then choose one and give it a try. Most newsletter providers allow you to trial their service for free. Then, you can communicate with your clients and students regularly. And you can also create a form for your website so people can sign up quickly and efficiently for your newsletter. Newsletter providers can send correspondence so that it doesn't get filtered out for your subscribers. And when your content is no longer right for the people on your list, they can easily unsubscribe. Don't be hurt if and when that happens. We are all at different stages of our growth. And sometimes we grow apart from even our keenest students or clients over time.

Canva/PicMonkey®

These services can be fun and provide wonderful professional photos and content for your website and social media. I don't have a great eye for photos, so I have a fantastic assistant who does this for me. Not only do these services provide some great images, templates, and content, but you can also upload your photos and add words, quotes, and other content to them. You can easily create posters, pamphlets, Facebook and Instagram posts, announcements, and book covers. Seriously, there is so much you can do. And they are a lot of fun to play with.

If they don't have the photos you need, you can check out several other sites which offer royalty-free images, such as Unsplash, Pixabay, Flickr, iStock, and PicJumbo.

I'll repeat this warning; it is essential not to use someone's copyrighted material in your postings. That includes music if you record a healing meditation. But check these out and have a bit of fun with them. There are sites for copyright-free music too. Or you can license music for your meditations. I had a local artist create beautiful music for me and licensed it from him. It wasn't inexpensive, but it is so handy for my podcast and other offerings that it was worth it.

Social Media
So many Reiki people dislike social media. But I think you get from social media what you put into it. I send a lot of Reiki and supportive messages through social media. And I find my social media feeds are equally loving and inspirational right back.

Now that said, social media can be a serious time sink. One of the things I had to do to carve out the time to finish this book was to refrain from using Facebook for a while. So how do you approach the social media dilemma? Would you need a full-time person to be on top of all of them, right? Possibly.

Instead of thrusting yourself into the steep learning curve of all types of social media, choose one or two that you enjoy using and be consistent with them. I'd take consistency over quantity. Social media gurus suggest you post daily or several times per day, depending upon the forum. I think it's better to post weekly content consistently so people begin to expect it or rely on you.

However, you choose to approach social media, be conscious of what you post. If you post rants or strong opinions, you will alienate potential clients or students, especially those looking for positivity in their feeds. At the same time, there's such a thing as toxic positivity. And you want to avoid that. Be genuine. People can feel it. It's OK to let people know that your life isn't perfect or that you're having a rough day. They will respect you more for it. Be yourself. Be authentic. Before posting, ask how your posts will help the people who see them. People appreciate posts that uplift them, consider them, and relate to them. Then have fun with whichever social media channel speaks to you the most.

If you can't post all the time. That's OK. Post when you can and when you are inspired. We all want to have consistent, prolific, thought-provoking, uplifting social media posts. But it's not practical for most of us, so it takes a back seat. And we post when we can.

But try to use this mostly free resource to reach as many people as you can. Think about how difficult and time-consuming it used to be to write letters or send emails to the large number of people we can now reach effortlessly with social media. This is a tool you can use. But have fun at the same time. And don't drive yourself crazy trying to post everywhere all the time.

I choose Facebook and YouTube for my social media posts - when I have the time. Then there's the podcast. And my assistant does her best to keep Instagram up to date for me. Eventually, I may add a blog to my website. And my assistant and I may roll out a great social media plan using Hootsuite, Cloud Campaign, Loomly, or some other tool to post to multiple social media platforms efficiently. But for now, our feeble attempts at social media are enough. When there's time, we will do more.

Facebook

I am just now realizing all that Facebook can do even though I don't use it as well as I could. Did you know there's a podcast button on the business page? And a way to post events (like classes and Reiki shares) and invite people to the events. Posts with photos or videos seem to do best on Facebook. But you can also post a significant amount of text if you need to.

If you don't have a Facebook account but think you'd like to explore Facebook, create one. It's free. Then go into the software and "friend" some people. Go ahead and follow my Reiki from the Farm™[1] page. Once you have looked around a bit, go ahead and create a business page. Then play with it to learn its capabilities.

Research shows that even a significant percentage of college students have a Facebook account. And it is the leading social media platform for older generations. So if this is the social media platform you choose to work with, you can reach a large audience. I don't pay to boost posts. I don't find it a good use of resources. But I intend to post ads on related pages when it's time to promote this book. Maybe you even found us through one!

Instagram

Instagram is very photo-heavy and is used for short, simple images, messages, and videos. It's beautiful, elegant, simple, and an excellent canvas for your Canva or PicMonkey creations. Go ahead and get a feel for it to see if it's something you enjoy. Follow some people who inspire you or whose posts you want to see. Then decide if you're going to use it. Then give some thought to how you want to show up there. Choose a photo filter you like to be consistent. Create some lovely posts with your branding. And enjoy! You can connect with me on Instagram.[2]

YouTube

If you enjoy video, YouTube is where you want to be. YouTube is popular. Creating your own YouTube channel and YouTube videos is relatively easy. You can offer any length of video. If you are using music, you must have licensed the music or use Royalty free music. There are videos on YouTube about how to start your own YouTube channel. You can record videos on your phone to share. Eventually, you may wish to invest in video editing software.

I knew I wanted to start my own YouTube channel, but it seemed like such a big deal in my mind that I never got around to it. Then I recorded a video with William Rand about a subject near and dear to our hearts, "Reiki and the Environment." He said, "Hey Pam, why don't we record this in video too?" Up until then, my podcasts were strictly audio. But I had combed my hair and wore a clean shirt, so I said "sure," and my YouTube channel was born. It wasn't nearly as complicated as I thought it would be. My videos are not professional quality, but they don't need to be. Yours may not be where you want them to be either but stick with it. It can be a great forum to share your work. You can follow us on YouTube.[3]

TikTok

TikTok allows us to upload personalized short videos. I have friends who are hooked on it, and my children enjoy it too. Check it out to see if it's for you. I haven't forayed into TikTok yet. There's only so much time. But it's something I will figure out someday. It's on my very long "to-do someday list."

Social Media and technology are constantly changing. I want to point out that you do not have to use social media with your Reiki practice. But if you choose to, choose just one or two platforms that appeal to you the most. And you don't have to post daily. Sure, that is what is recommended to gain traction. But once or twice per week works too. You can put together several posts simultaneously in the name of efficiency and schedule your posts too. Just don't get overwhelmed. And don't sink too much time into it. You can get clients from social media posts and platforms, but it's not usually the most efficient form of advertising. So spend as much time as you wish on the forums you like. But don't drive yourself crazy trying to be everywhere all of the time.

∼

ProTip
    Jules Davis, LRMT, California, USA
    Auralux[4]
    I think the first ingredient is just believing that it's going to work out. Then figure out one thing at a time so that it doesn't get overwhelming. You have to self-educate, you have to have some tools, but just know that Reiki is going to guide you and support you through the process.

WHEN I STARTED MY BUSINESS, it was a lot more complicated to make a website and customize it and figure out search engine optimization. Now there are tools to make it easy. So it doesn't matter how much you know about building websites. And that's how you'll get found because people go and search for "Reiki certification in my area" or "Reiki practitioner in my area" so your website is an essential ingredient.

INITIALLY, I was a licensed holistic health practitioner with multiple certifications so my website became "healingwithjules.com". But once I could focus a hundred percent on growing my Reiki business, it exploded. "Auralux" came in as my business name, but my website remains "healingwithjules.com" because it is what people know.

. . .

GET your early clients to write a review about their experiences is helpful because people will find your business through reviews. Then the review sites link back to your website, and everything gets interacted with your social media.

YELP IS REALLY IMPORTANT HERE. People use that to find practitioners or teachers. If you have a physical location, you can make a Google business page and you can have Google reviews for your business. If you have a Facebook business page, you can turn on reviews for that. Those are probably the three main areas where people will find your information. I simply asked some of my early clients, "Would you mind sharing about your experience?" Some people do post about you and what they experienced during this time.

BRANDING AND LOGO– who you are– are essential ingredients throughout the lifetime of your business. Canva is an amazing tool for creating banners for your event pages and website. You can also do newsletters with it. I'm always re-educating myself on how to get into better marketing tools. What's the latest trend?

WITH SOCIAL MEDIA, first set up an account and figure out what kind of content you want to share. Be authentic because people want to get a glimpse of who you are. I'm active enough to stay engaged, but I don't post as consistently as I would like to due to time constraints. Share positive things. Let Reiki be that bright light, a candle of energy that goes out into the world and ignites other people. People don't want to just see marketing. Ask what you can do to help people. And use the distance symbol to send Reiki to those who read your content.

. . .

PEOPLE ENJOY VIDEOS, which is why TikTok took off. A few years ago, TikTok asked me to be a creator for them, to create learning content. They had workshops on how to be successful on TikTok. To meet the requirements of their program I had to post every day and could see that with consistency, you can really build a following.

SO IT DEPENDS on what you want to do. If you use social media as a marketing platform, you want to be engaged in sharing a story or a post as often as you possibly can. And you'll reach different generations on different platforms. My younger students find me on social media.

I'VE ALSO LEARNED discernment about posting. Like who am I? What do I want to put out to the world? And what kind of clients and students do I want to attract into my world? I feel that level of professionalism and focus is important. I have business accounts where I post more business-oriented things. But you still can have a personal social media page going simultaneously where you might share different things. I'm engaged in my Instagram and Facebook, more than I am with TikTok.

IF YOU ARE FEELING OVERWHELMED, start with one thing at a time. You don't have to be on every social media platform or engage in everything at once. That is definitely overwhelming.

WHEN THE PANDEMIC STARTED, I thought, "How do I help? What can I do?" I decided to do a free meditation on Zoom, and we have a hundred or more people join consistently from all over the world, expanding my reach beyond what I had and growing the revenue of my business. People get to sample who I am and what I'm like as a practitioner and as a teacher.

. . .

It requires setting up these events in multiple locations and making sure people know about them. There's a lot of marketing effort that goes into offering a free event. But it's like an advertising tool in a way.

My biggest challenge is time. I saw a quote that entrepreneurs work 80 hours a week to be self-employed rather than 40-hours a week for somebody else. So time management is an issue. I've always been everything in my business, and I'm learning that it isn't the most productive way to operate. I probably should have started out sooner with some delegation. It might cost some money upfront, but then you are saving time, which can get reinvested in other aspects of your business. So that's where I'm in the middle of a big lesson.

I just got a new office space and I'm wondering, "Should I paint it myself to save a few hundred dollars or should I just have a painter paint it?" It's clear that I should have the painter paint it because they're going to do a much better job, and it will be less stressful for me. So I have to stop doing everything myself.

Start with the website and review sites. Help people locate your business, and set up Instagram and social media accounts so that you have the name registered that you want to use so no one can take it after you've started your business. And then engage with those things as you get more comfortable. Somebody may come in to help who is very comfortable with social media. Whatever you feel more drawn to work with initially is where you can get started. The other things can be learned or delegated over time.

. . .

Even writing newsletters can be overwhelming. I can't keep up with that. I'm really grateful that Eventbrite has a tool now where everybody that signed up can get these email marketing campaigns that just take me a few minutes to set up instead of a whole, beautiful newsletter, which takes a lot more time for me.

There are lots of different ways that you can navigate and set these things up without overwhelming yourself. Just get them organized so they're ready to go. When it comes to starting a spiritual business, there are a lot of logistical things to learn, but let Reiki guide you through the process and trust that you will be supported because we need more of us out there, and Reiki wants more of us out there.

You can always call on Reiki. I use that to make big decisions. I have to be proactive and productive as well, but I never feel like I'm working alone. I always have the support of Reiki and the beautiful spiritual beings that support me in my spiritual work. Reiki will help you choose the right platforms and tools for you and your business.

Know that you're supported unconditionally in this process; it makes you feel less alone as you go out there and start your own business. Everyone we help to bring to Reiki brings somebody else to Reiki, and so on. Or they spread Reiki through kindness as they interact with people out in the world, and that's helping us on a global level.

Ultimately, the best marketing tool we have is people experiencing Reiki and then going out into their communities and showing that transformation.

ProTip
Jill Thiel, LRMT, Minnesota, USA
Minnesota Reiki Center[5]

Use the book and use Reiki to help prioritize where to start so it doesn't seem so overwhelming because starting a business can be overwhelming. After your Reiki one and two classes, you're able to start working on people. In classes, we touch on these subjects, but people are ready at different times. The class is life-changing, so when people take Reiki levels one and two, sometimes we don't listen to all of the business tips. And then in the Master class, we don't think we want to start a business so again, we don't always pay attention to the tips. But then Reiki guides us to start a business, and we don't remember any of the things we learned. Do we need insurance? Do I get a table? Recently, a student told me she was treating five clients a day and her body was hurting and she asked, "Can I sit down?" She didn't remember that we covered that in class. Of course, you can. I even wrote an article about better body mechanics for Reiki. It's important to save our bodies with self-care and wellness.

I'VE BEEN DOING this professionally for close to 20 years. So I've gone through different versions of websites and branding just based on the time and how things have changed with having different types of websites for instance. It's a lot easier now, which is great because you don't need to necessarily hire somebody, pay a lot of money, and have it take months and months and months to have a really nice website. But depending on the sort of options that you're offering on your website, you might need to spend some money.

WHEN I FIRST STARTED, I had a very basic website. In your book, you talked about having a business name. So my original name was "Jill Thiel Massage." My Reiki business didn't do as well until I rebranded to "The Minnesota Reiki Center" which is focused on Reiki but if I wanted to incorporate a crystal store or other things, then I may have selected a different name.

WHEN I RE-BRANDED, authenticity was really, really important. I had been working a lot of different jobs and I felt like I was just getting pulled in too many directions. At some point it becomes too much. When I got sick, this voice said, "What is it that you really want to do with your life?" It was Reiki. I really wanted to do Reiki. So I understood it was time to let go of the other things. Because to open these doors, you need to close some doors. Then you can put a hundred percent into what you want to do.

AS I REBRANDED and wrote my story, I "listened" with Reiki for content. I didn't have that website done in a week or two, it took several months. Then I began listening for the right photos. I use my own photos and I love Canva! I use it for design. So when people go to my website, they can really feel me. Through the website they can feel the experience they're going to get in class. I think the best decision I made was to take the time to listen as I created my marketing. Some of it may have come faster if I hadn't, but allow the process that needs to take place, to take place, and not try to rush it. Then when you're ready to go, everything flows the way that it should. So after taking time to listen and develop the marketing and my materials, when I launched The Minnesota Reiki Center, I got results very quickly. I went from having one to three-person classes, to 16-person classes. Then I very quickly had to adapt.

COVID CHANGED things again and I've changed locations. I work from my house and so now I have nine people in person. But then I also have folks join online. So my hybrid classes are not limited and I'm able to reach more people.

. . .

AS THINGS EVOLVE and expand you learn a lot about yourself. And when you think, "I don't think I can do this. I need somebody else to do it for me" but you end up doing it anyway--it's really rewarding to realize, "I can do that now. And I didn't think that I could do that." So you become an expert in all of these things.

I THINK we all have different obstacles, and going through the LRMT program helps show you where that might be. Writing was an obstacle for me. I have dyslexia, so I was really scared to write articles and marketing content. My mentor said facing that fear has helped me become an expert in my field. And so it's important to do the things that really scare us. When I wrote my first article, "Reiki for Gardening" I received lovely feedback and was really surprised. This part of me is now healed. I've gone from feeling like I couldn't write at all to feeling confident writing.

I HAD to put social media aside for a bit and develop a healthier relationship with it. Through the Reiki community, I was able to determine the sort of frequencies I wanted in my social media. And when that piece healed, I became the manager of the ICRT social media. So it's kind of funny how you can go from, "I don't think I like social media at all" to, "I wonder what I can do with this?" If something feels uncomfortable, ask, why? It's usually an opportunity to heal something. And if you just take one step at a time, you will get better and better, and your business will continue to grow.

I ALSO THINK it's really important to make sure that your marketing and social media are very professional and that you're not creating trauma-based responses to things that could feel negative to people. We have to consider every person as a potential client or customer. And part of the unification consciousness is being open to helping all people to heal. I am very passionate about my beliefs and I think that's really important, but I think that when we're creating posts, I am really careful. I always go into that space of Reiki ahead of time to make sure that I'm creating this post from a place of Reiki energy versus creating this from a place that is unhealed and could potentially be harmful or hurtful to another individual.

AND THEN I always think about authenticity. Not looking at what other people are doing. What do I want to do? It's not really about how many people follow you, it's the content and the message that you're delivering and how you are helping people. I also find that you don't have to post every single day. Do what feels right to you. And if it's coming from this place of love and compassion, then that is where it needs to be. And so that's my strategy. Try not to get discouraged if you're not seeing immediate results. Look at those small steps. Maybe you didn't get a client, but maybe you planted a seed. Or they will refer their friends.

AND WHEN I'M scrolling other people's pages, I'm mindful of my thoughts and the energy that I'm putting out around their content. It can be easy to have negative thoughts and energy. Be very aware of that. And be aware of copyrights and trademarks when using logos and photos. Be mindful of licensed content. There are laws around that. Sometimes people aren't completely aware of that when they get started.

TAKE time to look back every now and then and celebrate how far you've come. Not everybody starts a business with Reiki. Believe in yourself and believe that there's a reason that you're doing this. Every little step you take is something to celebrate because having a Reiki business is a wonderful thing. And I can't think of anything else that I would want to be doing.

. . .

CHECK out our podcast on this chapter.⁶

STUDENT SUCCESS STORY **Jennifer Taylor**

Having a structure that kept me on task and breaking things down into measurable steps was helpful because it can be overwhelming. And the reminder that I can use Reiki for all of it.

THERE'S ALSO the spirit of your Reiki business, which is an entity itself and is being divinely led and supported. And the process of releasing the obstacles and resistance or any sort of blocks in the way. Being able to feel those things release and lift. And it is knowing that I can continue to do this for myself.

THIS LIT the fire that I needed, along with the idea that I had six sessions and this time to do what I've wanted to do for a long time. So I said this is the time I'm going to do it.

I DEDICATED myself to that time. I built a Wix website complete with a scheduler and scheduled all of my classes for the year. I wrote the descriptions. Then I taught an Animal Reiki level one and two class before this business class was even finished. I even taught people that I looked up to in the Reiki world as mentors and got incredible feedback which was very confidence boosting.

MY FACEBOOK PAGE now reflects the Reiki business. I changed the name of my business and have worked on branding. I use similar fonts and colors with everything I send out.

. . .

I HAVE AUTORESPONDER EMAILS. I have Zoom set up with a professional account. I was so proud of myself for figuring all of this stuff out.

I'VE HAD several paying clients. I've done multiple animal Reiki and human sessions in person or distance sessions. People are asking for Reiki for family members in ICU. I have repeat clients and referral clients.

IT'S JUST INCREDIBLE. One of the things that you had stressed that helped as far as the marketing was the idea that ultimately it mostly comes down to just word of mouth and people knowing people. So it's just letting people know what you're doing and then letting it take care of itself.

I SENT Reiki and asked for divine timing and the right people to find me. The people who would resonate with exactly what I offered.

WE DID an online Reiki and sound healing experience and had a lot of responses from that.

THERE WERE MANY OBSTACLES; the biggest hurdle was the website, building it from scratch. It was a huge learning curve and overwhelming with the volume that had to be written. But I didn't have much time to work with as I took care of kids and dealt with life; I tried to write things while making dinner. That added chaos that wouldn't be there if I was just an average adult without kids and household things. But the more I let go of the timelines, things flowed.

. . .

AND WHEN YOU SAID, "Teach before you're ready, or you may never be ready," that was really helpful. So I kept reminding myself with all of this stuff, "Do it before you're ready."

I DIDN'T REALIZE how scary the scheduler would be. The idea that somebody could book and I might miss it. What if somebody is sitting there waiting for an appointment, and I didn't even know, but I realized this was irrational.

I SPENT a lot of time on this and felt guilty about it. But my daughter told me how proud she was of me for making my dream come true and helping others. Having guilt turned into "Wow, I'm demonstrating that, as a mom, you can choose and prioritize yourself and your dreams." We did a mini Reiki and sound healing experience for her primary class at the Montessori school. It was incredible.

MY MIND WAS JUST BLOWN. I've created the field of dreams. If you build it, they will come. I made the space for people to find me, and it feels so good to be making this kind of difference, sharing Reiki and healing with people that I would never have had the opportunity to do—and starting to take off and grow. I feel like I'm finally living the kind of authentic and inspired life that was always in the future.

AND JUST THE idea that someone has a positive experience and tells someone else, it's such an honor.

I HAVE faith that the same forces that stirred in you this desire to have this business and to put Reiki into the world, that same force will support you and lead you and guide you through the process.

---

1. https://www.facebook.com/hiddenbrookfarmReikiHorsesOils
2. https://www.instagram.com/reikifromthefarm/
3. https://www.youtube.com/channel/UCW5ScR7ObSiPIpgnDkWkiQA
4. www.healingwithjules.com
5. www.mnreikicenter.com
6. *https://www.buzzsprout.com/1364386/10217670*

6
BUSINESS SKILLS

"I think the biggest obstacle is ourselves, really."
Karen Harrison, Senior ICRT LRMT

Business Consciousness

Many people struggle to bring business practices and principles together with the sacred nature of Reiki. I know I did. On the one hand, I wanted to share the beauty of Reiki with others. On the other hand, I had a negative image of business, believing it was aligned with corporate greed. I don't know why I had this impression because it didn't exist in my previous business life. I think it had more to do with the sacred nature of Reiki and whether the sacred could go together with the secular.

I ALSO STRUGGLED to accept money for spiritual work, making my clients uncomfortable. They simply wanted to pay for the service and move on. But I made it much more complicated by not accepting payment and being wishy-washy when I did. Consequently, clients didn't return. At least not until I healed my issues with my Reiki business.

IF ANY UNCOMFORTABLE feelings or beliefs exist within you, work with Reiki to heal them. Because sharing Reiki through a business has historical precedence. When he came down from Kurama Yama, a holy mountain north of Kyoto with Reiki, Usui Sensei started a Gakkai (school). People paid membership fees to belong and then attended weekly meetings to receive *reijus* or attunements. Usui also taught classes and worked with clients and students through a Reiki business. Usui Sensei was focused on Anshin Ritsu-Mei. This is also known as Satori, Personal Peace, or enlightenment. Healing was a side benefit because he felt that achieving this state would be much easier if a person was free of illness and physically strong.

AFTER RECEIVING the new state of consciousness, Usui wanted to tell his Zen master about it, so he ran down the mountain, tripped, and injured his toe. He spontaneously placed his hands on his toe, and healing energy began flowing and healed his toe. He then realized that healing was part of his ability. The Master level (Shinpiden), which means Mystery Teaching, is another way of saying Anshin Ritsu-Mei or Satori. And in fact, Usui's Shinpiden students did achieve Anshin Ritsu-Mei or Enlightenment.

WHEN DR. HAYASHI wanted to explore the healing aspects of Reiki further and pushed Usui Sensei to change his focus, Usui instead encouraged Hayashi to start his own Gakkai or business to develop this aspect of Reiki further. Hayashi did. And after his death, his wife and son continued working with it until their deaths.

. . .

Mrs. Takata, when she brought Reiki to North America, did so with a business. She taught classes and conducted sessions. Your business may look different from theirs. Their businesses looked different from each other. Reiki may weave into your current career path or a hobby or passion. But whatever it looks like for you, it's essential to heal any issues you may have around receiving an energetic exchange - whether in the form of money or barter (for goods and services that you require) to share Reiki with the world more easily. It benefits your clients and students to contribute to their healing with an energetic exchange. So determine what the best trade is for you, and use Reiki to heal any issues you have with business practices, principles, or ideals. Think of the companies you engage with that offer a fair exchange. A business is a way of creating offerings. It is a tool. It is neither good nor bad; instead, it is an extension of you and will be what you make of it. So create the best business you can. And then enjoy the expansion of Reiki energy and the learning that occurs when you say YES to sharing the gift of Reiki with the world.

Worthiness and the Imposter Syndrome

This is so common; I have to mention it here. Once we heal issues we have around starting a business, many struggle with worthiness and imposter syndrome. When I first met William Rand, I mispronounced my name - three times! Feeling downright foolish, I apologized and told him I didn't know why I had done that. I was in England for my Reiki Master class, and I was worried he would take one look at me, tell me I was not ready for Master's level training, and send me home. I explained to him that I didn't know why I had mispronounced my name; I was just so nervous. He asked why? I never even thought; with blunt honesty, I blurted, "Because Reiki Masters are wonderful and amazing people, and I'm not, I'm just me." William smiled and said, "And I'm just me. I'm glad you are here." Whew.

. . .

HONESTLY, though, I can't tell you how many of us do not feel worthy of being a Reiki Master or having a Reiki business. We wonder if people will see through us and see that we are not perfect. One of the things I loved about William as a Reiki teacher is that he did not let us put him on a pedestal. He said that if Reiki Masters had to be perfect, there would be very few in the World. In the Usui/Holy Fire®III Reiki Master Manual, William Rand says, "In the end, we must consider that a Reiki Master is not one who has mastered Reiki, but one who has allowed Reiki to master him or her."[1] So if you suffer from imposter syndrome or worthiness issues, don't let it get the best of you. Know that everyone who created a Reiki business has probably also struggled with that. Just send Reiki to the issue and allow it to heal. It may crop up several times. Understand that that, too, is normal.

WE DON'T NEED to be perfect to share the gift of Reiki. We just need to be our authentic selves, and the students who can learn best from us will find us. Of course, a Reiki business and a little marketing can help them do that!

Being Open to Success

Oddly, I did an exercise reasonably early on with my Reiki business and discovered that I was just as afraid of success as failure. I guess, in my previous life, business success was very stressful. I worked long hours and had very little time with my children. I was exhausted much of the time and struggled to find balance. So I deliberately kept my practice small. When I realized I was as afraid of success with my business as a failure, I sat down with Reiki and asked for guidance.

THE GUIDANCE that came was that I got to define what success looks like to me. I realized that the previous "version" of success did not feel successful to me. So I created my own version of success. My version contained balance. I set in my calendar the number of appointments I could easily accommodate at the time of the week that suited me. I also set aside time with my family and children and booked it in my calendar. And I set aside time for self-care to fill my cup. I love to travel. So traveling to teach became a part of my version of success.

I REALIZED I could teach as often or little as I pleased. Initially, I taught small classes monthly and found it time-consuming. Then I shifted to teaching every two months. The class size increased (which provided a better experience for my students), and I had more freedom with my schedule.

INTERESTINGLY, the more balanced my work-life balance became and the happier I became, the more abundance I received until my business became healthy and prosperous. It supports my family and my goals effortlessly. I have to pinch myself, as I didn't think this level of ease and success could go hand in hand. But they do.

EXERCISE: What Does Success Look Like to You?
So take a few moments now, activate Reiki and write down what success looks like to you.

Current vs. Future Clients
So often, with marketing and sales, we focus on marketing to future clients and forget about or ignore our current clients. Word of mouth is often the best way to grow your practice. So don't forget about your existing clients. Keep them engaged with newsletters, meditations, Reiki share groups, Reiki challenges, and networking

opportunities. Let them know what you have going on. Consider offering specials for them. Or giving them a discounted session when they provide referrals to you. If you have a Facebook or other social networking group for your current clients, stay engaged on the page. Comment on their posts. Let them know you are sending them Reiki regularly. I send Reiki to all of my students daily in my Reiki grid. I love to feel the connection with them when I do.

YOUR CURRENT CLIENTS are your foundation. And they form the foundation for your existing clients. Stay actively engaged with them.

Keeping the Conversation Current

One of the best ways to keep the conversation current is to keep yourself current. One of the things the ICRT encourages us to do is be continually involved in our own development to be of better service to ourselves and others. So stay in touch with what is going on.

You can stay in touch:

- With the free email newsletters from the various Reiki Associations
- By attending the Reiki shares of Reiki Masters in your region (or another area). Many Reiki Masters hold online Reiki shares or get-togethers now, so they are easily accessible.
- By checking out Reiki podcasts or YouTube videos. With my Reiki from the Farm™ podcast, I try to interview as many Reiki experts as possible. I find each one shares knowledge and a perspective or viewpoint that may differ from our own. And I include a healing meditation each week. There are some other great podcasts and YouTube videos out there too. Check them out when you can.
- With a mentor or a mentoring group. Suppose you can find someone with more experience than you have who

will agree to mentor you and set up regular meetings or appointments. I have a monthly appointment with my mentor. This not only keeps me current, but it also keeps me moving forward energetically and with my business.
- By reading Reiki books, news, the *Reiki News Magazine*, or other publications about Reiki. There are more and more becoming available.
- Working on your development, studying new courses, reviewing classes, or even learning something new can enhance your Reiki experience.
- By staying in touch with other Reiki professionals. Why not form a group for Reiki professionals in your region? Laurelle Gaia said that when they did this, not only did it feel very supportive, but as Reiki practitioners and Masters began working together, sharing their knowledge, everyone's businesses expanded, and everyone benefitted. There is no such thing as competition with Reiki.
- By listening to your guidance. Sometimes, the guidance that comes through you brings new information or ways of understanding.

One of the best things we can do for ourselves is create a space where we feel supported and can continue to grow. Go ahead and try out a few of these suggestions and then observe the growth of your vibration. This is the best way to keep the conversation current with your students.

Creating Boundaries

Boundaries. Boy. Creating and then holding boundaries with others can be TOUGH. Especially if you are an empath as I am. It is something I really struggled with and occasionally still do. Reiki is so powerful and effective; we want to help everyone. But you will come across clients who want you to shoulder their burdens. Or who want to blame you if things don't work out as they wish. Some don't respect the time you have allocated for a session. Or demand more than you are able or willing to give. And sometimes, people are desperate. And that desperation can spread out to you.

One of my friends shared a meme with me that said, "The only people who get upset about you setting boundaries are the ones who were benefiting from you having none." - Unknown.

Part of the ICRT philosophy is "Taking personal responsibility for one's situation in life."[2] And another is "Assuming that one has the resources to resolve any problem encountered, or the ability to develop these resources."

Sometimes, people reach out to you for help but do not wish to take responsibility for their life situation or don't want to make the necessary changes. Sometimes they are stuck in their story. Other times, they simply want to dump their burdens on you. It is essential as Reiki practitioners that we do not take on our clients' burdens. For one thing, that robs them of a learning opportunity. For another, it drains your energy without providing any benefit to you. How do we do this? Ask Reiki for help both with creating boundaries and balancing your empathy. And keep a very clear idea around what is yours and what is theirs. It serves no one if you shoulder their burdens. Let Reiki do the work instead. If you struggle with this, ask Reiki to protect your energy. And when you are done with a session, follow up with energetic hygiene.

I also want to address clients and friends with a victim or poverty mentality. If I feed into this mentality by providing lots of unpaid services or treating them as victims, I don't help them. They stay stuck in the story of poverty and victimhood. I don't empower them when I play along with these beliefs. The fact is that there are enough resources on the planet for everyone. And the victim and poverty mentalities serve no one. Reiki can empower people. But I need to get out of the way to allow that to happen.

So PAY ATTENTION. Any time you find yourself annoyed or even angry, there's a good chance that someone is not respecting a boundary you have set. Ask Reiki to help you set and hold the boundaries you need to. So many of us are people, pleasers, that this can be difficult. But the key to staying balanced and healthy in our work is setting and holding comfortable boundaries even when we upset people who don't wish to respect them.

What to Do with Unhappy Clients?

As I was writing my book and preparing to put it out in the world (which is another level of scary), I watched a video in my HayHouse writer's group by Nick Ortner, the author of *The Tapping Solution*. He said, "You haven't arrived until you have a hater."

No MATTER what we do or how hard we try, we occasionally have unhappy clients. Some of them don't tell us they are unhappy. They just don't come back. And that's OK. It's important to understand that your style is not for everyone. And everyone has the freedom to decide whom to get sessions and classes from. Sometimes, even if a client is happy, they don't return. That too is OK.

BUT WHAT DO we do with an unhappy client who lets us know they are unhappy? Or worse, lets other people know they are unhappy? It is going to happen. And when it does, send Reiki to the situation and ask for guidance. As long as we have maintained integrity in all that we do, followed the ICRT Code of Ethics and Standards of Practice, stayed within our scope of practice, and done our best, we must leave it at that.[3] Even if you are not a member of the ICRT Reiki Membership Association, the Code of Ethics is a great tool.

So if someone is unhappy, you can offer the client a refund. It is often worth it to do that and release the ties. I have a clear policy around my classes that deposits are non-refundable but can be applied to another course within the same calendar year. People pay for sessions once they are complete, and I don't think anyone has asked for a refund. But when classes were canceled due to Covid, I promptly sent refunds to students who had registered and decided not to attend the online class. And I have had friends offer refunds to clients who were not happy just to firmly cut ties with the type of client who would cause them headaches down the road. Understand that it is not possible to make everyone happy. And it's often their problem. But regardless of who is responsible, send Reiki and ask for healing, then move on. It is difficult but necessary. We can't please everyone.

I send Reiki to anyone who seems unhappy, even if they have been unreasonable with me or have sent a psychic or energetic attack. In a conversation with William Rand, he said, "it's important to understand that it is not that person's pure and beautiful soul attacking you. It is lower frequency energy attached to them that feels threatened which is attacking you." William said that he appreciates when these things happen because it shows him an area of his energetic grid that needs healing that he was previously unaware of. Like me, he then works on his energetic grid and sends love and Reiki to the unhappy person and the energies which caused the energetic/psychic attack. Whether they receive the Reiki energy is up to them. But we send it anyway.

. . .

ANOTHER ICRT PHILOSOPHY is "Willingness to recognize prejudice in oneself and replace it with truth and love."[4] This is followed by "Compassion for those who have decided not to do this." I think this is a beautiful principle that I do my best to live by. We can allow people not to be fans, send them Reiki, and move on.

Personal Attacks

What to do about clients, students, or other practitioners who talk badly about you behind your back? This, too, sometimes happens. My best advice is not to engage. People who gossip are often very insecure and may be jealous of your success.

IF THIS HAS HAPPENED to me in the Reiki world, I am unaware of it. But in the horse world, when what we were doing with horses was very different from what everyone else was doing (riding bareback without bits, using Reiki, essential oils, and Animal Communication), quite a lot of people in established horse businesses told people we were crazy and not to listen to us or to trust us. I think they felt threatened, but it was hurtful just the same. I decided not to engage. People can feel the energy in what they are doing and saying, and I had no interest in keeping the drama going.

ELEVEN YEARS LATER, our horse business is still here, stronger than ever. And many of the people who bad-mouthed us did not survive. I never wished them ill. But I think people were ready for a new way of doing things with horses, and so were we. So they gravitated to us and what we offered. And I think people saw through what the others were saying.

WE "[H]ONOR all Reiki practitioners and teachers regardless of lineage or organizational affiliation" in our code of ethics" and "[r]efrain from making negative statements about other Reiki practitioners or teachers." I love that we do this. So there is no stress. If someone has something negative to share about you, you let it be and let your work stand for itself.

ANOTHER THING I noticed is that the more I accepted and appreciated myself and my work, the less often these attacks came. When I was very new and experimenting with new ways of doing things with horses and wasn't sure of myself, I seemed to invite attack. Once I gained confidence, I was energetically stronger and noticed fewer and fewer people spoke ill of me. Especially as I didn't engage and never spoke ill of any of them. So look within yourself and ask, "Am I confident in what I am doing? Am I doing the best I can do?" If you are not confident, send Reiki to yourself to heal this. If you feel you could do better, ask Reiki to help, you do so. And to the person who is speaking ill of you, think to yourself, "Isn't that cute? I threaten them. And that's not my intention at all." Then send them Reiki.

Embracing Technology

Technology and I NEVER got along. My brain just doesn't work that way. I can't understand it easily. And I don't think it understands me. Technology sometimes breaks just from being in my presence. I could see some benefits from using technology, but we definitely weren't friends. Just as I felt "wrong" about using business practices and principles with Reiki, I also felt a little off about using technology in my Reiki business. And I didn't understand it well at all.

WHEN I STARTED WORKING with my mentor, Colleen Benelli, she said, "Pam, you have to heal your resistance to using technology. Technology allows us to reach more people and to do more - you need to embrace it and begin using it in your practice and your life."

. . .

THAT WAS SOME EXCELLENT ADVICE. I did as she said, sending Reiki daily to my fear and reluctance around using technology. Eventually, it healed. I got a big push in Heathrow airport at the beginning of Covid when I could feel that people needed help, so I sat down to do my first Facebook Live. I explained that it was my first Facebook Live, and I hoped people could hear me. I also explained that we were likely to be interrupted by announcements for flights in a beautiful British accent (we were) but that the meditation should work anyway.

Do you know that over 2000 people watched that video? And people told me afterward how much it helped them. Fortunately, the ICRT then moved our classes online. And I feel that the energy of technology aligned with Reiki in our ignitions and training. Indeed, I began to feel differently about technology. I aligned with it, my fear and reluctance let go, and I started embracing technology just as Colleen had advised. What a lovely thing it is.

WE ARE VERY fortunate to live in an age where technology does so much for us to make our lives easier. Technology washes my dishes, vacuums my floors, heats my house, allows me to email clients, record podcasts, and write and publish books. It provides transportation, lights, hot water, and cooks my food. I sometimes think this is the future our ancestors wished for us.

AS COLLEEN ADVISED, technology allows us to reach more people. When I can have people from 5 continents in my classes, all with a tiny environmental footprint, and we have an opportunity to get to know each other, understand each other and work together, I know she's right. I KNOW SHE'S RIGHT, too, when I can put out a podcast and a newsletter that reaches thousands of people each week. How incredible is that?

. . .

I make it a point to learn something new with technology every week. I decide what I want to learn, then watch tutorials and YouTube videos and play with it until it is figured out. If I get really stuck, I find a 10-year-old to explain it to me. Or one of my kids. It's a great sense of accomplishment once you master something new.

If you haven't already, embrace technology. And if you need the help of Reiki to do so, put Reiki to work for you. You will be happy to feel comfortable using technology in your business. And it can save you time and effort that you can use somewhere else!

Hiring Assistants

My mentor urged me to hire assistants when my business grew. I could see her point, but I didn't want anyone answering my emails or creating my newsletters, as I enjoy doing that. And I'm not very good at explaining what I want to an administrative assistant. So I decided to look at the other things in my life that take time. Ones that I don't enjoy doing. I have three businesses - a Reiki business, a horse business, and an essential oil business. It was getting busy, so I knew some of it had to go.

I made a list of the tasks I do and need to do. I realized that several things no longer fulfilled me and contributed to a feeling of overwhelm. So I hired an assistant to help in the gardens and with the house 3-4 hours per week. She's good at it, and my gardens and grounds have never looked better.

I have someone who helps me with social media–and my horse work. I asked her to take over teaching the riding lessons. It wasn't easy to let go of something I built, but I knew it was the right choice guided by Reiki, and she is doing a fantastic job with them.

I STILL CREATE THE OILS. It's something I do to relax, and I don't have extraordinarily demanding clients. They are happy to wait until creating their orders fits my schedule. I got help grooming the dogs. And mowing. And looking after the farm. And I upped my self-care.

As things continue to grow, I'll probably sit down with a new set of lists. And I realize that I can let go of the tasks that don't bring me joy. This letting go then provides an opportunity for someone else to grow and do what they are good at.

MY REIKI BUSINESS worked beautifully alongside my other two businesses for years. And I have friends whose business works alongside a part-time or full-time job. But at some point, if things get overwhelming, consider making a list of the things you love to do and the things you don't love to do. And then consider getting help with the tasks that no longer bring you joy. Send Reiki to attract just the right people or person to help. Sometimes, assistants are willing to work in exchange for Reiki sessions or classes or mentor training. Sometimes it is just simpler to pay them. With the time I have freed up by hiring help, I can see more clients and teach more classes. It has been a worthwhile investment.

KAREN HARRISON, an ICRT Mentor Teacher, says that "one of the secrets to her success is 'hiring it done.'" She pays others to do any task that is not required for her to do. Her Reiki assistant does all the administrative parts of producing a Reiki class, loads transactions into QuickBooks, balances and maintains payments, and balances the checkbook.

. . .

ANOTHER ASSISTANT CREATES the emails for Reiki Circle, Reiki Call, and her monthly Reiki newsletter. She also uploads podcasts. When Karen decided to add a mass texting program, her assistant learned how to use it, trained Karen, and then Karen could create her graphics and send out the messages easily.

ONE OF THE secrets of working with assistants is finding out what tasks they enjoy and are good at—and then having them do those things and not something they don't enjoy. Karen also hires help with yard work, maintenance, cleaning, organizing, and sometimes even shopping. Having assistants frees up her time for teaching, sessions, podcasts, Reiki Circle, writing, and working with the ICRT. And she's one of the busiest and most successful Reiki practitioners I know.

Record Keeping

You can get as complex or simple as you wish to keep records. I like to keep things simple. So I have a complete calendar where I keep a record of all income, mileage, clients seen, etc. Anything that I need to calculate my income and mileage for the coming year. It is paper-based and straightforward. But on those 52 pages, an accurate summary of my year is available and easy to refer to when I need it. I keep a record of any riding lessons or Reiki sessions held or canceled. Vacations. Class students. Income. And so on. And my expenses are stored in 2 folders (visa and cash expenses) until I am ready to put them into categories for my bookkeeper at the end of the year. I add my bank statements and put together my mileage and income statement. And my bookkeeper can put everything together for me for my HST claim and my taxes.

I NEVER MIND PAYING TAXES. My husband reminds me that if I am paying taxes, I must be doing well and making money. So I feel blessed to pay taxes, especially in light of all of the government's services for us. Clear roads. Garbage and recycle pick up. Public parks and spaces. Truly blessed. I smile when I write a check to the taxman and give thanks that I have the means to do so.

I ALSO KEEP records of every Reiki session I do. I use a paper copy of the Reiki documentation form from "Reiki the Healing Touch." When I see clients in person, I have them fill out the front page, and I fill out the back one. This helps me gauge progress with each client and remember what we were working on in the previous session. I highly recommend using something like this with your sessions.

AND FINALLY, in ICRT manuals, there is a class evaluation. I ask my students to fill these in after class to see how I did. I find these have helped me improve my classes over the years. As a Licensed Teacher with the ICRT, I am required to turn these into the ICRT. You may simply wish to have students fill them in for your own data.

Getting Paid

Set yourself up to receive automatic payments through Square or PayPal or another scheduling software that can accept payments. Set up your classes so that people can pay a deposit or in full when they register. And your sessions so that they can pre-pay or so you can send an invoice immediately after the session is complete. Try and make it as easy as possible for people to pay you. They will appreciate that. And so will you.

Accounting and Bookkeeping

During the first meeting I had with my accountant and bookkeeper, I was trying to decide whether to invest in their services or attempt to do taxes myself. My accountant gave me some fantastic advice. He asked what I charged per hour. And he suggested that I'd be better off paying him to do what he knows how to do and loves to do. Then take the hours I would save by not preparing my taxes and do what I'm good at with them. Boy, was he right! Because of his extensive knowledge of accounting, he has saved me a lot of money over the years, and his bookkeeper has saved me countless headaches. When we submit my taxes, I know that there are no errors.

On top of that, my accountant uses programs and information that I would never have known about. Unless you enjoy accounting and have a background in it, the assistance of an accountant and bookkeeper is priceless. Ask friends and family for referrals. Then get prices and interview your accounting team to see if they are a good match. You'll thank me for this.

Membership Associations

It can be helpful to join a Reiki Membership Association for added credibility and reach. Some organizations allow you to advertise your classes. Some also give you a logo you can use. A membership association may have a Code of Ethics or Standard of Practice that you are expected to follow. Being involved with a membership association can bring a new level of professionalism into your practice. Sometimes you can save money on Reiki insurance through the association too. Have a look at the different associations in your area - or some of the International Associations to see which ones you resonate with. Look at what they offer, their Purpose and their Philosophy to see if it aligns with you. Most associations charge a modest fee which is well worth it for what it brings to your business.

Meditation for Success Consciousness

Close your eyes, bring your hands into Gassho and activate your Reiki symbols. Then place one hand on your heart and one on your head, giving yourself Reiki.

Open your heart and your mind to receive the light of success consciousness.
Allow the light of confidence within success consciousness to flow through you.
Now allow the energy of trust to flow through you.
Trust in Reiki.
Trust in the higher power.
Trust in yourself.
And trust that you are on the path that you are on is the one you are meant to be on.
Understanding that when something is difficult or challenges you, it is an opportunity for growth and for stepping into your true path.
If something wasn't on your path and part of your purpose, you would feel apathetic about it. Fear, anxiety, nervousness, and excitement. These all indicate that something is important for you.
So allow any nervousness or anxiety or issues around self-worth issues or worries about your own talents and scope and abilities to transmute now into excitement. Into a surety that you are enough.
Into knowing that you are truly following your soul's purpose.
For what could be more important than spreading love and truth and joy and trust on the planet?
What could possibly be more important than helping to empower others to realize their authentic gifts and talents?
I invite you to relax into the light of success consciousness today in all the aspects of it. The confidence and trust and belief in yourself, all flow through you like water.
And if your inner critic is particularly active or harsh, we invite the light of compassion to flow through your inner critic now so that it can learn a new way of doing things.
And we're going to spend some time here just letting go of anything that would block you from receiving success and from being successful with your goals. Whether you are consciously aware of the blocks or not.
Pause

We are open to success, mentally physically, spiritually, and emotionally. We welcome the feeling of accomplishment that comes with purposeful existence.
We welcome Professional success and financial success.
Imagine now what that success looks like to you. Invite Reiki to assist you as you begin formulating those thoughts and intentions empowered by Reiki. And allow the Reiki energy to assist you in bringing form to the formless. Creating that which does not yet exist. Igniting the spark of the Reiki professional within you and allowing it to come to light. Bringing forth the practitioner and the teacher that are ready to come in to form at this moment in time.
Stepping into who you truly are. Empowered. Prepared.
Saying yes to Reiki and saying yes to success, whatever that looks like for you.
And allowing that energy to settle more firmly and deeply around and through you. Moving into every cell of your body and every part of your being in that deep knowing and deep understanding of your ability to manifest with Reiki.
And as you wish, so it is.

Remembering that just for today, I will not worry because I will keep my thoughts focused on the beauty and the positive. I will not be angry because I will view every challenge and every difficulty as an opportunity to learn and grow. I will be kind to all others as I spread the love of Reiki on the earth starting with me. Spreading kindness within me. I will be devoted to my work and devoted to the people around me and yet, will from enough boundaries that I will not take on the burdens of others. Not taking those growth opportunities away from them. And finally, I will be filled with gratitude. Gratitude for the gift that is Reiki. For the ability to share that gift. And for the beauty and wonder that exists in my life.

Today, as I look in the mirror, I say, "I love you. I really love you. You are the joy of my life." And today, I mean it.

Namaste.

ProTip
Karen Harrison, Sr LRMT, Missouri, USA
Whole Life Center[5]

Let me start by saying blessings to you, Pam, and all you've created.

Many of my students are so excited to start a Reiki business that they want to quit their job and jump on it full-time. And if you're independently wealthy, that's a great idea. But if you're not, it will take 18 months to five years to produce the kind of income you need to live on with a new business. So starting part-time is a great idea.

I began my counseling business in 1993 in private practice and had contract work with other places. At one point, my son said to me, "Mommy, won't anybody give you a full-time job?" So I started my Reiki business in 1998. I already had the structure in place for the business. I had an office, a bookkeeping system, and a payment system... all the things I needed. So I didn't need to add much for my Reiki business. I just started doing it alongside my counseling business.

I joke that I spent nine years in finance to overcome my math phobia. But I know there are many ways to set up your books. In your book, you talked about a simple way to do it, which is probably perfect for someone starting out. Keep it as simple as possible.

But going forward, as you have more transactions, it's helpful to have an accounting system set up, and having one online means that your CPA can check remotely. Your bookkeeper can enter transactions remotely. You can have your bank accounts linked to your program and have the transactions automatically downloaded into your accounting program, making the reconciliation process quicker and easier and giving you these wonderful reports. You can easily check your income and expenses and see your net worth. I think the reports are fun but admit I may geek out on that a bit. I use QuickBooks online. I've got my whole company set up there. It creates nice reports at the end of the year so I have all the information that I need for my CPA to do my taxes.

I had a bookkeeper set me up on QuickBooks and then teach me to enter things. I did that for about three years, and then I hired somebody to do it because one of my secrets of success is "hire it done." I have all the things around my house hired done that I can, including balancing my checkbooks, housework, and taking care of the lawn. Anything that I don't enjoy or I'm not good at, or if it will just allow me more time to devote to my Reiki business, then I hire it done.

In my Reiki business, I have an assistant to process students who register for classes, enter them into reiki.org to get their certificates, and track payments. Since COVID, she works remotely, so she created these cool online tracking sheets for me, and I can enter information into them. It's all kept online and up to date. Then I have somebody process payments, and someone handles QuickBooks and helps order supplies. For in-person classes, another assistant helps set everything up as I set my house up differently for classes. I also have an essential oil business and have an assistant to help process information and paperwork. I get help with technology.

RECENTLY I DECIDED to get online scheduling, so my assistant did the research and presented me with a spreadsheet of the kinds, costs, what they do, and don't do. Then we chose a system, and she trained me on how to use it. I've got five different assistants, and each of them does what they are good at. Different people have different skills and abilities, so I let them choose the things they like to do.

Sometimes my assistants need long periods of time off so I have them each write a procedure manual for their position. Then if they are out, one of us can read it and figure out how to cover for them, so the tasks are still getting done. In the beginning, you may not be able to hire as much done, but as your business gets more established, the more that you can hire done, the more that allows you time to teach the classes, post to Reiki circles, write articles, etc. To do the things that only you can do.

When I look for help, I think, "What sort of things do I need to get done?" Then I think, "Who do I know that might be open to doing that?" And interestingly enough, most of my assistants are either my friends or Reiki students. Working with friends can be challenging, but it can also be fun and rewarding. Working with my assistants becomes my social time. We work together and catch up as part of what we're doing.

You talked about the worthiness issue in the book. Whenever I talk to people who are new at offering Reiki, they think, "My Reiki is not good enough," and they're worried about themselves. But I tell them to focus on being of service to others. Focus on them, not you, and get yourself out of the way. Then your issues clear away.

My only goal is to do the best job I can with each session to help the client in the best way I can. Am I going to be able to perform a miracle? Probably not. Can I provide some comfort? Can I provide some help and support? Probably. That is my goal. So just focus on being a service rather than your abilities and worthiness.

And around success consciousness, I offer the same advice. I remind Reiki practitioners to focus on being of service. And trust that with the help of Reiki, you'll be able to do the best job that you can.

Start small with teaching. Start by just teaching Reiki level one. You don't need to teach Reiki levels one and two at the same time. And you can find someone to share the teaching with you if you want. Perhaps each of you brings a friend, and each of you teaches half the material. That makes it easier. Or you can divide the material up for Reiki one and two over three or four nights. Then each week, you just have to prepare two or three hours of material. Try it out first on your friends and have them give you some feedback. Charge a lower fee or offer your first classes for free or trade or something. Just so you can get out there and start. You'll get better with time, but you won't get better if you don't start somewhere.

When I started, there were so many experienced Reiki master teachers in Kansas City, it was intimidating. I just want to be the best Reiki teacher I could be. So I reviewed ICRT classes which helped a lot because I learned so much when I reviewed with an ICRT teacher. I learned things that I hadn't in my first Reiki level one and two class. That gave me more information about teaching. Also, the ICRT manual is a great resource. Just jump in, be brave, and try it.

Having this all in a book is so convenient. And having your personal experience shared here, I think, will help bolster people's confidence. Some people will be drawn to sessions and some to teaching. If you're going to teach, do some sessions to inform your teaching. There are so many different ways to go with it.

Sometimes when students start giving Reiki sessions; some give an unlimited amount of time in their sessions. That can be a challenge, both for you and the person receiving. So if you've scheduled an hour, keep to that.

Technology is constantly changing. I mean, who knew that we

would be teaching classes on Zoom? So stay current with technology and make technology your friend and ally.

Entrepreneurs need a different mindset than the employee mindset. So learn to make that shift from employee consciousness to entrepreneur consciousness and business ownership. Learn how to set your business up, start a bank account, etc. Do you want a sole proprietorship, corporation, LLC? Register the name. Your state or province generally requires a name; search to make sure nobody else has that name, then register it. When I started in 1993, I made my website my name, and I am so glad that I did because, for years, the focus of my business was counseling. And I still love counseling. But now, the main focus is Reiki. By having my name, I had the flexibility to shift that focus and redo my website with the same domain name.

The biggest obstacles to creating a Reiki business are usually around our mindset: our fears, the things that we don't know how to do, and things we think we're not good enough at. But I think having this book as a resource will help people organize the things they need to think about. And then, they can create a plan for themselves. Best wishes to you as you do!

Here are some of Karen's fantastic Reiki business articles:

- Reiki Business Practices[6]
- Developing Clients and Students for Your Reiki Business Part I[7]
- Developing Clients and Students for Your Reiki Business Part II[8]
- Things to Consider When Starting a Business[9]
- Reiki for Tax Time[10]

Check out our podcast on this chapter.[11]

STUDENT SUCCESS STORY Steve Hansen

Having Reiki has been an enormous blessing to my life. Although my business started to take off from initiatives I began during the course, I experienced a significant loss recently and pulled back from that. I understand that these experiences are growth experiences and need my full attention.

THE COMING TOGETHER of multiple people with the same intention allowed some steps to happen energetically. I was surprised at how big that was. I approached the course with a sense of curiosity and was ready to learn, but what I imagined was that I would pick up business insights.

BUT I WAS REALLY surprised that the Reiki energy was the teacher and that we were coming together for that purpose and providing a space for these huge things to happen. Having some of those experiences with the meditations and interacting with classmates shifted things for me.

THE BIG LESSON for me was to follow Reiki. It is the best guide.

I WAS able to overcome a fear of being seen. Reiki gently came in and offered the perfect inroad for me to begin in a small way. I created short Facebook live videos, holding simple and approachable meditations and experiences. It was exciting that the energy was there to support me.

. . .

REIKI NUDGED me to take a break when I needed to. The message came in to stop worrying about anything else before my personal life became complicated with loss.

SHIFTING out of comfort and into a place where I can be seen and visible helped fulfill a purpose that aligned with my business, and you allowed me to access my intuition. I released energetic blocks.

CURRENTLY, my business is in winter dormancy, but there's no urgency about starting anything or continuing what I had been doing. It's all in place and ready to go when Divine timing and guidance point me in that direction again.

I WAS able to find an ideal place to practice. So I'm ready once my healing is complete. I like that I can trust that it will work out.

I'M EXCITED TO TEACH, but I'll start small. I think that's what's next.

IT'S hard to put into words how much the course helped me. I feel a little inadequate there, but it's just surprising how much I could have walked with it and had the healing happen. Reiki and the course provided a perfect avenue to do the healing work that needed to happen to shift me into business mode and recovery.

EVERY WEEK, I saw how you would be in tune with the guidance you were receiving, and it just played perfectly into our needs as a class. I just loved being a part of that. I loved coming to class and seeing that sometimes, it was not what I expected, but it was dead on to what I needed that week.

. . .

YOU FOLLOWED your guidance and brought us just what we needed. It was beautiful.

REIKI WILL GUIDE you through every step. The temptation is to go into the logical part of "What do I need for my business?" But don't forget to let Reiki lead. It will lead you exactly where you need to be, one step at a time.

---

1. Rand, William Lee. *Reiki: The Healing Touch*. Southfield, MI: International Center for Reiki Training, 2019. 118.
2. https://www.reiki.org/center-purpose-and-philosophy
3. https://www.reiki.org/code-ethics
4. https://www.reiki.org/center-purpose-and-philosophy
5. www.karenharrison.net
6. https://www.karenharrison.net/wp-content/uploads/2017/04/ReikiBusinessPractices.pdf
7. https://www.karenharrison.net/wp-content/uploads/2016/09/Build-and-Maintain-your-Reiki-Client-Relationships.pdf
8. https://www.karenharrison.net/wp-content/uploads/2017/05/SocialMedia.pdf
9. https://www.karenharrison.net/things-to-consider-when-starting-a-business/
10. https://www.karenharrison.net/reiki-for-tax-time/
11. https://www.buzzsprout.com/1364386/10263010

7
TEACHING REIKI

"I'm passionate about teaching. Empowering people with Reiki then watching them become who they came here to be, that's what fires me up!"
Pam Allen-LeBlanc - ICRT LRMT

I find it funny that I never intended to teach - EVER! Because now it is my greatest joy. So even if you don't think you want to teach, I encourage you to read this chapter. Reiki may change your mind...

I PLANNED to do attunements for animals (yes, you can do that), and I wanted to teach children (yes, you can do that, too). And I'll discuss how to do both in this chapter. But I never ever wanted to teach Reiki to adults.

THE MAIN REASON I didn't want to teach was that I didn't particularly like people. I'm an animal lover and an empath, though. And directly after I finished my Reiki Master class, as I was flying home from England, I awoke from a light sleep and, in that lucid state, realized that people are animals, and I love animals; therefore, I must love people.

ONE OF THE unique things about empaths is that we always know the truth once we hear it. Once the truth of that statement sank into me, a wave of love for people and the human race washed over me, and I knew it to be true. I understood that what I didn't love was picking up the dense layers of energy and emotion I tended to pick up when I was around people. But I realized that I had the Master level energy and a host of tools from my recent class to address that going forward, so that reservation left me.

I DIDN'T KNOW if I would be any good as a teacher. So there was that. But I thought my lineage was so closely tied to Usui Sensei's after studying with William Rand, and I liked the thoroughness and evidence-based teachings of the ICRT lineage. So I wondered, "How can I not share that?" And immediately set up a class.

MY FIRST CLASS WAS INTERESTING. I was terrified. I don't know many people who aren't scared to teach their first class. I was fine as we were planning it. And as we kept changing the date to work around people's schedules. Five people wanted to take the class. But when we set a date, one couldn't make it because of work. Then another couldn't find a babysitter. So I changed the date about four times.

FINALLY, we decided on June 21, 2011, for my first ever Reiki class. It had been less than a month since I had returned from my Master's class. But this date worked for four of the five people. The day before I was to teach, my level 3 teacher came for a visit. She said, "I never know who will show up for my Reiki classes." I asked why. She said, "Because the ego gets involved and convinces students that they don't want to grow, they shouldn't attend, so people sign up but don't always show up. Sometimes I have five registered for a class, and only one shows up. Especially for level 1 classes."

I WAS happy she shared that with me because of the four people who planned to attend; one arrived shortly after we were due to start. One messaged that she had had a panic attack and wouldn't attend. Another messaged that she was having car trouble. And I never heard a thing from the fourth person!

THAT LEFT me with one student. She was my horse work apprentice, so I felt really comfortable with her. We waited 1/2 hour for the no-show, then I breathed a sigh of relief and began teaching the class. I didn't know the no-show or the lady with car issues. And was nervous about teaching them. But I felt utterly comfortable teaching my apprentice. I knew I didn't have to be perfect, that I could make a mistake, and we would laugh about it. So I was able to completely relax and get comfortable teaching the material.

I WONDERED how I could create the magical attunement William Rand had created at Stonehenge on my little farm in New Brunswick, Canada? I needn't have worried. It really was not about me as a teacher. It was about connecting my student to the Reiki energy and allowing her to have her own experience with it. When it came to the attunement, I could feel the same magic happening. It wasn't from me; it was from Reiki. I invited her to step outside to process once the attunement was complete. And to take her time writing in nature with the horses. And then come back inside when the process felt complete.

. . .

When she returned, she explained that her senses were heightened and that it was like she could hear and sense what the wind was saying. That it felt as if she had received superpowers. She had. I often refer to Reiki as my superpower because we are never, ever helpless when we have Reiki. The magic transferred just fine. It was all about getting out of the way and allowing Reiki to do what it needed to do.

We are fortunate with the ICRT that we have a comprehensive manual and well-organized class outlines, so teaching is much easier. I simply followed the manual for the first several years when I taught. And my classes were exactly right for the students who attended. As I gained more experience with Reiki, I was able to add personal stories and examples. And eventually, over time and after I took the 1000+ extra hours of training to become a Licensed Reiki Master Teacher with the ICRT, I formed a new relationship with the energy where I had become so comfortable with the material and the energy that my classes became richer and more evolved.

After that first class, I went on to teach another level 1 class the following week at a friend's house. And all four people who registered DID show up. But I was more confident this time so that I could teach easily. Then I taught a children's class using Barbara McKell's "Child Reiki" material. My three children and several other children from our neighborhood attended with their parents. It was a magical, wonderful class. And shortly after that, I taught level 2.

Meanwhile, I attuned animals and just got to know Reiki at the Master level. I believe *"if you want to learn, teach,"* and in teaching Reiki, I learned. I'm still learning today in my sessions and classes!

. . .

It was a few years before I was asked to teach level 3 and Masters. But eventually, they became part of my repertoire. In 2013, I studied Karuna Reiki®, the advanced Reiki Master class, and began teaching that. At some point, I discovered that if I sent Reiki to my students once they signed up, intending to help them get to class, they did. And I could count on their attendance. Everyone shifts once they sign up for class, and the shifting can be uncomfortable. When I explained that in my class write-up, sending Reiki to my students to assist in the process, they showed up and told me that it helped them.

Types of Classes

Although we typically teach level 1&2 classes together in my lineage, my teacher suggested that we teach them separately until we become comfortable with each one and then put them together. Our Master class can no longer be broken up into two parts because we also give the Holy Fire® Reiki symbol and energy and teach the Usui Reiki Masters, and Holy Fire® Reiki takes three full days to install. So the Master class is now only taught as one class.

We can also teach children. When teaching children, William Rand recommends that we teach no further than levels 1&2. I never really understood this but followed William's recommendation. I discovered that this was appropriate for my children, two who studied level 1 and one who attended a full-length level 2 class with adults because she really wanted to learn level 2. Indeed, my youngest daughter, who studied level 2 in an adult class at nine years of age, was so diligent with the energy and understood it on a level that most adults do not that if anyone would have been a candidate for going further, it would have been her. And yet, all of the children went through phases of self-discovery where they pushed both their parents and Reiki away.

. . .

I HAVE COME to realize that this is a normal part of growing up. It helps children become their own people. They need to push their parents away to figure out who they are. My daughters both returned to Reiki around 18 years of age and reviewed the adult level 1&2 classes. My son just asked for another attunement, declining the full class. When my daughters took the class as adults, they were completely different people from the nine and 12-year-old who took my children's class. And so, I could then understand William's recommendation on so many levels.

WE CAN TEACH IN-PERSON, in-person, online distance, and hybrid classes in my lineage. You can also "teach" animals and children. Let's take a look at what all of these classes involve.

IN-PERSON CLASSES

Every lineage teaches in-person classes. That means the teacher either rents space or holds a class at their home. There are different things to consider. If you have pets, will some of the attendees be allergic? Will you have children returning from school during the class? Do you have enough bathrooms to accommodate your students? If not, the breaks will have to be a bit longer. Is your kitchen and dining space large enough to accommodate your students? Are there restaurants close by? If so, you may have to allocate additional time for lunch. Can you be easily found? Is your home free of clutter to provide a safe and comfortable environment? Do you have comfortable seating for your students?

IF NOT, you can always rent a space to teach. If you rent a space, you will want to ensure comfortable seating. You need to bring snacks, tea, water, and drinks. You will need to transport your Reiki tables and any crystals, decorations, music, speakers, etc. you need for class. But it can work well in a suitable space.

. . .

AND THERE ARE a few things you need to do to prepare in addition to advertising the class (unless you have enough students through word of mouth), ordering or creating manuals for everyone, and preparing light snacks (e.g., fruit and granola bars– being conscious of nut allergies and gluten and remembering that some of your students will be vegan or vegetarian). Prepare your space with Reiki by putting the symbols all around the room. You may wish to send Reiki ahead to the students to help them get to class and assist them as they shift getting ready for class.

IN-PERSON CLASSES ARE LOVELY. You have to manage the chatting during the breaks to get people back in their seats in time for class to begin again. I found it helps to simply tell people: "We are breaking for 15 minutes, and we have a lot to cover, so I'll need you to come back at __ o'clock."

But if you are inclined to hold in-person classes, they are lovely. There's nothing like a real, in-person hug!

DISTANCE CLASSES

These are not available for all Reiki lineages but are a possibility for those teaching from the ICRT Reiki lineage and some others. Here's the scoop. During the Covid pandemic, William Rand, the president of the ICRT, got very clear guidance to move our classes online so that we could help people during the pandemic and beyond. I was both delighted and terrified. I have this thing with technology in that it doesn't like me. I can stump really knowledgeable tech people with the "fixes" I get in. But at the same time, I had been in Heathrow airport at the beginning of Covid and recognized that everyone needs Reiki at difficult times like this–and suddenly, there was a way to make it happen.

. . .

It is interesting that this came through because until that point, the ICRT did not recognize online courses. The main reason they didn't is that until that point, most online classes offered were pre-recorded and did not include "real-time" attunements. Pre-recorded attunements were found to be less effective.

With the ICRT Holy Fire® Reiki classes, the attunements had shifted back in 2014 when Holy Fire® Reiki was introduced to a hands-off style of attunement called an ignition at the Master level. In 2016, when the frequency of the Holy Fire®, Reiki energy shifted again, it brought a hands-off style of attunement to levels 1, 2, and Usui Reiki Masters called a placement.

The attunements were much more potent when the teacher backed out of the process and allowed the Holy Fire® Reiki energy to interact directly with each student. Some unexpected benefits were that people with physical disabilities could conduct this style of attunement. It simplified the complicated attunement process so that more and more people felt confident enough to teach. It also set us up so that in 2020 when Covid required us to think of another way of teaching, we were ready. Who knew?

ICRT online classes are offered online but in real-time, in-person, instead of as a pre-recorded class. They are conducted exactly like in-person classes, except some of the techniques were adapted to be taught online.

Upon making the announcement, William and Colleen Benelli, together with their staff, created clear guidelines and tutorials to help us teach online. At the same time, William worked with the energy daily, strengthening his connection with both the Usui Reiki and

Holy Fire® energies and with the energy of technology so that they could pass along a stronger ability to attune over a distance to all of us. And there is something in the Reiki experiences they brought forward to prepare us to use technology and teach online because I somehow became aligned with technology after all of the years of difficulty I've had with it. My Master students say the same thing. Many who were not comfortable with technology before class have begun teaching effortlessly online.

WE USE the Zoom platform to teach as it is the one that has shown itself to be the most stable, accessible, and user-friendly to date. While we wondered if the attunements would be as strong at a distance, we discovered that, if anything, they are stronger.

THERE ARE some benefits to teaching online. Your students no longer have the stress and expense of travel to get to your class. You no longer need a classroom with several massage tables, as a virtual classroom works just fine. Introverted students are much more comfortable attending online. In fact, most students are more comfortable because they can become completely relaxed in the privacy of their own environment during class. And in the experiences, they seem to be able to relax more deeply.

I WORRIED that the camaraderie the students sometimes experience would not be possible, but if anything, it is more robust. Some of my students stay in touch, sharing distance Reiki with their class partners and supporting each other for several months after the class. And when they are ready to build their own Reiki businesses, the support continues.

. . .

THERE IS MORE comfort with distance Reiki afterward, too. Even though we practiced distance Reiki during in-person classes, students generally lacked confidence in their abilities to conduct distance sessions. Now, they are utterly confident because they get so much practice with it.

ANOTHER BEAUTIFUL ADVANTAGE is that you can have students from all over the world in your class. I have had students from Australia, Singapore, China, Canada, Hong Kong, the United States, and the United Kingdom all in the same class. It is a beautiful gift to experience Reiki with such a diverse group. People sometimes show up for a class at 4 am in their time zone. I've even had people stay up all night to take classes from me. They are dedicated! And afterward, they all said it wasn't that bad.

OF COURSE, the main advantage of distance classes is that even when it is not possible to meet in person, you can still hold classes, and students can still become connected with the gift of Reiki. What a tremendous blessing that has been.

IF YOU HAVEN'T TRIED a distance class yet, register for one and check it out. You will experience firsthand how smooth, comfortable, and effective they are. Another terrific benefit of the online classes is that you can study with teachers (and students) from everywhere. So you can learn with a teacher who may be a considerable distance from you—someone you have always wanted to work with. Go ahead and find them online and see if they offer distance classes. Nothing can be easier!

. . .

One of the things I recently realized regarding online classes is that they have a much lower carbon footprint than in-person classes. It makes me even more delighted to teach them than I already am!

Hybrid

Hybrid classes are pretty cool. There are a few ways to teach hybrid classes. LRMT Jill Thiel breaks some of her classes up so that students study online from their homes in the morning while she covers theory and some of the experiences. Then they break for lunch and resume after lunch at her home/classroom for more experiences and practice time. It works perfectly for Jill, who doesn't have adequate seating for people to distance themselves during lunch. And it still allows her students to practice in person.

You can also teach Hybrid classes where some students are online and others are in-person. This is the type of class I will teach. The students in my home will see the online students on the television set in the living room. And as people share, I will spin my camera and microphone to each student so the students online can meet the in-person students. The in-person students will practice Reiki with each other in person, while the online students will practice online. I haven't taught this class yet, but I have a clear plan and will teach it soon.

Teaching **Children**

When you teach children, you do not need to go into as much detail as you do with adults. They also don't need to be "still" during the attunement or meditations. Although the children I have taught have managed to remain still(ish) during attunements, other teachers, when leading children in a hands-off style of attunement, allow them to complete a craft or some other project which holds their attention as the Reiki energy connects with them.

. . .

One of William Rand's suggestions when I first asked him about teaching children was to invite the parents to the class. That way, the parent is also attuned to Reiki and, therefore, better able to support the children. And looking after the children is then not your responsibility either. It is beautiful for a parent and child to experience Reiki together. I have always taught my classes that way and highly recommend it.

I priced my class full price for the parent and 1/2 price or less for the child. Then invited the parent to attend a full-length class at another time for no additional charge. It has been well received. And parents seemed to benefit from this additional exposure to Reiki with their children.

When teaching children, they don't need ALL of the information we would teach in a full-length class. And you don't want your class to be more than 4 hours. I usually time mine to be 5 hours in total. 2 hours before lunch, an hour for lunch, and 2 hours after lunch. I typically have a "Reiki coloring book" for the children and invite them to color and draw as I teach.

If you can cover the following, it is usually sufficient:

- A basic history of Reiki (make it fun)
- What Reiki is (and isn't)
- Getting permission before doing Reiki
- How to do a self Reiki session with hand positions
- How to beam Reiki
- How to use Reiki to empower goals or to send ahead
- How to give Reiki to animals, people, trees, plants, and the Earth
- You may wish to cover some Japanese techniques such as

Kenyoku (dry bathing) or Byosen scanning if there's time.
- I also teach children to make Reiki balls of light and throw them around places that need "lightening" up. Little boys particularly enjoy throwing Reiki balls at each other; it's a lot of fun. One of my students still asks her little brother to do this for her in her workplace when it needs help. Even though he is almost grown now, it has remained his favorite way to spread Reiki, and I'm told it's incredibly effective!

"Teaching" Animals

Animals seem to know what to do with Reiki energy. So it is possible to attune them to the energy, regardless of what lineage or system of Reiki you use. The important thing when working with animals is that you have the animal's permission to connect them to Reiki as well as the animal's caretaker/owner's permission. We talk about this in detail in the ICRT Animal Reiki course. But suffice it to say that it's essential that the animal gets to choose whether or not they want to be connected to Reiki (some don't want to be, and that's just fine) and that we honor the wishes of the animal's person as well.

It is also essential that if an animal chooses to receive a Reiki attunement, we do not place any expectations on what they will do with that energy. They decide how, when, why, and where to use Reiki. Many will use it for themselves. If they choose to use it on their person or others, it must be entirely up to them and at their discretion.

How do you know if the animal wants to be attuned? Well, they will show signs in their body language. They will come toward you or lean toward you when you ask mentally; they may become calm, remaining in your space. You may get a clear sense of "yes" through the energy. You can dowse or use your pendulum to be sure you understand correctly. (Even though I am an animal communicator, I always dowse this to ensure I understood the animal correctly as I would never want to go against an animal's wishes). Or you may feel the energy activate through you.

An animal will indicate no by walking or turning away, becoming agitated, or you may get a clear sense of "no" through the energy. When an animal says yes, it can be ambiguous. But their "no" is usually very clear.

If you get a clear sense of "yes" from the animal and the animal's person also wants them to receive an attunement, then you can go ahead. For physical attunements, simply substitute your hands for theirs. Everything can be done the same way, but place your hands at the heart and above the head, etc., as their feet must remain on the ground. When it's time to draw symbols in the hands, simply lift the hooves or paws to draw symbols or draw them in the air over the top of the paws/hooves and motion them in. For animals without legs, simply imagine hands or allow yours to stand in for theirs. Simply substitute your hands for the "hands" of the animal. Most animals will stay still or mostly still for an attunement. If not, work around them.

Too much movement could mean you misunderstood their interest in receiving an attunement, so check back in. During a clinic, I had horses in for training who did not know how to stand still tied. Everyone in the clinic remarked on how they were agitated and uncomfortable. Then, I sent everyone but the Reiki Masters who were helping me with attunements inside. As we set the energy and intention, these untrained horses became so silent and still that you could hear a pin drop. Once the attunements were complete and we invited the other participants to join us once more, they were amazed at the difference in the horses who were standing quietly absorbing the energy.

CONNECTING animals to Reiki (if they chose) became one part of my training methods which allowed the horses to process past trauma and injuries so that we could connect and bring them forward effortlessly into a way of life that would support them and their goals.

PLACEMENT AND IGNITION styles of attunements are simpler. You can simply read the meditation from the manual aloud if no one is around or silently if you're not alone, with the intention that the animal receives the attunement. You can do this in person or at a distance. And simply say the same or similar prayers that you would use if you were doing a placement or ignition for a person.

ANIMALS OFTEN DO NOT NEED to stay in the meditation as long as humans do. The energy seems to connect and process quite quickly. And there is no need to "teach" them anything. Once they are connected to the energy, they tend to know what to do with it, so you can conduct the placement or attunement and leave understanding what to do with the energy up to the animal.

WHY WOULD you want to attune an animal? Although animals understand energy and already work with it, it can be nice for them to be connected to an energy source independent of their personal energy. They can then use it for their own healing. And sometimes they may choose to use it to help other animals or people. The important thing is not to impose our will on them. If they wish to use Reiki energy on themselves or us, they can, but we never ask them to.

It is up to them how they choose to use the connection. Reiki can never cause harm, though, so what have we got to lose?

Many of the animals I have asked have said that they wished to be connected to this outside energy source so that they do not have to use their personal energy to support their person, herd, or pack. Animals I have worked with said they use Reiki to keep their vibration clearer and higher, thus supporting their health. My animals choose to work on my family, the land, and my students. The choice is always theirs. And I have been amazed at the remarkable ways the horses, dogs, cats, and poultry at Hidden Brook Farm have continued to support my work and Reiki journey.

I used to think that Reiki was my idea. At one point, I came to the powerful realization that my horses brought me to Reiki. They introduced me to it through a student, then brought my first teacher to the farm through animal communication. Later, they provided the financial means to attend the Master class in England when my finances were a mess. My horses even helped me become a writer when William Rand asked me to write my first article about attuning horses! And it just kept growing from there.

People's animals often bring them to Reiki. And just as often, they enjoy being part of the journey with their human caretaker.

Getting Started

Here's a checklist for teaching your first class:

1. Reach out to friends, relatives, clients, or acquaintances to see if they are interested in learning about Reiki. If even just one is, set a date for your first class.

. . .

2. Answer a few questions:

- Will you teach online or in-person? Are you trained to teach online? If not, could you be?
- How will you break the class up? Will you teach levels 1&2 together or separately? Will you teach over a full day or break the class up?
- Will you offer a manual such as *Reiki: The Healing Touch* from reiki.org? Or will you create your own reference materials?
- If in-person, will you provide snacks and breaks? If online, do you need to practice to get used to leading sessions online?

3. Teach that first class even if only one person shows up. One person you feel comfortable with is perhaps the best way to teach that class. It allows you to get over the jitters, understand the flow of the class, get to know the energy better, and see that, indeed, it works. It helps build your confidence.

4. Go ahead and review the material. ICRT manuals provide class outlines that walk you through how and what you will teach. And the manuals back it up. If you have another type of manual, create your own outline so you will have an idea about the flow of the class.

NOW YOU ARE ready to teach. Go into that first class knowing that it may not be perfect and doesn't need to be. The most important part of the class is creating curiosity in your student to learn more, the openness to receive the Reiki connection, and connecting them to Reiki. It's not about us. It's about Reiki and your student becoming connected. Once your student is connected to Reiki energy, it is done. I often tell my students that the energy is not responding to MY intention for the student in class but to THEIR intention to work with the energy.

ONCE YOU HAVE TAUGHT that first class, in my lineage, that makes you a true "Reiki Master" or a "Reiki Master Teacher" in other lineages; it also increases your connection with Reiki and with Source. Enjoy!

REVIEWING **Classes**

One of the best ways to get ready to teach a class is to review it. Review the class you are going to teach. You can review it with your own Reiki Master-teacher or another if you'd like to get new ideas and see how other classes are taught.

SEVERAL STUDENTS TAKE my classes because they wish to see what a class from a Licensed Reiki Master Teacher (LRMT) who has the additional 1000+ hours of training is like. Many enjoy this, as these classes give them fresh ideas about how to teach their own classes and contribute toward their Professional Membership in the ICRT Reiki Membership Association.

NOW, with online classes, it has become effortless to review classes. So go ahead and sign up for a class that you are considering teaching. Every time you review a class, not only do you learn more, but your vibration rises. Usui Sensei used to do reijus or attunements with his students every time they met. So while there is a school of thought that says we only need to receive an attunement once, and that's enough (and it's true), I find that every time a student reviews classes, their energetic frequency rises. It's not sequential either.

. . .

I HAVE REVIEWED every Reiki class 3-4 times. And I intend to continue to sign up for classes with my LRMT colleagues to continue learning more and experience other teaching styles. Three years ago in January, when I reviewed Reiki levels 1&2 with Colleen Benelli at the beginning of my LRMT training, even though I had taught that class for ten years and knew it well, it rocked my world. So make reviewing classes part of your personal development plan. You'll be glad you did.

PROFESSIONAL ASSOCIATIONS

Several organizations support Reiki. I love the ICRT or International Center for Reiki Training for its openness and support and the balance between information, evidence, and intuition. Although evidence-based information is provided, you are encouraged to form your own ideas and beliefs. This works well with my style of working and intuition. You may also resonate with that, or you may not. You may resonate with a different type of professional organization.

YOU CAN'T GO wrong being aligned with a Professional Association. It can add credibility to you and to what you do. It gives you backup and support. And some even offer group insurance discounts. So go ahead and research the different Professional Associations available in your region - or internationally- and see the advantages of becoming a member. Then make a decision based on the organization that seems to be the most in alignment with you.

CREATE a Reiki Support Group

Once you have taught several classes, or maybe even before you teach classes, it's a great idea to create a Reiki support group. Once people begin experiencing the magic of Reiki in their daily lives, they want to be connected to people they can talk with and share about it.

There are several ways to create a Reiki support group. I have a private Facebook group just for the people who studied with me. We ask each other questions, ask for help when needed, and share our remarkable stories. The group is incredibly supportive, has facilitated several miracles, and helped us realize we are never alone. This incredible group of people always has our back. And they are always there to support us, no matter what we need!

In addition to this lovely group, I offer free monthly online Reiki shares to anyone who wishes to attend, even if they have not yet been attuned to Reiki. It is open to people from any lineage. And those who have not yet been attuned simply channel love when we get to the "sharing" part. But it is a low-risk way for people to experience and understand Reiki.

Prior to Covid, I offered in-person Reiki shares four times per year just to my students. People would bring their Reiki tables and crowd into the house, or if weather allowed, we would set up outside. I would lead people in a Reiki talk and meditation of some kind. And then, we would break up into groups dependent on the number of tables we had. And do hands-on Reiki sessions for each other. Afterward, we shared coffee, tea, sweets, conversation, and camaraderie. It was lovely. But for me, it took up most of my day on the weekend. And though people requested shares more often, I could not fit them into my schedule. As I started teaching in Australia, the US, and the United Kingdom, students from away were disappointed that they could not attend. So I set them up as a Facebook Live and recorded and shared the meditation part with my Private Facebook Group.

. . .

During Covid, I realized Reiki shares could be online and required only a few evening hours for myself and the participants. I graduated to monthly online Reiki shares. We don't often have time to share much Reiki as we only spend 90 minutes together, and the talk and meditation mostly take that up. But once I finish whatever talk Reiki has guided me to and the corresponding meditation, we sometimes have 5-15 minutes to beam energy to each other.

I have a regular following that shows up whenever they can. And I still record the share, as there are still students who can't make the dates and times. Now I share it as a podcast for everyone.

However you decide to set this up, once you start to teach, it's really important to create a support group. It gives your students a "tribe" or a place to call "home." It is a group to belong to where they can be completely open and completely themselves. If you are teaching, you are stepping into a lovely leadership role with Reiki. So give your students a place to belong where they can be comfortable as they explore all that Reiki offers.

Tips to prepare for classes

- Class details: Decide how you will teach. How will you break up the class? How many people can you teach at one time? If you need to order or print manuals, get that done. Unless you have a certificate provided by your professional association, create a certificate for your classes.
- Logistics: Set the time, date, and space for the class. Book anything you need to book.
- Advertise classes: Once you become established, advertise

your classes in your newsletter or email list, on your website, and on social media. Create a Facebook event or use Meetup or Eventbrite. Get the word out. Don't copy other people's words about Reiki classes. Write about your classes in your voice. The student will connect with YOU, so they need to hear what the Reiki class is about, as you would explain it.

- Registration: Set up a registration process that allows your students to sign up for class and send payment or partial payment. This helps people to show up. So often, people decide to take a Reiki class, then the unhealed ego becomes nervous or afraid, and they choose to cancel. If they have sent in a payment, they are more likely to show up. I make the payment non-refundable, though it can be applied to any other class that year if a student cannot attend. It happens.
- Respond to those who register in a timely way, letting them know you have received their information and that you will be in touch closer to the date of the class with additional information. Stay in touch if they have questions. If they have a lot of detailed questions, it's OK to let them know you will be covering the details in class.
- Class items: Get together anything you need to support the class. Music, crystals, sacred objects, incense or smudge (be aware of scent sensitivities, though), chairs, speakers, printers, etc. Anything you need to teach your class, put it together so you can just grab it as you are heading out the door or as the class begins. I keep mine in a tub.
- It's time for class. Be sure to let each student introduce themselves. This allows everyone to get to know each other, breaks the ice, and brings the group energetically together. You may wish to open the class with an opening prayer, smudge/energy clearing, or a Reiki experience. But bring the

group together and begin teaching from your outline. If you need to change the order of your outline to accommodate questions or queries that come up from class, remain flexible to do so. LRMTs need to have students fill in an evaluation at the end of class. I teach with both the outline and evaluation to ensure that I cover everything that needs to be covered, especially as I can get off track as I answer questions.

- Managing your class: As you manage your classes, ask Reiki to help. Sometimes we get over-sharers who have so many questions and spend a lot of time on stories during the time to share. When I notice that, I ask Reiki to help. And while I want everyone to be heard, if the stories or opinions shared are not around the course material, I let the student know I am happy to stay after class to discuss it with them. We also get under sharers. I never force anyone to share. Some people feel more comfortable keeping their experiences to themselves. But to ensure that everyone feels included in the class, I usually start by asking if anyone would like to share. And in smaller classes, if a few consistently don't, I sometimes circle back to them once everyone else has shared and ask if there was anything they noticed in the experience they want to share.

- Time: It's important to start your class on time, though you may need to wait a few minutes for students who got lost or online who misunderstood the time zone. I also used to have difficulty finishing classes on time. There was always SO much I wanted to share with my students. But in addition to getting familiar with the class material and getting used to how long each thing took to review and teach, I began asking Reiki to help me finish on time. I find that as long as I set clear expectations about the break, e.g., we are breaking for an hour for lunch, that means everyone needs to be back at 5 minutes after the hour... or we are taking a 10-minute comfort break, so be back at 30 minutes after the hour... people respect that, and I can begin even if they are still making their way back.

- Understanding the experiences: It's important to note that while everyone wants beautiful and remarkable experiences, it doesn't always show up that way. Sometimes the experiences are downright uncomfortable or even frightening for the student. I always let students know that they will experience the meditations and attunements in the way that is exactly right for them. It will always work even if they have monkey mind. Or if they experience unrolls differently from what they expect. If and when a student shares that their experience was less than positive, I am usually aware that what they are describing is a large amount of stagnant or negative feeling energy releasing and letting them know that. I also tell them that we begin the experience during class, but it often keeps developing long after class. So I let students know that their outer world always resembles the inner world. And so they will have a better indication of what happened in the experience when they see how it unfolds in their outer world. An example I use is how BEFORE every Reiki class, I look around at my home and think how beautiful it is and how much I love it. AFTER every Reiki class, I look around my house and wonder where the clutter came from. My husband knows that there will be a big decluttering event in our home after every Reiki class, even when I review classes. That's how I know that internal clutter was cleared in the class.
- Challenging students: Sometimes, you will get a student who feels out of alignment with you. I pray as I set my calendar and classes, asking that exactly the right students find exactly the right class for them. This activates Reiki and allows it to bring groups of resonant students together. And it helps me to know that every person who

finds my sessions or classes was meant to. So if, after that, I get a student who challenges me, I know that they are there to teach me something. I can enjoy the process of teaching the student with an open mind and heart and with curiosity about what I am to learn! Sometimes it is patience. Sometimes it is a new way of looking at things. Sometimes the student is there to challenge the way I do things so that I can become a better teacher. So let go and let Reiki decide who needs to be in your classes. And trust that they are precisely where they are meant to be - and so are you!

Transition to a Reiki Career

Reiki can so profoundly affect people's lives that they often want to leave the career they have and begin working with Reiki. I have found that it's best to transition to a Reiki career more gradually. For several reasons.

1. If you need to make a living from Reiki right away, it puts pressure on you that can make it uncomfortable and rob the beauty of the learning process.
2. We grow gradually in our connections with Reiki. And our businesses often have a more solid foundation if they grow at the same rate as our connection with Reiki.
3. Maybe, instead of teaching classes and performing Reiki sessions as we traditionally think of as a Reiki career, Reiki has something else in mind for you. Perhaps you are to work with Reiki in a very different way. Maybe it is meant to roll into the career you already have.
4. Many people are passionate about their careers, but often, by the time they find Reiki, they are burned out, disappointed or exhausted. Allow Reiki the time needed to heal the burnout or exhaustion or to show you a

different way of doing things, and you may find that as you heal, your passion returns, and then Reiki blends together with your passion to show you a new way of doing and approaching things.
5. If you allow Reiki to lead, you will see that it is often a very gradual process. And we seldom know the endpoint. William Rand once said in class that if he had known what he was creating, he would have believed it to be impossible and limited himself. But because Reiki just showed him one step at a time, it did not cause him to question and where he ended up was so far beyond what he could have ever conceived. Allow Reiki to lead you. We often limit ourselves otherwise.

Fit Reiki in where you can and follow the guidance of Reiki. Don't get stressed. Reiki will lead and guide you. Check out my article Start a Reiki Business by letting Reiki Lead the Way.[1]

Plan Your Calendar

Now you are a teacher. I take a paper calendar—note the full and new moons and any significant astrological events–and then, I ask Reiki to show me where to place my classes. As a Licensed Teacher, I may teach more often than you do. Decide how many classes you wish to teach in the coming year. And then space them out accordingly. Every two months, I teach Usui/Holy Fire® Reiki level 1&2 and Master classes and ICRT Animal Reiki level 1&2 and Master Training. And 3-to 4 times per year, I teach the advanced Karuna Reiki classes as well as my Animal Communication classes. You may only wish to teach levels 1&2 at first. Until you have taught several levels 1&2 students, you often don't have Master students. You may want to teach only a few times per year.

. . .

THE THING I encourage my students to do is teach when it works for you. You don't only have to teach on weekends. I teach primarily through the week, and it works for the students who find me. Often they have to take a few days off from their regular work to attend classes. I find that means I get more dedicated and invested students. And they are not as tired as if they are trying to fit the classes in on the weekend during their time off. If you have a regular job, you don't want to be teaching every weekend.

I USED to teach small classes every month. When I began teaching fewer classes, my class size grew, and I became more efficient and enjoyed the classes more. So figure out what works for you, and then ask Reiki to help you set your calendar.

WHILE IT IS up to you, one thing I decided to do with my in-person classes was to teach them even if only one person showed up. That way, people could count on me. So if they took time off to attend a class, I wasn't going to cancel the class at the last minute. It was imperative to build up that reliability. Even before I entered the Licensed Teacher Program, people would sometimes fly a considerable distance to attend my classes, book hotels, etc. I had to be reliable.

ONCE, we were surprised by the arrival of a foal (new baby horse) during the lunch break of my Reiki classes. I had three students in the class—one from Massachusetts, one from Wisconsin, and one from New Brunswick, about an hour away. The students asked if I needed to cancel the class. I laughed and said, if they could give me the lunch break to get the baby settled, we would proceed with class just a few minutes behind schedule. They had come so far that I needed to ensure they experienced everything.

. . .

I GOT mom and baby in the barn and tended to them. I was in shock as we had not realized mama was pregnant. The baby was healthy and beautiful, so I went back inside once I had done everything I could for the horses. We had a great class. And that evening, once it was complete, I retired to the barn again to spend the evening with mama and baby.

WITH ONLINE CLASSES, I have had to cancel a few as I felt the students would feel uncomfortable with that amount of scrutiny from me if only one registered. I also think it is more fun to have partners to practice with. I've only had to cancel two classes to date. Both times I let the student know it was a possibility ahead of time so they could prepare, and they both enrolled in the following class - which had lots of students. Both shared that perhaps they were not ready earlier, and the group they joined in the latter class was exactly right for them.

ONCE YOUR CALENDAR IS SET, if you happen to have a class where no one enrolls (it happens to all of us), enjoy your free time and do something extraordinary with it.

TRAVEL TO TEACH

Once you have begun teaching, you will have the teaching "bug." It is one of the most beautiful things to witness another person or animal's Reiki journey. I began traveling to teach because of the teaching requirements of the LRMT program. We have to teach a certain number of classes with a certain number of students in each 12-month period. I live in a very small community where it was difficult to get the numbers I needed to meet the requirements. When I asked for guidance from Reiki, I heard, "No problem, travel to teach."

. . .

I HAVE ALWAYS LOVED to travel and experience new places. And in fact, I wanted to visit a horse partway across the country in Edmonton, Alberta, which my dear friend had purchased from me. My friend offered to host a Reiki level 1&2 class and an Animal Communication class and have me stay with them while. The classes paid for my flight. When another friend heard, she said, "I'd like to host a class for you in Ottawa. Can you stop here on the way?" It was on the way, and broke up my flights beautifully. Then another friend said, "I've always wanted to take your Reiki classes. Can I host you in Colorado?" I've always wanted to go to Colorado, so I did a cross-continent tour and met my LRMT requirements!

I TAUGHT a small class in Ottawa, two moderate-sized classes in Edmonton, and two larger classes in Colorado. It covered 1/2 of my LRMT requirements for that program segment in just a few weeks, allowed me to visit my friends, and showed me that teaching Reiki classes could become an economical way to travel and share the gift of Reiki at the same time!

BECAUSE I STAYED with my friends and they held the classes in their homes, there was no pressure for me to cover the expenses of hotels or meeting rooms. I only had to cover airfare. They all picked me up at the airport, so I didn't even have to rent a car. It took all of the risk out of traveling to teach. I have even traveled to teach in Australia and the United Kingdom that way!

OTHER LRMTs TRAVEL to teach when invited, renting a meeting room and hotel space. Some ask people to organize classes for them and advertise them on their websites. Some say they will travel for a certain number of students, setting the goal for the size of class they will travel for. Most teachers offer the people that organize the classes a discount. And for a certain size class, the organizer can often take the class for free.

Is there someplace you'd like to travel to? Where do you have a contact who could help you arrange a class? The sky's the limit!

Expand Your Reach

There are several ways to expand your reach once you have begun teaching.

1. Create a newsletter and ask friends, family, and students to share
2. Start making social media posts. Try not to sell anything in the posts. Make the type of posts your friends might want to share. But put your name, logo, or website discreetly at the bottom.
3. Form strategic alliances with other health care professionals like chiropractors, massage therapists, health food store owners, essential oil therapists, new age bookstores, Rolfing instructors, etc. Offer them a free Reiki session and ask if they would allow your business card or pamphlet on their bulletin board.
4. Attend a trade show, particularly one offering complementary healing or new age events. You may wish to offer free sample Reiki sessions. Or you may even want to charge for full sessions at the show if you feel there will be enough people who wish to take you upon it. People usually offer "show specials" to invite people to try Reiki at these.
5. Offer to do Reiki talks. I have been invited to speak about Reiki at Universities, Aesthetic schools, City Hall, new age trade shows, horse events, etc. Any gathering where people want to learn something new. Often it is the

wellness committee for workplaces that reaches out to me. See if you can reach out to some of them and offer to speak and offer sample Reiki sessions to their staff. Several clients and students came to me through these channels.

6. Write an article for the *Reiki News Magazine* or another publication. I often hear from people who gained something from my articles. Some of them turn into clients; many don't. But it feels great to share new insights and information with other Reiki practitioners.
7. Create a Reiki circle with the other Reiki practitioners in your area. It could be a forum for practitioners and teachers to get together and share questions, information, and insights. Or you may wish to create a special event. A local Reiki Master here creates an event where people can receive a Reiki session from 3 well-known Reiki Masters. It promotes all of them. And they get to work together and learn from each other.
8. Find influencers in your area and engage with them on social media, etc. Study what they do. And don't copy it, but consider what works for them as you create your own strategies, then reach out with your own social media posts.

Pricing Your Classes

This is something that many people struggle with. What should I charge? I've heard people say, "Well, I can't charge as much as so and so; they are well known/have done this for a long time/have a large following...." You get the gist. And to that, I say, "Why not?" Reiki is about connecting people to the energy. And the student who needs you will find you! Indeed, suppose you are working with friends and family at first to gain experience. In that case, it is appropriate to charge less for your initial classes, to barter for something you want or need (this is always appropriate), or to charge nothing at all. But eventually, you will want to set prices for the public.

WHEN IT IS time to put your prices down on paper, on your website, or anywhere else, be forthcoming. People feel more comfortable with modern business practices. If you don't feel comfortable charging for your classes, do self Reiki to heal your issues with money. It is not fair to pass those issues along to your clients. And your client will get from the class an equitable exchange for what they put into it. So don't rob them of the opportunity to contribute to their own personal, professional, and spiritual development.

WHAT TO CHARGE? Do some research and choose a middle-of-the-road price. When I started, I priced my first classes pretty much the same as what others in my region were charging. A few teachers charged way less than others and held large classes. But their classes were only a few hours long. And when I met their students afterward, they did not seem to be as connected with the Reiki energy as students were. It reinforced that the students get a fair value for what they invest.

I ALSO DIDN'T WANT to charge more than other teachers. After studying Reiki with William Rand, I realized my lineage was closely aligned with Usui Sensei, Reiki's founder. And also that the ICRT classes were a bit more detailed and involved than some of the other classes. And that the classes came with a very professional and complete manual. But I also did not feel my classes were "better" than any of the other teachers. And I didn't want to insult these experienced professionals in any way. I knew the students who found my classes were meant to be there, and those who found theirs were meant to be there. So I set middle-of-the-road prices and held them.

. . .

As an LRMT, all of our classes are priced the same. And they are middle-of-the-road prices. Check what we charge for classes, and you can base your class prices on that. You don't need to discount classes because you are not an LRMT. And, in your region, you may find that people charge much more than we do. If that's the case, charge accordingly.

Recording Classes

As I mentioned earlier, technology and I never got along. We do much better together now, especially since I received an ignition style attunement to teach online classes. But even before that, I noticed that my Mentor, Colleen Benelli, recorded the important parts of her Reiki classes. Not the sharing/conversation, but the experiences and theory. I loved that students could return afterward and re-listen to anything they really liked or didn't get the first time through. I did so much healing in my first Reiki level 1&2 class that I don't remember the details of the class at all. It's a blur. Did we cover the Japanese Reiki techniques? I couldn't tell you. So when I saw that Colleen recorded her class on the voice memo app on her phone and then sent them to students as we wrote in our journals, I thought it was brilliant. Think about doing the same for your students.

If you are teaching online, Zoom makes recording classes easy. Immediately after every class, I send my students a follow-up email thanking them for attending the class, including any additional details or information needed and a link to their recordings. I also ask them to download them that week so that I can erase them and they don't continue taking up valuable storage space.

Create a Reiki Challenge

One way to engage your students, bring them together and help them have fun with Reiki is to create a Reiki challenge. The first

Reiki challenge I made was 21 days long. I set it to begin in March, which is a pretty dreary month here. Over 50 people actively participated and completed the full 21 days. And yet others did their best.

I OFFERED crystals and essential oil prizes to the 3 top winners. I sent out 2 Bingo cards. One invited people to do self Reiki every day, send Reiki to their Reiki grid, and then use a Bingo dauber to track their progress. The other card was for people who wanted to stretch themselves. I had things like:

- Tell someone who doesn't know that you are a Reiki practitioner
- Do Gyoshi Ho (Japanese Reiki technique) the next time you are out in public and see what you notice
- Do Koki Ho (Japanese Reiki technique) 3 days in a row on a problem area of your body
- Send Reiki to a situation with someone you don't like
- Use Reiki to repair a relationship
- Offer to do a Reiki session for a friend
- Offer to do a Reiki session for a friends' pet
- Exchange Reiki sessions with a friend who has Reiki

You get the idea. It can include anything you wish. I had 21 different challenges that stretched people out of their comfort zones with Reiki. I asked people to take photos of their cards at the end of 21 days and then did a draw for three prizes from those who had completed the cards!

IT GENERATED a lot of conversation and excitement in our Facebook group. And it stretched a lot of people out of their comfort zones. It helped them discover tools and techniques that they didn't use. Set up your challenge however it suits you. And have fun with it. I did the challenge myself, and I must say, it stretched me out of my comfort zone too!

Become a Mentor

"*If you want to learn, teach*" has become my mantra. And by teaching others, you will become a stronger, more accomplished Reiki Master and Practitioner. You may have figured out enough things that you can save others time in their journeys. Or people may ask you to mentor them. Maybe even before you think you are ready to become a mentor. If you have the time, say yes.

You will want to set the parameters. Perhaps you mentor them with a monthly phone call or a regular Reiki session. Will you charge for your services? Ask Reiki to guide you and consider what it will look like and how much time you need to devote to it. Then hold your boundaries to what is comfortable to you.

And if you are in a position to mentor several people, consider setting up a formal mentoring program. It will cause you to become more organized and deliberate in your presentations; it brings students together with their peers, provides support, and allows you to make the best use of your time. If this appeals to you, check out the chapter in this book on creating a mentoring group. And enjoy! You will learn as much as your students as it will push you to learn and become the best you can be.

~

ProTip

Author's note: Dianne and her husband have "retired" and live on a boat. But she still teaches Reiki. She travels to different locations to teach or teaches Reiki online from her ship. She explains that the boat is constantly moving. So she has to teach indoors because if she were outdoors with the horizon and ocean in the background, people would get seasick. Inside, because the camera moves with her, she looks perfectly still when she sets herself up with a large scarf in the background, teaching in her boat! My classes are "Reiki from the Farm™," while Dianne's are "Reiki from the Boat."

~

DIANNE THOMAS, LRMT, South Carolina, USA
Fifth Dimension Reiki Classes[2]

We're all terrified to teach our first class. We are terrified in stages along the way, too. You don't get past that. When I did my co-teach with Laurelle Shanti Gaia, she was watching me, and I was so afraid of messing up. And she had such a beautiful energy of support and said, "Diane, don't worry, you can't mess it up."

TEACHING my first level one class, I was scared to death. And again for my first level two class, first level three class, first masters class. Then there was Holy Fire®. But the most terrifying thing was my co-teach classes (part of the thousand hours plus of training we need to become a Licensed Reiki Master Teacher), where we co-teach with our mentor. We teach together, and it's terrifying.

WHEN I LEFT MY BUSINESS, I had to decide what to do. It was overwhelming, but I told my daughter-in-law, "I'll tell you what I'm not going to do; I'm not going to teach." That was in the year 2000, which is also when I received my first Reiki session. After that, I had to know more. So I found Laurelle Gaia online in 2001 and went to her class in Myrtle Beach. Then a year later, I took her Master class and within six months, I was teaching Reiki.

. . .

I WAS PETRIFIED TO TEACH. I thought, "I just know these attunements are not going to work."

But Reiki helps you to gain that confidence. Reiki validated that it was working because I did the attunement, and one student said she was painting a wall with symbols. The other was out in space. I thought, "I don't think it worked." Then I handed them the symbols, and one said, oh my gosh, this is what I was painting on the wall. And the other said, "This is what I saw in outer space."

SO TO ME, that was Reiki saying, "See, I told you it was going to work." They saw the symbols in their attunements. They just didn't recognize them because they hadn't seen the symbols yet. It was fabulous.

EVERY TIME YOU TEACH, you may doubt, but you kind of push through it. Reiki will help you, show you and support you. I hit that wall again when it came to teaching online. Even after all of the classes I had taught in person! Suddenly we were teaching online, and I wasn't worried about the material; it was all about "How do I get music?" And I could not figure out how to do breakout rooms. I melted down and said, "I can't even do this." So I gave myself Reiki, and two hours later, I went back and had all of the answers.

WHEN YOU START TEACHING, teach someone you know, that you are comfortable with. Because someone you've never met before can be more challenging so you add a level of discomfort that you don't need, in that first class. And set it up the way it works best for you. Some students are uncomfortable teaching levels 1&2 together. One of my students taught level one separately. Then when her students said, "When are we going to have a level two class?" it pushed her into teaching the next level. We always need those nudges.

. . .

I LOVE THE NUDGES. I've taught several classes after somebody texts me and says, "When will you teach another class here?" And I say, "Well, I hadn't planned on it." But then, lo and behold, three or four people will suddenly show up and say, ``I was looking, but you're not teaching a class here." So I say, "Okay, Reiki, I get the message. I'm supposed to teach a class there." But what's funny is that the person who started the whole thing seldom attends!

BEFORE I TEACH, I set the energy in the space using the distance symbol to send it to the students there so they can feel the space ahead of time. Then, when they walk in, they're already connected. If you are teaching online and do this, you send Reiki to their space so that their spaces are set. Everybody comes to class a bit more at ease.

AND NOW, I teach on the boat. When we moved to the boat, it never dawned on me that I couldn't continue to teach. So that was my attitude. But, when you say, "Oh, well, I don't have this, or I don't have that," you're holding yourself in that place of not having it. So you need to just kind of rethink that and just say, how do I make this work? And the answer will come.

BUT IF IT hadn't been for COVID, I would have never learned to teach online. So it wouldn't have been possible. How beautiful it was that Holy Fire® set everything up for us ahead of time? So stepping into that happened seamlessly. To me, it's phenomenal to be online. I have classes that are just as intimate, if not more so with online experiences than in-person classes. Everyone gels. I hear, "Can we stay in touch with each other?" So, it's been a fantastic thing.

NEXT YEAR IN JANUARY, February, and March, I hope to be in the Turks and Caicos, where you can swim with the whales. So I will hold a destination class there.

OUR MIND IS the best search engine in the world. But if you keep Google "not having something," you'll get those search results. So we need to reword the search to "How do I make this happen?" and the answer will appear. Move out of the space of lack and into the space of solution. I guess that's what William did when he brought the classes online; he just stayed in the space of solution.

WHEN MY MASTER-TEACHERS are ready to teach, we get together on Zoom, and I show them how to do things. I make them the host, and they can figure out breakout rooms and practice the crazy little things that can be monumental unless you know how to do them. Don't let technology intimidate you. If I can do it and I'm in my seventies, you can too.

I CREATE little videos of me charging my Reiki grid for the masterclass and doing a Byosen scan for teaching levels one and two ahead of time when I have the space because teaching on the boat, I don't even have to have a Reiki table here and couldn't get one on the boat if I wanted to. But I made some videos to show in class. Go ahead and teach. Just be open to possibilities. And ask, "How can I make this work?" Because what you'll receive then is Reiki-guided, and it will turn out to be fabulous.

AND I THINK the most stubborn obstacle can be feeling worthy. I really, really butted heads with that feeling. I thought, "Who am I to teach somebody else?" I looked at my mentor teacher and thought, she's just this fantastic person; I can't measure up to that. But you have students out there waiting for you. They're waiting for your way of teaching. Even though Laurelle influenced how I teach, I teach in a very different way.

I TEACH about vibrational energy and frequencies and like to talk about the science behind this. So I teach differently from some of the other teachers, but those students who come to me are looking for my method. They may not know it. But the energy brought them there for that reason. Students are waiting for you to come up with your special secret recipe, which is what they want because that is what will inspire them.

SO WHEN YOU START TEACHING, just trust that you have everything you need because you do. I used the ICRT manuals when I started to teach, so I didn't have to develop my own. Anyone from any lineage can use the ICRT "Reiki; The Healing Touch First and Second Degree Manual" and class outline.

AND IF YOU'VE learned from another lineage, go ahead and look and see what's available, so you don't have to create a manual as there are some generic manuals available online. If you want to use what your teacher created and gave you, you have their permission to use it. Don't infringe on their copyrighted material; even if they didn't officially copyright their material.

IT'S the most amazing feeling to teach. I love sharing Reiki with clients and watching them change with Reiki. I'm just the conduit. The class channels through you and you will get the students who need what you have.

CHECK out our podcast on this chapter.[3]

STUDENT SUCCESS STORY **Patricia Giannasi**

My objective with the Mentoring course was to find out how far I could go in my journey with Reiki and the ICRT with whom I've been involved since 1990. I wanted to know what expanding my business entailed.

THE COURSE MOTIVATED me to integrate Reiki with my meditation development and the development in mediumship classes I teach. They never used to blend. But, my Reiki and mediumship have now started to blend. We talk about Reiki and use it in my mediumship classes, and then people want to study it, so they book a class. So I'm teaching. As I'm expanding now, clients are coming in at my pace. I think the student finds the teacher when they need them.

I HAD a website that wasn't very good. But the program explained why I needed a better website and gave me a little push. Now I have a great guy to help me. We make trades. I give him a reading, and he does my website.

THE MARKETING PORTION made me realize that it's okay to put yourself out there more because before the class, I was working with just personal recommendations. I had a business name, but I wasn't doing anything with marketing. This class made me more comfortable in my skin and gave me the confidence to go forward and put it out there a little bit and attract more people. I've had tons of responses.

ATTENDING the mentor group helped me realize that there's another world outside British Columbia. It's given me the ability to reach out further. It gave me an opening into the rest of the world and taught me to step outside my box. To think bigger and be more competent in what I was doing.

It made me expand my thinking and think more about every part of my life. I also try to make time for myself now with no apologies. Getting my nails and hair done, time with my grandkids. It's nurturing. You instilled into me that self-care is essential. I pass that on when I'm teaching. I ask, "How can you look after others if you're not looking after yourself? How can you love others if you do not love yourself?"

I started expanding my Reiki teaching and teaching online. I feel a fire in my belly. I taught in person but this has given me the confidence to teach online. It's just changing the method a little bit.

Another thing I learned is about incorporating Reiki into every aspect of my life. So I'm using it in more places and blending Reiki into different things. It's a business, but we're now becoming one.

To others, I say, just take it slowly and don't expect too much. And when you don't expect too much, that's when you receive. We're all different. Go forward. If you feel like you can expand, then do it.

And start to teach. Your students will push you to grow. My students are now asking me to put on a mentor course. It's like a mushroom effect, you taught me that I could mentor. It's all about pushing yourself a few steps at a time. The mentor group wasn't stuffy; it was lighthearted. It was relaxing yet fulfilling.

. . .

AND NOW THAT I feel confident in my own business, I have the gift of being able to encourage my students and say, "If I can do it, you can do it. Open your own business." It's made a big difference in every way. Clients are coming organically, naturally, and effortlessly now. It's still word of mouth. And when the student becomes the teacher, I'm happy for them. I'm following my guidance and keep doing it. I look forward to your book and admire you. The course has been a big help. Huge. In my business, my teaching, and my connection with Reiki.

---

1. https://www.hiddenbrook.ca/wp-content/uploads/2021/06/StartReikiBusiness.pdf
2. http://www.5dreikiclasses.com/
3. https://www.buzzsprout.com/1364386/10263087

8

YOUR EVOLUTION WITH REIKI - THE PATH TO ENLIGHTENMENT AND BEYOND

"Reiki has evolved for me in ways that I never thought would be possible. I call it life on the skinny branches, and that's where life is the best."
Kris Valentine, LRMT

Reiki causes our connection with the Divine to grow. Therefore, I picture my connection with Reiki and Divine energy as a beam of light coming from the Divine to and through my crown chakra. But I am aware that the bandwidth of this energy continues to grow. And in fact, it can grow infinitely.

DURING MY FIRST Reiki Master class with William Rand, the students came back from one of the fantastic exercises discouraged that we all still had work to do. We wondered when we would be perfect? When would we be done?

. . .

WILLIAM SAID with a smile that we would never be done. He said the potential for connection to God is "unlimited" and explained that "becoming a Reiki Master differs from other traditions where the word Master is used to indicate mastery over a subject. It is not about "mastering" Reiki but is about allowing Reiki to master you." And that this opportunity is the great joy of Reiki; there will never be an end to the ever-increasing experience of improved health, love, peace, abundance, and happiness. He said, "Our unhealed ego wants to be 'done' but enlightenment is the beginning of the spiritual path," and asked, "why would we want an end to the beautiful gifts Reiki can continually give to you?"[1]

THERE ARE a lot of fantastic ways to continue to grow your connection with Reiki and with the Divine. So many that I wrote an article about it "Allowing Reiki to Guide Your Life."[2]

Reiki Self Care

There are several ways to grow your connection with Reiki, but self-care cannot be underestimated. I would call it the first pillar of growing our connection.

DOING daily self-Reiki grows your connection with Reiki as it heals issues that arise and helps bring the next level of healing to the surface. Daily self Reiki also improves the health and well-being of our mind, body, soul, and emotions. It spreads out into our day, helping everything go smoother. We approach our daily lives from a more balanced and solid foundation. And yet, many of us struggle to fit our daily self-Reiki into our lives. One of my teachers, Carolyn Musial, acknowledged our busy lives and yet showed us it was possible to do our self Reiki sessions in as little as 5 minutes per day.

1. She begins with a hand position over the eyes and face, treating the eyes, third eye, and sinuses.
2. Then she moves one hand to her brow chakra and the other to her base chakra.
3. Then one hand to her throat as the other is on the sacral chakra.
4. Then one hand at the heart, the other at the solar plexus.
5. Finally, she wraps up with a minute on the crown chakra.

Often, I do my self-Reiki in bed at night. I simply place my hands where I am guided and then move them again as I am guided using the Japanese style of Reiki with Reiji ho followed by Chiryo. I also chant or sing the symbols, invoking them as I take a Reiki walk. There are several ways we can work daily self-Reiki into our lives. Try and do your best to fit it in. Your day will improve as a result. Don't let it feel like a chore. Work it in, in a way that works for you.

Reiki Sessions from Others

One of the ways I prevent moving into crisis and keep things going forward in my spiritual journey is by ensuring I receive Reiki sessions from others. I book a Reiki session with my mentor once per month. Although a session from anyone would be of benefit, I love working with my mentor because she has more experience than I do. And so, if I have a question or need advice, she is happy to accommodate me within the session.

But it is very liberating when you get a session from someone else. They may notice energies you have become familiar with or are not within your scope to release. You have no responsibility. You can relax during the session. And if you work with Reiki Masters who have more experience than you, they may offer helpful insights. So consider setting up a regular Reiki session for yourself. Book it into your calendar along with your self-care. I'll talk about that later.

Meditation with Reiki

Another way I like to bring Reiki into my life every day is through meditation. In our level 1&2 class, we learn the Gassho meditation. It is a way to meditate as we activate the Reiki energy and let it course through us. Even when I cannot fit a full 10-15 minute Gassho meditation into my day, I can fit several short sessions in as I am in between tasks. It is remarkable. At the Master level, we learn how to meditate with Holy Fire Reiki. And in the Animal Reiki classes, we learn to meditate with the Tree of Life.

One of my favorite ways to meditate with Reiki energy is to play Jonathan Goldman and Laurelle Gaia's Reiki Chants CD. It has a musical ensemble for each Usui Reiki symbol 15-18 minutes in length. I enjoy sitting with a different symbol each day and getting to know it better. If you can fit some form of meditation with Reiki into your life, your connection will continue to grow. If you have other forms of Reiki, you can spend time with each symbol, one at a time, with soft music in the background as you get to know each of those symbols better. I have done this with the Karuna Reiki® symbols as well as the Animal Reiki® symbol.

Walking Meditation with Reiki

In addition to a quiet/seated meditation, I do a walking meditation with Reiki each day. I invoke or call in my Reiki symbols, then head out for a walk as I listen. I listen to the sounds of nature around me. I listen with inner awareness to my intuition and the thoughts that flow through my mind. This is a lovely way to receive guidance, and I have to admit that most of my guidance comes from my twice-per-day "Reiki walks" with the dogs.

Sometimes, I have questions or am working on a solution to a problem, and I notice that the answers or solutions enter my conscious awareness. Other times, I simply enjoy the moment allowing Reiki to flow through me as I walk and to remain behind on the Reiki trails I create. Sometimes I find myself singing or chanting the names of the symbols as I walk. Other times, I am guided to stop and share Reiki with a tree. Sometimes I ask for inspiration. Or to be guided to where I am to go next. I use William Rand's prayer, "Please guide me and heal me so I may be of greater service to myself and others," then I listen. One day it said, "Create a book to help people spread Reiki in the world…"

Admittedly, I walk in nature with no one else around. But wherever you walk, go ahead and invite your Reiki energy to flow. Then connect with your guidance and see what you notice! It's a lot of fun.

Other Forms of Self Care

Reiki practitioners often think that self-care means doing self-Reiki. And perhaps getting a Reiki session from someone. And it does. But it also means doing the things that bring you joy. The belief in the need to "sacrifice" for another to become well is very dualistic and unnecessary. So to be the best Reiki Master and Practitioner I could be, I recognized at one point (with the guidance of Reiki) that I needed to fill my cup with things that give me joy. This allows me to be more present for my clients, and I do a better job for them. It helps me feel rested and joyful. And that is the place my clients need me to be coming from.

Think about what brings you joy, then make a list. It might be something simple like spending time with children or animals or going for a walk. Or it might be something more elaborate like attending a yoga class or getting a mani/pedicure. Whatever it is, make a list. I'll give you a few ideas from my list–in no particular order:

Daily:

- Tea, journaling, and planning my day
- Morning smoothie
- Self-Reiki
- Reiki Meditations
- Reiki walks with dogs
- Quick bike rides to break up the day when weather permits
- Yoga and stretching
- Kombucha break
- Read

Weekly:

- Yoga classes
- Reiki clients (I LOVE doing sessions for my clients)
- Date with my husband and/or children
- Camping or visits with friends

Bi-weekly or Monthly:

- Reflexology
- Massage
- Surface floats
- Physiotherapy
- Acupuncture
- Hair appointments
- Long bike rides
- Lead a Monthly Reiki Share

Semi-annually or Seasonally

- Medical check-ups
- Dental appointments
- Eye appointments
- Teaching Reiki (I also get a boost from doing this–it is so rewarding)
- Travel

I know I do a lot of self-care. I believe it's a big part of what makes me good at what I do. It allows me to show up for my clients and students from a place of joy, balance, and fulfillment. And besides, it helps me live a more joyous and rewarding life.

SELF CARE EXERCISE PART 1:
So what I challenge you to do today is list the things that feed your soul. What do you love to do? Do you love to dance? Camp? Spend time in nature? Or do you love to travel? Set a timer for 5 minutes and begin writing down all of the things you love to do that bring you joy. This exercise was challenging for some of my students. It had been so long since they had experienced joy that they had no idea what brought them joy. It wound up being a powerful exercise, as they realized they needed to make some significant changes in their lives to get them back in touch with joy.

IF THIS SHOWS up for you, I'd like you to think about what you enjoyed doing as a child. What brought you joy then? Just get started and see what flows.

SELF CARE EXERCISE PART 2:
Once you have the list, I'd like you to take your calendar out and schedule at least 5 of the things that give you joy. Try and do some-

thing joyful each day. Take some of the things you'd love to include in your life and schedule them into your week. Then FOLLOW up with them. If a client asks if you are free Wednesday afternoon as it's the only time they can fit a session in, but you have planned a bike ride, let them know you are busy and find an alternate time for their session. It is as important to honor these commitments to yourself as anything else you have on your calendar.

AND IF YOU are committed to self-care like I am–and if your calendar can get a bit complicated–you may want to take some of the monthly and seasonal appointments and schedule 6-12 months of them. When I do that, I can work my massage, hair appointment, and sometimes something else into the same day, saving me a trip to town. It's not only efficient, but it's a full day of self-care that I look forward to!

DAILY LIFE

You can also weave Reiki into your daily life. Sit down and think of some ways. Here are a few options:

- Can you do 5 minutes of Reiki meditation or a Reiki walk on your lunch break?
- Between clients or appointments, can you do Kenyoku to cleanse your energy and even a minute or two of Gassho, bringing your Reiki energy through you?
- Can you Reiki your food and drinks so that they become the exact right chemistry for you?
- Can you chant or draw your Reiki symbols into your office each morning, asking them to be with you throughout the day?
- Can you do self Reiki as you travel to work? Can you surround the vehicle you are in with the Power symbol, inviting it to help everyone travel safely?

- Can you do a moving meditation each morning while activating your symbols for the entire day?
- Can you send Reiki ahead to meetings and appointments throughout your day?
- Can you Reiki the files or equipment you are working with?
- Can you send Reiki with your eyes (Gassho) whenever you shake hands or meet someone new?
- Can you send Reiki to your voice box, asking Reiki to help you with discernment, so you know what words to use and connect with your authentic voice?
- Can you create a Reiki grid for your work, putting important projects in it, and charging them with a continual supply of Reiki each day?
- Can you cleanse your whole workplace? I have students who do this in hospitals, schools, and office buildings, and they say it has made a considerable difference in their working environment.

However you integrate Reiki into your daily life, remember to do Kenyoku and a brief Gassho before you leave work for the day. This helps leave work at work so that you do not bring it home. So you can enjoy your home life separate from work.

YOU ARE ONLY LIMITED by your imagination, and Reiki can never cause harm, so what have you got to lose? Begin experimenting with the different ways you can weave Reiki into your daily life.

Reiki Guidance

One of Reiki's unique and valuable aspects is that it can connect us with Divine Guidance. I often use William Rand's mantra, "Please guide me and heal me so that I may be of greater service to myself and others." Initially, when I heard that mantra, it did not include "to myself." It only spoke of being of greater service to others. Later on, William added "to myself and others," and I think the statement became more complete. So many of us are over-givers. But we are an essential part of the equation as well. We need to be healthy in order to help others. So be sure to include yourself in this.

I OFTEN ASK for my guidance with the statement above at the beginning of the day and simply pay attention when it shows up. Because I am kinesthetic and love movement, guidance often shows up for me when I walk. It can also show up when I travel. Or meditate. And sometimes, it shows up during client sessions. Spirit often brings us clients who are working through similar questions/issues/problems to those we are working through. It is often very easy to see the solution for your client, even when it is difficult to see it for yourself. Then your solutions become more evident. Sometimes, I journey with Reiki if I have a specific issue or question I want an answer to. If this speaks to you, Colleen Benelli wrote some excellent articles about using "Reiki for Spiritual Guidance"[3] and "How to Journey with Reiki."[4]

DAILY EXERCISE FOR GUIDANCE:
Begin your day with the statement, "Please guide me and heal me so that I may be of greater service to myself and others," or something similar. Then plan to try one of the ways described above to open yourself to receiving guidance.

IF YOU HAVE difficulty tapping into your intuition, it could be that you just don't know what type of intuitive you are. There are several types of intuition. Clairaudients hear messages. Clairvoyants see energy/messages. Claircognizants have knowledge about the message though they don't know why. Clairempaths get information through emotions. Clairsentients get messages through touch or physical feeling. Clairintellects get messages through their thoughts. At the same time, people with clair-imagination (creative types) get messages through their imagination (don't knock it, this is how all new creation comes into being). We all have a combination of these, but there is often one type of intuition that is stronger. And everyone is different.

AND REIKI CAN HELP you discern whether a thought or idea is your own or if your intuition is attempting to work with you. Until you are sure, it can help to use a pendulum, dowsing rods, or muscle testing to ask the question, "Is this my thought? Or my intuition?" After a while, you will start to understand better how your intuition works for you. And as you continue to work with your intuition, you will find that not only does it get stronger and easier to understand, but it also gets broader so that you sometimes begin to notice that in addition to one clair, another one is making itself available to you.

AS I MENTIONED, much of my Reiki guidance comes when I walk. I am a kinesthetic learner who loves movement. Walking is my moving meditation. My mind becomes still as I observe the natural environment around me. And thoughts, ideas, and pictures just float into my mind. I have become adept at listening to my intuition, and over time, its breadth has expanded so that I can make use of most of the clairs. To me, it feels like truth. Simple. Easy to understand. It has become a gut feeling.

AT ONE TIME in my Reiki journey, I spent time arguing with my Reiki guidance. However, I've learned over time that the guidance I receive is always right. And always in my best interest. Even and especially when it doesn't seem to be, enjoy tapping into your Reiki guidance!

THE WAY of Reiki

In his Reiki Master manual, William Rand says, "Over time, you will learn from experience that the guidance of Reiki is worthy of your trust. Once you have surrendered completely, you will have entered The Way of Reiki."[5] And "[w]e must consider that a Reiki Master is not one who has mastered Reiki, but one who has allowed Reiki to master him or her. This requires that we surrender completely to the spirit of Reiki, allowing it to guide every area of our lives."[6]

NOT LONG AFTER becoming a Reiki Master, I decided to enter "The Way of Reiki." I still get to make choices - but I turn my issues and problems over to Reiki and ask Reiki to lead and guide every aspect of my life. Since Reiki has moved into the driver's seat, I have experienced more and more grace, joy, peace and synchronicity in my life. It is not necessary to follow the way of Reiki, but if you would like to, this meditation may help.

The Way of Reiki Meditation

Make yourself really comfortable, close your eyes and take a deep breath, bringing your hands into Gassho and activating your Reiki symbols.

"Today, I surrender to the way of Reiki, accepting divine guidance and divine timing in all that I do. I understand that I always get to choose, but I invite Reiki to guide every aspect of my life now.

As Reiki flows, I am ready and willing to release everything that is no longer necessary in my life. All of the burdens I carry on behalf of myself and others. My culturally created self. The expectations I and others have of me. Old injuries, trauma, beliefs. Anything that would hold me back."

Take another deep breath as you place your hands comfortably on your body, giving yourself Reiki.

I invite you to imagine that it's a beautiful, warm sunny day and that you're walking through a trail in a beautiful forest. As you walk along and as you breathe into yourself, you breathe in the life essence of the forest, and the energy of the earth flows up through the bottoms of your feet.

You walk along until you come to a clearing in the forest and in the middle of the clearing is a small hill covered with soft grass and beautiful wildflowers.

I invite you to climb up the hill. And as you do, you feel the grass and the wildflowers brushing against your legs. When you get to the top of the hill, lie down and feel the earth and the grass beneath your body.

The earth beneath you begins to glow, and you realize this is the light of the Divine Earth. It completely supports you, nurtures you, and holds you in this material existence. And as you allow the light of the earth to hold you, you feel held and protected, cared for, secure in the arms of the earth.

And as you're lying there, held and safe and secure, a beautiful beam of light pierces the clouds and shines down directly upon you. And this is the light from the highest heavens. This is about your spirit, your breath, filling your body.

And as the lights shine on you, from below and above, balancing your chakras, balancing every part of you, helping you align and to tune into the higher frequencies and vibration available to you, the energies begin to focus on the blocks, injuries, resistance and frequencies that are holding you back. And so I invite you to focus on them, yourself, with a willingness to let them go.

And at the same time, surrender to the way of Reiki, allowing Reiki to lead, and guide every aspect of your life.

Imagine that there's a wheelbarrow beside you. Think about all the things that have been troubling you or that are not sitting well. Think about the burdens that you are carrying. Some of these burdens are very old. Some of them might be injuries or traumas that you experienced a long time ago. Some of them are current.

As you consider them, begin unpacking your burdens and moving them into the wheelbarrow. The wheelbarrow will remain there for the entire time you are in meditation today. At the end, you will have left all of your burdens, issues, and problems with Reiki, allowing Reiki to sort them out.

And all of these burdens and problems and decisions and issues will only be returned to you from a space of solution that Reiki can offer.

Breathe into this energy, allow it to hold that vibration of surrender and solution as this unfoldment process takes place.

I invite you to stay in this space as long as you need, and when you are ready, you can return.

~

Energetic Hygiene

When you are sensitive, as most Reiki practitioners are, you are more aware of the energy and energies around you. And not all of them are healthy and positive. So energetic hygiene becomes essential. Particularly for empaths–which so many of us are. Typically, empaths have an imbalanced empathy which causes them to take on the energy and issues of others. It's something I have been working through for much of my Reiki journey.

. . .

IT IS NOT usual that we will pick up negative energies from our clients because the energy we are channeling comes from a higher power. But it is essential not to use your own energy as you are doing Reiki sessions. Say a prayer asking your ego and personal energy to step to the side so that only the pure energy of Reiki and God's love can flow through you to the client. Once the session is complete, remember to use Kenyoku (dry bathing) to release anything in your field. Or give yourself a quick Reiki session. Or ask CKR to flow through you, releasing anything you picked up. And imagine all energies that have been released returning to Source.

OCCASIONALLY, though, even when we are careful, we can feel drained after a session, after an interaction with a friend or loved one, or due to life events. When this happens, it is essential to remember that the person or situation the negative energy or feelings seem to have come from is NOT where negative energies come from. Everyone has a beautiful, pure spirit. But our spirits get covered by layers of the ways and worries of the world. And sometimes, these layers become so dense that energies attach to us. This is where the uncomfortable energies come from. Not from the person or event.

AND THE OTHER thing that is important to remember in these situations is that if these dense energies find their way to us, we have created the opening on some level of our consciousness.

IN HIS ARTICLE "Solutions to Improve Your Practice," William Rand said, "When a practitioner takes on a client's negative energy during a healing session or feels drained afterward, it is usually due to something that the practitioner is doing energetically within the self, either consciously or unconsciously, to allow this to happen. There is usually a misunderstanding or a misalignment of energy within the practitioner's energy field that invites the client's symptoms in."[7]

. . .

So if this happens, it is an excellent opportunity to address your energetic field and discover what is within you that is inviting the energy in. So while our self Reiki and basic energetic hygiene are often enough to keep our energies clear, if ever they are not, regard it as an opportunity for your own healing. And be sure to send love and Reiki to the source for assisting you in seeing an area of your own field that needs help.

Psychic Attack

It had been such a long time since I had been psychically attacked that it came as a surprise as I was leading a meditation in a yoga studio a few years ago–and afterward, once everyone left, I did not feel myself. I knew immediately that I was in the midst of a psychic attack. When I asked energetically where it came from, I sensed that it came from a lady who had left partway through the meditation. She left just as I was about to do spirit release. I was happy to catch it before it sent me spiraling. Immediately, I did a release of the attack and then sent Reiki and love to the lady from whence it came.

A few weeks later, I was at an ICRT LRMT Reiki retreat with William Rand and asked him about it. He said that he appreciates that psychic attacks show him an area of his own energy field that needs to be healed. He then heals that area and releases the energy that is attached to him. He says thank you to the source of the energetic attack and sends the person Reiki.

I had never met anyone with such an enlightened attitude toward this, and I share this outlook with my students, doing my best to emulate it myself.

. . .

Handling Stress

Reiki is a Japanese form of stress reduction. And yet, sometimes, as we manage our Reiki business, we experience stress. I recently laughed with another Reiki Master-Teacher that doing what we do is not always as zen as you would think. It often is relaxing, but sometimes, our clients are pretty wound up. Sometimes, they are not satisfied with our work, or their lives, etc., but we are a convenient person on whom to take out their frustration. Sometimes, we cannot help as much as we would like. Occasionally, we take on our clients' stress or issues. Sometimes, we become stressed from working with technology or dealing with taxes or tasks that we don't enjoy. It happens to every small business owner.

WHEN STRESS HAPPENS TO YOU, the important thing to remember is that you have Reiki to help. The first thing to do when you are feeling stressed is:

1. Ask yourself, "Is this mine?" If it is not, do a Reiki session and release the stress. If it is, go to step 2.
2. If the stress is yours, take some time for self-Reiki. If possible, while listening to a guided meditation or some beautiful music. If you still feel stressed when this is done, go to step 3.
3. If you still feel stressed, reach out to a mentor, peer, or peer group. Discuss the source of your stress and ask for their advice; then make a plan of action. If you still feel stressed, go to step 4.
4. Book a Reiki session with another practitioner. Take a Reiki walk in nature. Book some self-care or some downtime. And one thing I notice is that it always feels better in the morning. So even if I go to sleep feeling a bit wonky, I do Reiki as I sleep, and the stress is almost always significantly diminished once I have slept on it.

Reiki Sessions from Others

It's a great idea to book a regular Reiki session with someone else. I book a session with my mentor once per month. And I would not miss it for the world. One of the things I notice is that it keeps me on an even keel. I never go into crisis anymore. Seriously. Never. And it keeps me moving forward in my spirituality.

I gladly pay for my session. It's some of the best money I spend. But if that isn't in your budget, consider setting up a sharing opportunity with a peer you respect. Take the sessions seriously, though. Fill in the paperwork. Once it is booked, treat it like any other session in your calendar. Take the time. But this is an excellent investment in yourself, your business, and your spiritual growth.

Past Life Work

Sometimes there are things in our lives that hold us back. Things like fears, phobias, victim mentality, destructive patterns, or tendencies. These issues and patterns don't always make sense based on our experiences from this lifetime, and they are sometimes difficult to surmount. In these instances, sometimes, they are related to past life trauma or injuries.

Some of the patterns I see coming up as we step forward in our Reiki path are a reluctance to step into our power or use our intuition. Fears and phobias sometimes show up out of the blue. Prejudice and judgment. And others. Sometimes they are even physical, such as rashes, etc.

. . .

ONE CLIENT who had to travel for his work suddenly developed a fear of heights and had difficulty going over the many bridges he had to traverse daily in his work, suffering panic attacks each time he did. It made no sense to him because he did not have an issue with heights before. I explained to him that perhaps something traumatic had happened regarding heights at that age in another life, such as falling from a cliff, etc. Understanding that, he was able to isolate the incident causing his issue and heal it so that he could travel for his work again.

IF AN ISSUE CROPS UP for you that doesn't make sense, go ahead and send Reiki with the distance symbol to the source of this issue, and be aware that it may not come from this lifetime. I also did a podcast on this which includes a Reiki-infused past life regression with Julie Russell to dig in further.[8]

SPIRIT RELEASE WORK

Sometimes the energies that cause issues contain consciousness. And this can make them more difficult to release than the layers of energy and the ways and worries of the world which do not. But even energies with consciousness will respond to Reiki over time.

IN OUR HOLY FIRE® Reiki classes, we teach a Spirit Release technique which is more efficient as it is often helpful to release this type of attachment for people. Everyone has the right to be sovereign in their bodies, and this type of attachment can negatively impact their (or our) health. It's important to understand that this type of energy is common. It is rare to find people who don't have something attached somewhere.

. . .

BUT IF YOU don't have Holy Fire® energy and would like a technique to deal with this efficiently and effectively, William Rand gives us one in his article "Solutions to Improve Your Practice".[9] Check it out.

The Kingdom Within

I found an article by Colleen Benelli when I was teaching my Reiki Master Mentor class called "Reiki and the Kingdom of God Within," which deeply affected me and played with my mind a bit.[10]

IN THE ARTICLE originally published in the *Reiki News Magazine* in Spring 2015, Colleen explained that almost every spiritual tradition discusses that the Kingdom of God is within. And that Reiki awakens this consciousness within us. She has a beautiful meditation in her article to help you access this. And I admit that the concept plays with my mind a bit. Although I understand it, I don't yet have a firm grasp of it.

STILL, it inspired me. With Holy Fire® Reiki, at the Master level, we discuss 12 Heavens and the different energy frequencies from each of them. With my Reiki Master Mentor group, I was guided to lead a meditation that takes us into each of these Heavenly frequencies within us, using the distance symbol to access and get to know each one. My students said it was incredibly powerful, so I decided to record it and turn it into a podcast for everyone.[11]

Expanding Your Intuition

I work with intuition regularly, especially as I teach telepathic Animal Communication. But also in my Reiki practice. It is interesting that I was initially petrified to open my intuition. And many of my students are too. But I understand them. Really.

We all experience our intuition differently. As I mentioned in another section, some people see energy. Some hear it. Others have a knowing. Some feel it. There are many ways to experience our intuition. But one thing that happens naturally with Reiki is that our intuition expands. Initially reluctant to open up to my intuition because it frightened me as a child, I am so happy that I overcame this reluctance and began to embrace and listen to my intuition. It now governs much of my life. Of course, my brain is trained logically, as is yours. But logic can work together with intuition to give you a complete picture of what is happening.

So speaking as someone who was VERY reluctant to embrace my intuition, one of the things I will encourage you to do is to let go of any fear around opening up to your intuition. And to focus on listening and integrating it. Get to know how your intuition works. What are your strengths? Then engage every chakra, your mind, body, spirit, emotions, imagination, intellect, and every part of your being into listening with Reiki. When we listen, we learn. And Reiki has much to teach us.

In fact, in the Animal Reiki course, particularly at the Master level, listening is one of the skills we develop to listen more effectively to and for the animals. I have noticed that "listening" with all the parts of myself has positively impacted several areas of my life. Not just my Reiki practice. So go ahead and activate Reiki, and listen. You are connecting with your intuition and getting to know it. Place your hands over your third eye, asking your intuition to reconnect with you if you feel disconnected from it. And then listen. You won't be disappointed as you learn to tap into the Divine guidance of Reiki and use it to make decisions in your life.

Release Duality

Finally, if you listen to my podcasts, you have probably heard me talk about duality at one point. I believe we are entering a time on the Earth where we are ready to release duality.

DUALITY IS the combination of both love and hate or love and fear. It exists here on earth—a balance of both. But according to our understanding, in the higher heavens, there is no duality; there is only love.

WHEN HOLY FIRE® first arrived, it came with the indication that one of the purposes of the energy is to create a higher heaven reality here on the Earth. In other words, to release the duality on the Earth so that there is only love.

I BELIEVE that as we continue to practice Reiki and share it with others, spreading the love on the planet, we are contributing to this great awakening of the earth. In other words, we are contributing to creating Heaven on Earth.

SO THANK you for your willingness to spread Reiki and love on the planet. Thank you for taking part in this great awakening that is happening. I believe that with every person that we introduce to the power and love of Reiki, the vibration of the planet rises. It releases more hate and fear, leaving more room for love. Invite that love into your life, releasing duality wherever you find it simply by applying Reiki. As you do this, the vibration of the planet rises. And then allow it to spread out to your family, friends, clients, and students who are interested in doing the same. We don't need to be pushy. The people who are ready and willing will come to us. Thank you, thank you for answering the call.

~

Meditation

Bring your hands into Gassho, activating your Reiki energy.
Then hold Reiki out in front of your heart chakra and just fill your heart chakra with Reiki.
Then go below your heart, chakra to your solar plexus. Stay here until it is filled with Reiki.
Now the sacral chakra.
And the base chakra.
We are activating all of our chakras today as we learn to listen to Reiki and let go of our agendas.
Now we'll go to the throat chakra and activate that.
Next is our third eye.
And then the crown at the top of your head.
Now come back into Gassho. Thank you.
Today we are letting Reiki lead. And if it feels comfortable to you, you can even decide to adopt "the way of Reiki," which is surrendering completely to the Reiki energy.
We invite Reiki to Guide us and heal us so that we may be of greater service to ourselves and others. And now, we open ourselves to listen to the energy.
Listen with your chakras open.
Listen with your mind.
Listen with your body.
Listen with your emotions.
Listen with your imagination.
Listen with every part of your being.
Listen for your path.
Listen for your next step.
Listen to the guidance of Reiki.
Remain here for 15-20 minutes, listening to your Reiki guidance.
Namaste. Thank you.

ProTip

Kris Valentine, LRMT, Texas, USA
Kris D. Valentine Wellness[12]

I love this chapter. So thank you for writing it. The first thing that I noticed with the book is that you can apply Reiki to just about any point-of-view aspect of your life and watch that aspect grow. Adding the vibration of Reiki to anything is like giving it an extra boost of love or higher vibration.

WHEN WE FIRST COME OUT OF our classes, we go back and practice exactly what we learned. And then we might be in that speculative or curious state of, "I wonder what would happen if I applied Reiki to this?"

THAT'S what I love about this book because there are so many things that you can apply Reiki to. The whole thing about walking with Reiki, I do that. And it's one of the ways that I like to meditate. Of course, you might have your laundry list of things going through your mind as you walk. But when I walk with Reiki, it's more peaceful. It either sets up my day in the morning or gives away what is unnecessary at the end of the day.

ONE OF THE other things that stood out to me from the book is the self-care of Reiki. And using Reiki to release stress and anxiety. During the pandemic, I used Reiki for clarity and self-care.

THIS BOOK IS SO necessary and needed because many of us are not really business-oriented. I am a physical therapist, but I don't have my own clinic; I work for someone. So how do you set up your own business?

. . .

I TELL my students they will go to areas they never thought they would or could go to. That they will learn things that I don't know. And they say, "No, you're a master." but I tell them "You will teach me."

THIS CHAPTER PERMITS you to look at different ways to use Reiki for yourself and others. To apply Reiki to anything in your life. Reiki has evolved for me in ways that I never thought would be possible. I had a mentor in the ICRT licensed teacher program. Each level is different. In my Karuna year, it was interesting how different the energy felt.

BUT I WAS in a quandary of how to expand my business? So I started doing Facebook Live shares. I wanted to play music during the shares and I wanted the group to hear the same music. I didn't know how to do that as we can only play royalty-free music on social media. There was none I liked and it wasn't very long. I wanted a continuous song.

SO I THOUGHT, "I can play music. It won't be a problem." But trying to lead a meditation and play music at the same time is tricky. I did it in the beginning but it was stressful. So I learned to record music. Then I turned on my Reiki and waited for inspiration. The next thing you know, I was writing music! It was so much fun that I started playing with it because I thought, "Wow, this is Reiki-infused music."

I PLAYED that music with my meditations in my Reiki shares. Then people asked to buy it. I thought, "Are you kidding me?" But loads of people wanted to buy my music. So my website designer helped me put it up on my website.

. . .

I LISTEN to that music throughout the day as I travel between clients. It helps me stay relaxed. I never thought I could do that but Reiki led me to write Reiki-infused music. Now I write compositions for others. That was a natural evolution of this process because other people wanted royalty-free music for their Reiki and spiritual sessions.

I COMPOSE for them and they own the rights to it. Karen Harrison, the co-director of the LRMT program asked me, how do you do that? And I said, I just apply Reiki to it. That's really all I do. Then I set a timer because I might not be aware of how long I've been playing. And I play. It just flows through me. It goes around my logical brain to my intuition.

REIKI LED ME TO MUSIC, but for you, it could be something else. It could be painting with Reiki. What is it that you love? I've always loved music. But where is it in your life that you are creative? You can use Reiki to increase your creativity. It's about asking that question and allowing Reiki to answer. What does the future hold? I don't know. I'm excited to find out.

THE GUIDANCE I am the most reluctant to follow is usually the guidance that creates growth. That growth isn't always comfortable. You're stepping into the unknown. I call it life on the skinny branches, and that's where life is the best.

CHECK out our podcast on this chapter.[13]

∽

STUDENT SUCCESS STORY **Amy Butler**

The effort you made with the course was empowering for all of us, and we feel the freedom in a straightforward, beautiful, succinct way. We felt free to explore and figure out the best practices for us and understand that it's a continuous process, not a static experience.

THERE'S a lot of confidence and support in the energy. And so, what you've given us is the foundation for what we're building. It's going from one lineage to the next so we are ambassadors for that energy of empowerment. And it creates energy around us that frees everyone in our lives. Reiki creates an invitation and opportunity for everyone and everything. It's all-inclusive.

THERE WAS simplicity and beauty in what you delivered and the way you empowered us so that we could explore what Reiki means to us. And in that exploration and that ownership of who we are, our authentic selves came forward. There's no restrictions so we're continually exploring what that means. The net energy gets passed on to our students and the people in our lives. And it just flows from that. I believe it will impact thousands and thousands of lives and the vibration on the planet.

WHEN THEY SAY one person can make a difference, it's true. When you step into your authentic self, you honor all of life around you. It's never defined in black and white because it's also a moving picture like a movie, constantly changing. It's not static, and we're not fixed, and we're not limited. And that's Reiki. That's what gives us the ability and the inspiration to teach or share, or be a vehicle for Reiki because of the power of that and how it impacts everybody.

. . .

AND THERE'S SO much love in that. Of course, we benefit from the healing and the love from Reiki continually; we're held by it. It's like a cradle. It's not apron strings because it changes shape with who you are and as you evolve. It's multi-dimensional energy. Even though our conscious minds can't fully grasp it, we can feel it.

I HAVE no idea what it will be for me, but I feel like I can trust it, and I don't have any history of trust at all, but I can trust in Reiki. And I feel like I have hope for my future and for all of life.

I FEEL like it's a reliable source of love that's available to me. It's real. I didn't have that reliability or stability in my life. But Reiki is the safe spot where you can be yourself and give of, and to, yourself without holding back. Creating your life without holding back. If it's baby steps, that's perfect. Whatever our timing is perfect. Reiki has no judgment.

OUR POTENTIAL IS UNFOLDING ALL the time. Reiki is just waiting for us to step into it. I didn't have a voice for myself before or a clear way of voicing support for others because I didn't have that language or the tools. But Reiki brings us access to a million zillion different creative voices with unlimited options. You can step into your happiest, most joyful, peaceful self to whatever degree you can embody that. And if your capacity can't hold a whole bunch, that's okay too.

IT'S TOTAL TRUST. It's tapping into the balance of life. Unconditionally loving, holistic, and just waiting for us to wake up. It's a gentle knock on your shoulder when you're not present. It brings you to a place where you can get just enough distance or perspective and objectivity to embrace yourself and embrace the moment and realize "I'm going to be okay" in every situation.

. . .

It has paved the way for me to be okay with not steaming ahead into my business. Reiki supports "You be You and take whatever time you need." So for me, with my Reiki business and my creative businesses, Reiki is showing me that it's all integrated because that's all of who I am. So the way Reiki shows up in my life isn't going to look like the way it's going to be in anybody else's life.

I had developed my own personal Reiki practice and was ready to teach, but I needed to honor myself and slow down. The course taught me that's okay. Follow Divine timing. And I'm more empowered. And I have more faith and belief in what I'm going to bring forward in my Reiki practice. I'm honoring my capacity and what I'm being asked to take care of within myself to grow and develop as a practitioner and in my own life.

I have two clients in my Reiki business right now, and I'm okay with that because it fits where I'm supposed to be. Reiki is showing me to take the time and space to do the things I need to do to get ready for the expansion.

You've taught us that there's no measurement or comparison. There's no rule book on how your practice is supposed to develop. That's the biggest freeing thing. It's Reiki your way.

I REMEMBER THAT when I'm tempted to compare myself to someone else's Reiki practice.

. . .

I ASK what feels true to me right now? What do I need right now? And I honor all these other aspects that need attention and love in my life that I've neglected because I didn't have the tools until I had Reiki.

FEEL into what's possible with what you can create in a business. You can start a unique business based on what inspires you, what you love, and your passions in your unique perspective of how Reiki is expressed through you for other people. Slow down and allow that to happen.

REIKI IS ALWAYS behind the scenes, moving things forward in a big way, even if we're resisting it because we're not ready to embrace certain aspects of the energy.

IT'S JUST PATIENT, generous, and loving. And that rings through the course for me.

I SEE myself having Reiki guide me into service with people and animals. I don't know what that looks like. So I'm just trying to be gentle with myself and respect divine timing.

IT GIVES the roadmap of how to get started down the path, and then Reiki takes over. But the course is potent that way, showing us how to get guidance and what steps to take to get your energy moving. It helps you set your intentions and take action. And that's all going to look different for everybody.

---

1. https://www.hiddenbrook.ca/wp-content/uploads/2020/09/AllowingReikiToGuide-1.pdf
2. https://www.hiddenbrook.ca/wp-content/uploads/2020/09/AllowingReikiToGuide-1.pdf
3. https://reikilifestyle.com/reiki-for-spiritual-guidance/
4. https://reikilifestyle.com/reiki-journey-techniques/
5. Rand, William Lee. *Usui/Holy Fire® III Reiki Master Manual Online and In-Person*. Southfield, MI: International Center for Reiki Training, 2020. 117.
6. Rand, William Lee. *Usui/Holy Fire® III Reiki Master Manual Online and In-Person*. Southfield, MI: International Center for Reiki Training, 2020. 117.
7. https://www.reiki.org/articles/solutions-improve-your-reiki-practice
8. https://www.buzzsprout.com/1364386/8278488
9. https://www.reiki.org/articles/solutions-improve-your-reiki-practice
10. http://reikilifestyle.wpengine.com/wp-content/uploads/2015/02/Colleen-B-Reiki34-54.pdf
11. https://www.buzzsprout.com/1364386/7138201
12. https://www.krisdvalentine.com/
13. https://www.buzzsprout.com/1364386/10263206

9

BECOMING A REIKI MENTOR

"If somebody asks you to do a session for them, you're ready to become a practitioner. If somebody asks you to teach; you're ready to teach. If somebody asks you to be a mentor, I think you're ready to be a mentor."
Joan Mauté, LRMT

As I was completing the requirements of the first block or level of the ICRT LRMT program, people came out of the woodwork asking me to mentor them. Several didn't even know I was in the program. Others had never studied with me. Most just knew I was an experienced Reiki Master. I think a dozen people from various backgrounds approached me, explicitly asking me to mentor them. I understood this as Reiki's guidance at work. But the ICRT program was intense and time-consuming. And I had my businesses to run. I didn't know how I could find the time to mentor even one student, never mind the dozen who asked me. I knew I would be a mentor someday, but not today. So I put it off, but the seed was planted, and I knew it would germinate when the time was right.

. . .

AT SOME POINT, once you have created a successful Reiki business, you get a calling to share it with others. Sometimes, people will ask you to mentor them. Other times, you will suggest it to students you want to see go further. Maybe you will mentor other Reiki Masters. Or practitioners. Perhaps you will simply provide guidance. Or perhaps you will set up a class or a formal mentoring program. As with everything else, Reiki will guide you.

IF YOU PLAN to mentor students individually, you need to determine the framework. Will you receive compensation? How often will you meet? Will you set it up as a Reiki session? Will it include guidance, or will it also include healing work? What are some of the things you want to share? Do you prefer to keep it informal? Or will you work from an outline? Be conscious of not taking over your student's journey. Instead, let them find their way with it.

MY GUIDANCE CAME in loud and clear in England during Covid as I realized "everyone needs Reiki at times like these" and that my role was to "teach the teachers." The seed that germinated sprang to life. And what a life it had. I understood that perhaps I didn't have the time to mentor people one-on-one. But if I created a program, I could mentor several people in a few hours per month.

So I SAT DOWN and created my first 6-month program. The class filled immediately, demonstrating how much Reiki practitioners and teachers need mentors! I followed that up with two more 6-month courses for a total of 20 sessions. Some of the sessions were focused entirely on business. At the same time, others were about personal development.

. . .

THE STUDENTS SHARED that the sessions were always exactly what they needed. And everyone got different things from them. I held each 2-hour meeting on Zoom. It consisted of an opening prayer and a talk or discussion, followed by a healing session or a group session. I assigned homework which included at least one group assignment each month. And the designated groups were expected to support and work together. We had a private FaceBook group where we could connect, share our work, and ask questions. I don't know who looked forward to the sessions more each month--the students or me. My husband always said I was glowing when I wrapped it up.

I OFFERED the sessions from 7-9 pm in my time zone, allowing my North American and Australian students to attend. I had some European students stay up very late at night to join us as well.

I ACTIVATED my voice box with Reiki and asked Reiki and Source to guide each session. The prayers and some of the meditations were very guided. Although I often had a plan going into the meeting, I always listened for guidance, and it always came in clearly and powerfully. So after the sessions, people said they felt like I was talking just to them.
I'll outline what we did.

CREATING a **Reiki Master Mentor Class**

When I got home from England, knowing that more people needed Reiki and that I was in a unique position to "teach the teachers" so that could happen, I immediately created a Reiki Master Mentor group so I could help Reiki Masters who simply haven't "gotten themselves out there" or who would like help "getting themselves out there more effectively" to do so. That way, more people could be reached by Reiki. That was my ultimate goal.

. . .

I HADN'T COUNTED on how much the class would benefit me. I learned so much while teaching that class. I also didn't expect the financial abundance that showed up when I needed it. During Covid, my horse business shut down, but the horses' considerable expenses continued. I had large hay bills to cover, not to mention vet and farrier expenses, etc. Another benefit is that the class allowed my practice to grow. As people got to know me through the lower-cost Reiki Master Mentor group and as I was able to add value to their lives, they began to want to take classes from me or book sessions with me. Or to tell friends and students to do the same.

I WAS BLESSED that the course took off immediately. I offered six monthly 2-hour sessions online from 7-9 pm. The session was filled within days of announcing it. I held the classes online and introduced the topic, an opening prayer, discussion/teaching, Q&A, and a closing prayer. And it wasn't just my students who signed up. Somehow word got around. And so my first sessions included students from 5 different countries and three continents. It became a time I looked forward to each month. I was connecting with these lovely "experts" in the field of Reiki and listening to the energy and where it was guiding us. It was beautiful. You have the results in your hands. This book is the result of what came from the course. We all learned and grew in the process.

I RECORDED the sessions so that those who could not attend in person could still enjoy them, but the in-person attendance was strong. The students looked forward to the sessions each month as much as I did. They didn't always get as far as they wanted or expected each month (we are often our own harshest critics), but everyone made progress in some form or another. People who had websites "under construction" for years developed a website; some started to teach, others started Reiki shares, and one student even purchased land she plans to develop into a retreat center. Some people realized their "unique way" of practicing Reiki blended fully into what they are already doing and took the pressure off of themselves to "start a practice" that looks more like mine. Everyone became more comfortable and confident in what they were doing with Reiki. Even those who became a bit overwhelmed and found it challenging to complete the sessions had the recordings and knew they would proceed in their own time. I considered it an unmitigated success.

In addition to conducting a monthly session, I assigned homework and working groups and created a private Facebook group for people to share. The group that joined me felt supported and stayed in touch. It was a wonderful process.

One of the great things about being a mentor is passing on hard-won knowledge. I remember explaining a complicated energetic concept to a group one day, saying it took me nine years to learn this, but I should be able to get you up to speed in 15-20 minutes! That is the beautiful thing about both being and having a mentor.

I once read a horse book by Bill Dorrance. He was in his 90s and collaborating with a writer to get the book written. He said he had learned a lot about horses in his 90 years (he was one of the top horse trainers in the world and well ahead of his time), and he hoped that by passing along what he learned, it would shorten our learning curve so that maybe we could accomplish more with horses in our lifetimes even than he had been able to. That has been my philosophy ever since, and it is my hope with my mentor program that by passing along the knowledge that took me years to sort through and accumulate, I can shorten the learning curves of others. Perhaps they can take things even further than I did. Indeed, some of my students got going on their websites and got them published even as my website revisions languished. They created YouTube channels, held

Reiki shares, advertised sessions, created Reiki spaces, and created their own Reiki Master Mentor groups. I was a proud mama.

AND WHILE I created my course for Reiki Masters, it occurred to me that I could just have easily created a course for level 1&2 Reiki Practitioners to help them begin offering sessions. I will be putting a course together on that shortly, and I hope you will consider doing that too.

I CREATED the first 6-month session based on what I needed when I started, and I asked my students what would have helped them or what assistance they needed. After that, I asked my Reiki Master Mentor students to help me design the class they wanted. And that continued. The most challenging part was coming up with content that supported everyone, regardless of their stage. Some of my students were new Masters; some had been Reiki Masters for a while but hadn't taught. Others were actively teaching a large number of students. But when I listened to the energy, I was always guided into deeply healing meditations that left everyone motivated and able to move forward regardless of what stage they found themselves in. I have shared a number of these meditations with you in the course of this book. The hours spent with my group were my favorite time all week! I hope it will be yours too.

EXERCISE TO GET STARTED:

Activate your Reiki energy. Move into the Gassho meditation. Then ask yourself the following questions:

1. First, think about to whom you might offer this class. Do you have a Facebook group, Newsletter, Instagram, or YouTube following who would be interested?

2. How will you communicate with them? Will you send an email or announce it during a Reiki share or a video?
3. How many people do you want in your group? I cut my group off at 24.
4. Will you offer the course online or in-person?
5. How often will you meet? Monthly? Weekly? Every two weeks? Initially, I met monthly, but I found we lost some momentum. So the next session will run bi-weekly.
6. What time of day is best for you? For your clients? By offering it in the evening in my time zone, it is late afternoon for my West coast students, morning for my Australian students, and late evening for my European students, but it worked well so that they could all attend.

SOME PEOPLE CONTINUED for the next session. Others found that between life changes, becoming overwhelmed, or realizing they were not quite ready to continue, they needed to drop out part way through or could not attend the next group of sessions. But I still sent the recordings, and when they are ready, they can pick them back up again. And for the nominal price of the class, everyone appreciated that.

TAKE some time to write down topics you think would interest your clients and students. You might consider creating the course based on the chapters in this book. Some examples might be:

- Identifying your goals
- Understanding your own unique Reiki practice
- Identify the obstacles
- Creating a Reiki business
- Marketing
- Branding

- Develop your practice
- Business skills
- Teaching Reiki
- Grow your connection

You might even add some fun topics like:

- Spirit Release
- Dispelling Psychic Attack
- The 12 Heavens
- The Kingdom Within
- Expand your Intuition, etc.

I tried to balance two serious classes with one fun one.

Let's go into meditation now, which will help you formulate your own Reiki Master Mentor class.

Exercise: **Choose the topics for your own Reiki Mentoring class**
Close your eyes, and take a deep breath. Activate your Reiki energy and use HSZSN to connect with yourself when you were a brand new Reiki Master just starting out. Stay in the Reiki energy as you ask yourself the following questions. Then after meditating with each one, write down the responses you receive.

1. What advice would you give to yourself?
2. What do you wish you had known?
3. What are some of your skills and talents?
4. What are the topics you would like to share as a mentor?

Take some time to journal your responses and ideas.

SAMPLE SESSIONS:
  Session 1: Setting the Direction & Goals of Your Practice

- Identify the direction of your Reiki practice
- Goal setting exercise
- Reiki guidance & grids
- Identify obstacles
- Meditation to release obstacles
- Closing prayer
- Question and Answer

Session 2: Growing Your Community

- Identify your community
- Marketing
- How to introduce Reiki in discussions
- Discernment and language
- Growing a practice in a Covid environment
- Reiki shares
- Reiki talks, etc.
- Closing prayer
- Question and Answer

Session 3: Ready to Launch

- Sessions
- Teaching
- Professional Associations
- Best business practices
- Reiki support group
- Transitioning into a Reiki career

Session 4: Strengthen Your Guidance

- Reiki in your daily life
- Reiki guides
- Energetic Hygiene
- Reiki when you are stressed
- What to do with an unhappy client
- Self-care
- Closing prayer
- Question and Answer

Session 5: Spirit Release Work

- Spirit Release - what is it?
- Techniques
- Spirit guides
- Energetic Attack
- Psychic Attack
- Closing prayer
- Question and Answer

Session 6: Other Styles of Reiki

- Child Reiki
- Animal Reiki
- Karuna Reiki®
- Medical Reiki
- Reiki in Hospice, etc.
- Following your guidance
- ICRT Code of Ethics

Bonus session: My gift to you

- Introduction to the "Lights"
- Journey to the 12 Heavens
- Question and Answer
- Closing Prayer

Session 7: Refining the Goals of Your Practice

- Reviewing & Refining the Goal
- Creating an identity & name
- Reiki sessions - plan (calendar)
- Self sessions (formal and informal)
- Reiki partner
- Closing prayer
- Question and Answer
- Homework: Write an article about your identity/name
- Connect with your Reiki partner and share your plan & article
- Arrange a complete distance Reiki session with your partner

Session 8: Marketing and Growth

- Marketing & Branding
- Newsletter - frequency, style, what you are sharing
- Website; Facebook; social media
- Canva
- Reiki shares & Reiki challenges
- Book a speaking event (handout)
- Reiki partner
- Closing prayer
- Question and Answer
- Homework: write down three marketing things you plan to do and give them the dates
- Connect with your Reiki partner and share your marketing plan

Session 9: Past Life Healing

- Explanation of past lives
- Discernment: recognizing when past lives are causing a

problem
- Cord-cutting, releasing trauma, phobias, and allergies
- Reiki partner
- Healing past lives
- Homework: connect with your Reiki partner to practice past life healing

Session 10: Teaching Reiki

- Tips to prepare for classes
- Teaching online or "hybrid" classes
- Traveling to teach
- Already teaching? Expanding your reach.
- Plan a class (or classes) - calendar
- Reiki partner
- Self-care
- Closing prayer
- Question and Answer
- Homework: connect with your Reiki partner to plan a class or an expansion

Session 11: Business Skills

- Responding to correspondence
- Keeping the conversation current
- Record keeping
- Accounting & bookkeeping
- Enlisting help
- Reiki partner
- Closing prayer
- Question and Answer
- Homework: make a plan, connect with your Reiki partner to share

Session 12: Expansion of Intuition

- Developing Discernment
- Balancing Compassion and Over-Empathy
- Disconnecting from 2nd Heaven influence
- Releasing Fear
- Living from a space of Love & 3rd Heaven
- Following your guidance
- Reiki partner
- Homework: connect with your Reiki partner to practice intuitive Reiki

SOME BASICS:

Now you have to decide how to set up your class. How much to charge? When to offer the class, etc.

I OFFERED six monthly sessions for $240. And threw in a bonus session for the first class. I provided the course on Zoom, so I wasn't limited to who could attend. I had over 20 people register immediately after I opened the session. And had even more for the second session.

IT MIGHT BE a good idea to create a group of some sort so you can stay in touch. And have fun with it. Everyone involved will learn and grow, including you. I hope you enjoy it!

ProTip
Joan Mauté, LRMT, Hawaii, USA
Rising Light Reiki[1]

I think this chapter will inspire a lot of people who've thought about mentoring but didn't have the confidence or thought they didn't know enough to move forward with that. It also doesn't have to be a big, huge, complicated thing. I wrote up sample sessions of what you could offer in each mentoring session that would be super helpful for students to know. Like different options of what can be included in sessions. Help people to recognize what it is that they want to focus on.

I DID my first Reiki training in the mid-nineties. It was in the old style: Oral, no manuals, no handouts, no nothing. You were expected to memorize everything, and afterward, I just didn't have a clue. The teacher was not available. They had come over to Hawaii to teach the class, and then they were gone. So I felt pretty lost. I didn't use Reiki much for several years and really wished I had had some kind of mentor. Some sort of guidance. I think my Reiki practice would have developed much sooner and would have been better in every way.

SO I DIDN'T KNOW what to do. And I didn't have the internet. So about a year and a half ago, I started thinking about offering a program with a slightly different focus than yours, Pam. It's more for students to connect on a deeper level personally with Reiki. And if they have a Reiki business, it can apply to that. I called it the Reiki deepening program.

AND I NOTICED that the level one and two students, in particular, needed support and help because they felt like Reiki orphans, like, "Okay, I did this training, I have these skills now, what do I do?" Even though our training is very comprehensive, suddenly, you are out in the world by yourself, wondering what's next.

WE ARE Reiki teachers who have been doing this for a while. And also we both have a lot of life experience. We've made a lot of mistakes and learned a lot of things through trial and error and education. So it would be beneficial to take all of this information that we spent our lifetimes learning and compiling and sorting out what's good and what isn't and share this with people so they don't have to go through this whole long, incredibly evolved process of trying to figure out what to do.

So I started one program for level two students and one for master students because they have different needs, focuses, and skills. I offer the programs three times a year. They're a little shorter than yours, Pam. They're four-month programs. Then I can offer these classes three times a year, so students don't have to wait if they missed the one that just started.

I got ideas and insights from our LRMT program. The students have Reiki buddies, and they pair up, and they'll stay together for at least a couple of months. And they are expected to do Reiki activities during the month. Like expressing gratitude. Students are sent a prayer of gratitude they can use if they don't already have something. Or they are connecting with Source or putting themselves first. So many practitioners put themselves last, which doesn't work very well. Over time you get depleted. Or Self-healing. Or using Reiki in everyday life. And they're sent suggestions on how they could do these things and encouraged to develop their own ways of using Reiki.

Receiving sessions is so important because none of us receive enough. That's one of the reasons for the Reiki buddies. Not just to practice on someone, but so you can receive and remember what you're doing and why. And we did journaling and accountability. So students were asked to send me a monthly progress report and tracking form.

. . .

THEY HAD a monthly assignment that they were expected to do. It's nothing complicated. It's just something to focus on. For the level-two group, I like to start with either the symbols and deepen their connection with the symbols or the Five Reiki Ideals.

AND THEN, with the Master group, the first-month assignment was to strengthen their energy by placing Holy Fire® Reiki on their chakras and in their energy field. There's a process you use for that with the Moving Meditation.

THE SECOND MONTH has been for manifesting from a place of wholeness. We all want to manifest things, but sometimes the place we do it is not from a place of wholeness, it's from a place of lack, and that just doesn't work so well. And then, they also have access to me during the month via email if they have any questions or if anything comes up. Whether personal or business-wise or whatever, I'm happy to help them individually. I've had students say, "Oh my gosh, I just wish I'd had this a long time ago," so I feel like I've turned into the mentor I wish I had had so many years ago.

ONE YOUNG STUDENT SAID, "Wow, you're so wise." And I just looked at her like, "I'm just a surfer girl from Hawaii." But I guess I've learned a couple of things over the decades, you know?

YOU MAY NOT FEEL that you're wise enough, or you know enough, or you may think you don't have something to offer. But keep in mind that whoever shows up for your program needs you. There's a reason why they're there. So really embody that sense that these people are here for a reason, and they need you, and you have exactly the right information to share with them.

. . .

AT THE MONTHLY MEETINGS, the other thing that we do is an attunement or an experience or something along those lines that helps deepen the connection with the Reiki. I'll let them choose what they feel they want each month.

ONE MONTH I only had four students in the master group. It was a cozy little group. They all had different needs. So one month, they all had individual assignments based on what they needed that month.

EVERYBODY JUST APPRECIATES it so much, and it changes people's lives in ways you would never expect and helps people feel that they're not Reiki orphans anymore.

THE MOST POPULAR part of the program is having a Reiki peer, someone to share with and talk to who are on the same level. In my first class, I had a student from Virginia and one from New York, and they were like long-lost sisters. They've become lifelong friends, and they even came down to do their Master's training together with me in person.

ONE STUDENT just studied at the master's level and said she was so taken with the deepening program that it was just the nudge she needed to instill confidence, gain experience, and take the next step to pursue her purpose of healing.

AND IT'S JUST SO heartwarming to know that you're making such a meaningful difference in people's lives. I had a meeting last week, and everybody looked like zombies.

. . .

So we just did the Tree of Life experience from ICRT Animal Reiki. And the feedback I got afterward was incredible. So even if your group doesn't seem to be engaged that month, you're still doing a world of good. Allowing someone to be immersed in Reiki for this period can be incredibly healing. I don't micromanage their experience.

The other really helpful thing was the Q&A. Just having the opportunity to ask questions. I'm constantly amazed at how connected people are in these. They connect so deeply.

The main thing that prevents people from becoming mentors is their minds and self-limiting beliefs. I think if you've gone through the master training and taken all the levels, you feel comfortable with the material. You've been practicing (you don't have to have been teaching), have life experience, and want to help people; you can become a mentor. If you believe you can, you can; if you believe you can't, that's your reality. So it's up to you. Being a mentor doesn't mean you have to have the answers to everything.

If somebody asks you to do a session for them, you're ready to become a practitioner. Somebody asks you to teach; you're ready to teach. If somebody asks you to be a mentor, I think you're ready to be a mentor.

I also think it would be helpful to take a mentoring program, like something you and I offer and a lot of the other teachers do. Having the experience as a participant will deepen your connection and answer a lot of questions and give you a sense of how to run a program like that.

. . .

When you're a Licensed Teacher, there are expectations that aren't always realistic. I've been an entrepreneur and self-employed all my life. I've had several different types of businesses, but this is the first time I've had a business that involved all this technology. Everything was much more tangible in the past, and I knew what to do and how to do it. But honestly, I'm struggling to learn how to run a business in this format. And I need help. So I am so thrilled that Pam wrote this book because I will read it from cover to cover. I don't have an MBA or anything like that. I have a degree in ornamental horticulture, and I was not focused on the business aspect. I just wanted to play with the plants. So just because you do whatever you do, doesn't mean that you know everything about how to do it. Don't be shy about seeking help in whatever areas you're not good at.

I'm an excellent Reiki teacher. I know that from the feedback I get from my students. But the business. Not so much. So this book is really, really helpful, and I appreciate it from the bottom of my heart.

Check out our podcast on this chapter.[2]

~

Student Success Story **Charlotte Tomyn**

I was guided to create a mentoring course called "Blueprint for Teaching Reiki Levels One and Two." I'm creating the fourth generation now, and last week, I realized that I wanted to create a master class for teaching Levels I and II.

I had that beautiful experience with you, mentoring all of us month after month. As I progressed forward in my knowledge, tiny bubbles of inspiration would percolate. They just sat over to one side. Then there was this moment of complete alignment with what I knew I wanted to do. I've always been a teacher. I have a Reiki studio. I've been teaching classes and doing sessions for years.

I HAVE experience as a teacher teaching in ways that present different learning viewpoints for students. My focus became how we can create a deeper connection to learning for students when we teach Reiki classes. I looked at creating deeper and more practical experiences for the students to learn how to use Reiki in their everyday lives.

I WAS GUIDED to help teachers with the overwhelm, so I created a blueprint that breaks down teaching. It is intended to enhance the teacher's ability to see the Reiki class from the student's side of things.

ONE OF THE biggest things I learned in your mentoring class is that it's not about me when I teach a class. It's about the student. You empowered us to see that it didn't have to be complicated.

I AM a retired elementary school teacher and principal. I enjoyed teaching students. It helped me be a better teacher for teachers. I was a national language arts consultant, which allows me opportunities to speak internationally at educational conferences. I worked all over Canada supporting teachers on teaching-learning strategies and techniques.

MY COURSE IS about observing your class through the eyes of the student. It's a transformational shift because you remember what it was like for you as a student and what you liked and what didn't. The teaching in the class is very much on how to make those deeper learning connections and experiences with students.

We review the entire curriculum for levels one and two from the eyes of a teacher teaching the class. We keep it simple. The purpose of the class is to develop a level of confidence, skill, and know-how for the teacher so that the Reiki class they teach will be a wonderful learning experience for their students.

During your mentorship class, I had two students who wanted to review levels one and two because they were ready to teach the course but couldn't remember it. So instead of setting up a review class, I set up a class with the specific intention of preparing the students to teach. I created templates with talking points and a digital manual. At the end of the class, they're equipped to go. Everything is teacher-guided.

You got me on the path. You got me on the train ... I didn't get off the train and didn't it get awesome! You supported each of us in our own way and empowered us. You gave us suggestions about how we would meet with different people, which would give us different experiences. We had a little smorgasbord to test our interests. We discovered our strengths and the things that spoke to us and things that did not.

You empowered us to do that without any parameters or barriers. You were just accepting everything from everyone at every level, which is not easy. How you were mentoring all of us is so different yet complementary to how I mentor in these teaching classes. Everybody has their own style. That's the beauty of it. Find what's aligned with you because everyone has that capacity. You don't have to know everything about a subject to mentor. You just have to know a little more than your students.

STUDENTS SAY, "I know what Reiki is. I know how to explain it, but how do I teach it? I have no idea." We break learning down for different types of learners and different types of learning styles. People are wired for stories, and that's one of the teaching tips. What example or story would you bring in here? How can we have learning be as participatory as possible?

I STARTED AS A REIKI PRACTITIONER, loving self-Reiki. Then I ventured on to a studio and a business with clients, still doing self-Reiki. Then I became a Reiki master-teacher and taught classes. I still had a studio and was doing client work and self-practice. Now I'm teaching teachers and am still doing all the other stuff. Nothing has been left behind. It has just developed and accumulated.

THANK YOU FOR BEING YOU, being so open, and putting the mentorship class together. You probably have no concept of how you have supported and empowered us because you don't hear everything. You just will never know the tiny ripples that turned into big waves of Reiki in the world. I could just see everybody opening in the group. I saw the obstacles let go, and it's so rewarding.

---

1. https://risinglightreiki.com/
2. https://www.buzzsprout.com/1364386/10263405

10

BLENDING REIKI WITH OTHER MODALITIES

"The more you let go and allow the energy to guide you, things will come in that you will say, if somebody told me I was going to do this, I would have never imagined it."
Julie Russell, LRMT

Reiki blends with everything. And I mean EVERYTHING! Reiki is Grace. Love. Joy. Peace. Is there anything in your life that is not compatible with that? Then apply Reiki, and it will become compatible. And in addition to applying Reiki to every aspect of our daily lives, we can apply Reiki in our work lives. No matter what we do. The use of Reiki is only limited by our imagination. So this list is not comprehensive. Its purpose is to give you ideas. To get you to consider how you can apply Reiki to what you do.

SOMETIMES WE GET HUNG up on permission. But Reiki is spiritually guided life force energy that comes from a Source that would never disrespect a person's free will. Because we can never impose Reiki on someone against their will, we can feel free to spread Reiki liberally throughout our work lives. Medical practitioners are surprised that, at times, while treating patients, their Reiki energy activates without their intention, while with other patients, it is still. Our Reiki energy responds to the intention of the patient. From these examples, we realize that it is completely appropriate to spread Reiki liberally within our workplace without intending to impose on people's free will. And then simply relax and enjoy the results.

REIKI CAN NEVER CAUSE HARM. And will never go against anyone's free will. So what have you got to lose? Try it. Here are a few examples of what you can do. Feel free to expand on these! I'd love to hear how you make out.

HERE ARE some things that everyone can do:

- Clear the space where you work
- Use the distance symbol to send Reiki ahead to appointments, meetings, or your day.
- Reiki customer files or bills
- Place Reiki and your symbols around your workplace
- Use Reiki on equipment and electronics
- Send intentions with Reiki and place them in a Reiki grid which you charge regularly
- Send Reiki to clients, patients, or customers
- Offer Reiki to co-workers who are struggling
- Use Reiki to assist with large projects

REIKI AND MEDICINE

Doctors, nurses, and other medical practitioners often report that

Reiki begins flowing spontaneously throughout their day, without their intention. Some worry about this unintentional flow. They don't mind the energy flowing, but they question if they are sending Reiki without permission or against someone's will. When we go to a medical practitioner for healing, we don't tell them, "I want you to use ONLY what you learned in 3rd year, not in 4th year." We expect them to use whatever they have in their toolbox to help patients. Because it is divinely guided, Reiki has the intelligence to know who wants to receive it and who doesn't. That is why it activates in some instances and not in others. So it is OK to use Reiki energy in all that you do. It will not go where it is not wanted. We asked William Rand about permission in class. He said it's not so different from praying for someone. Sometimes they want our prayers. Other times, they don't. Reiki will only go where it is welcomed.

SOME OF THE things you can do with Reiki in the medical field are:

- Clear your office/hospital/clinic/space with Reiki regularly. One of my Reiki students began clearing her medical center regularly. She said that not only did it feel better to everyone in the space, but staffing issues sorted themselves out, and patients and clients were happier and less agitated or frustrated. The entire dynamic of the center shifted.
- Clear your energy at the end of the day so you won't take energy home with you.
- Activate Reiki at the beginning of your day and ask for its guidance throughout the day, so you are in your highest state of consciousness.
- With the distance symbol, send Reiki ahead to your day and to the clients you will see that day. You may not know the clients or whom you will see that day, but the distance symbol acts as a homing device and sends energy where it is directed.

- Ask Reiki to work for the highest good of everyone you interact with.
- Use Reiki with your calendar so that things go smoothly and efficiently.
- Reiki any medications or equipment you use.
- If you are in surgery, ask Reiki to support everyone involved in the surgery.
- Ask Reiki to assist clients, patients, and family members who are overwhelmed or distressed.

Reiki and Business

There is a business aspect to almost everything. And you might think that Reiki and business are not a match, but they are. Imagine if all businesses were aligned with the Reiki Principles and with the love and light that is Reiki. Reiki can assist us in many aspects of business. Here are a few:

- Reiki the files you are working on.
- Use Reiki with any projects you are managing or designing
- Clear your space with Reiki. One store owner had me come in regularly to clear her crystal shop because the cash register receipts were 30% higher than usual every time I did.
- Send Reiki to colleagues and clients.
- Send Reiki to attract the type of client who is aligned with your business.
- Use Reiki to develop new concepts and ideas.

Reiki and Management

Managing people can be challenging. And many managers

wind up in management because they are good at their jobs. But managing people is not necessarily what they love to do. Reiki can help us manage people, however. And sometimes, it can simplify things so that we can once more incorporate the parts of our job that we love back into our daily lives. When you have people in positions where they can do what they are good at, it simplifies management considerably. Reiki can help you identify and align with this. And it can help in other areas too. Here are some ideas to start with:

- Clear your space, employees, and clients regularly.
- If employees struggle with their jobs or with other colleagues, send Reiki and understand that you don't need to "fix" it. It will work out as it is supposed to. Sometimes, Reiki even helps people who are not a good fit with an organization or their culture to smoothly exit into an opportunity that is a better fit for them.
- Reiki your projects and the files of your clients.
- Reiki your reports, projects, correspondence, etc.

Reiki and Holistic Health (Massage, Chiro, Acupuncture, Reflexology, Cranial Sacral, etc.)

Reiki is compatible with just about every other form of healthcare. Massage therapists who activate Reiki as they conduct a massage find that they can achieve better results with less effort. And that they do not suffer the burnout that many of their clients do. I enjoy working with a reflexologist who activates Reiki before she begins her work. I don't have the "hangover" processing the energy as I did before working with a "Reiki Reflexologist." I feel great right away. Here are some things you can do with Reiki:

- Reiki your equipment, acupuncture needles, table, etc.
- Clear your space regularly.
- Clear yourself between clients.

- Send Reiki to your calendar so that it fills, intending to attract clients who are compatible with you and your style.
- Use Reiki as you conduct your healing work, whatever it is.

Reiki and Beauty

Some of the most successful aestheticians, hairdressers, and cosmeticians I know use Reiki alongside all they do. Have you ever had a Reiki facial? A Reiki hair appointment? A Reiki massage or pedicure? You might have been unaware of it if you did. Some people in the beauty industry advertise that they blend Reiki and intuition into what they do. Others don't. After a Reiki facial, people commented that I looked younger and less stressed. I felt that way too! Many people in the beauty industry activate Reiki in what they do with the knowledge that it will only go where it is welcome. But it helps them discern better what their clients want. And it keeps their day stress free. So if you work in this industry, go ahead and try a few of these tips--along with any others that you think of:

- Reiki all products, tools, and equipment before and after using them.
- Clear yourself between appointments.
- Clear your space regularly.
- Send Reiki to your appointment book, asking that it be filled exactly as will be comfortable to you, still allowing you to achieve your goals.
- Send Reiki to draw the right clients and mix of clients for you.
- Send Reiki ahead to your day, asking that the timing of your appointments works out. You will notice that if you are running a few minutes behind, so is your next client.
- Send Reiki to your clients ahead of time, so they are in a lovely space before they even get to you, so they get to you

easily, and so that you will have already developed a gentle camaraderie before they arrive.
- Send Reiki to new clients so that the "get to know you" appointment goes smoothly and you more easily understand each other.
- If you do your own marketing, activate Reiki and ask for its assistance before creating your ads or campaigns.

Reiki, Teaching, and Children

I have several students who work with children either in schools or daycares. They noticed that things go more smoothly when they activate Reiki in their classrooms. So much so that their colleagues and managers comment on how calm the students are, how peaceful it seems to be in their classroom, and how happy the children appear. It is safe to use Reiki in your classroom, as any students who are not aligned with Reiki or whose parents are not aligned with Reiki will not receive it. But those who are will. Here are some ways Reiki can help make your day and your students' day better:

- Clear your classroom and yourself regularly, especially before you go home for the day.
- Use Reiki at the beginning of the year, asking that the students who align with you and each other come together to form the best class possible. Reiki can help you orchestrate a divinely ordered group of individuals who will inspire each other and get along. Then, even if you have a disruptive student, you know they are supposed to be there.
- Send Reiki ahead to your classroom, students, and your day as you travel to work.
- Use Reiki when you are planning and developing your curriculum.
- Place Reiki symbols around the room and ask them to help any child open to Reiki when they need assistance.

- Place intentions in your teaching or working environment. You may wish to make it a positive learning experience. To help the class get along. To assist any children who are struggling to reach their potential. Allow Reiki to help you bring your intentions to fruition.
- Use Reiki if you are planning special events. For parent interviews. When marking or grading tests and assignments.
- Reiki your voice box, asking Reiki to help you with the words and explanations your students need.
- If you need to ask things of management, use Reiki before you ask and send Reiki ahead of the request.
- If you work with budgets within your school, ask Reiki for assistance so that there is always enough to do what you need to do. If there are choices to be made, ask Reiki to assist with the discernment here.

Reiki and Animals

Animals love Reiki and know how to use it and what to do with it. They love to receive Reiki sessions. And many animals enjoy Reiki attunements as well. But there are all kinds of other ways to use Reiki with animals. Here are a few:

- When training animals, clear the space, place symbols around it, activate Reiki, and ask it to help you form clear pictures in your mind of what you want to achieve and that these be easily transmitted to the animal. Ask Reiki to help the animal become comfortable in the environment and willing to work with you.
- Whenever you feel frustrated, breathe and activate Reiki. Allow Reiki energy to flow through and around you and the frustrating situation. Take a time out to release whatever has caused the frustration. And if possible, don't step back into the situation until you have released it fully.

- When working with animals you don't know, allow Reiki to flow between you, making the introduction. Animals are so aware of Reiki that many animals are immediately drawn to my hands and begin sniffing and sometimes licking them.
- Clear the space and bed animals spend time in regularly.
- If you have had difficulty with an animal, sit down with the distance symbol and send Reiki to every difficult situation you have had with the animal in the past. Ask Reiki to show you patterns and ask if there is anything you were meant to learn from the difficulty. Then let them go so you can start fresh with that animal the next time you work with them.
- Use Reiki to check and see if you have a heart wall. Many sensitive people place heart walls around their hearts. But these heart walls significantly distort communication with every animal species (including other humans). If you have a heart wall, use Reiki to release it. It may release all at once. Or it may release by degrees. Reiki will know what is best for you.
- If an animal has difficulty settling into a new environment, ask Reiki to help.
- For rescue animals, in addition to clearing their space and helping to release trauma, Reiki can actively go out and bring the best person forward to adopt the animal.
- Set intentions with Reiki and ask it to communicate the intentions to the animal to determine whether they are in alignment with them.
- Send Reiki to wild animals to help them with rough winters, natural disasters, or the destruction of their environment.
- If you are an animal activist, empower your activism with Reiki. If there is a brace or judgment within your activism that negatively affects you or the results you achieve, ask that it be healed. And then empower your goals with

Reiki, love, and understanding. You will find you reach your goals much more successfully.

Reiki Products and Manufacturing

When you create a unique product, whether on a small or industrial scale, Reiki can work for you. There are so many ways you can use it. Here are a few:

- Reiki your raw materials when they arrive.
- If you have difficulty sourcing materials, ask Reiki to assist you. A source of them will probably come out of the woodwork. Or the timing of their arrival will shift positively.
- Clear your space regularly.
- As you create or manufacture the products, use Reiki. Ask that they are made to the best of your ability, work to their intended purpose, and never cause harm.
- If you have staff, send Reiki to them and the schedule to help it work out smoothly.
- Send Reiki to your potential customers, helping those who need and are aligned with your product to find it.
- Reiki your bills and give gratitude that you always have enough to cover them.
- Reiki invoices with the intention that they are paid promptly.
- If you are in a growth phase of your business, ask Reiki to help you plan and manage the growth.
- If there is discord among staff members, ask Reiki to assist.

Reiki and the Environment

Working with the environment is challenging. It can be difficult not to get angry and frustrated. It's not uncommon to burn out in this field. And losing hope is common as well. But Reiki can help in so many ways. Here are a few.

- Use daily self-Reiki to keep yourself motivated, grounded, and calm.
- Use Reiki with your messages, asking for assistance in getting heard.
- Create a Reiki grid with your goals.
- Send Reiki to your to-do list, asking it to help you accomplish all that is on it.
- If you feel pressured by a sense of urgency, ask Reiki to mitigate it for you and to move everything into divine timing. You will be amazed that things will fall into place beautifully as if orchestrated by a Divine conductor - because it is.
- Send Reiki to people and organizations that are helping to advance progress with the environment.
- If you need donations to conduct your work, use the distance symbol to reach out to those who will donate and send them love and gratitude ahead of time. It will facilitate the donation process and allow donors to feel your appreciation.
- Remember that the solutions to all of the world's problems exist. Ask Reiki to help bring these solutions to the forefront.
- If you feel overwhelmed or under-appreciated, turn it all over to Reiki.

Reiki and Science

As a scientist, I initially thought that Science and Reiki were not on the same wavelength. Boy, was I wrong! There is so much science supporting Reiki–and conversely, Reiki supports so much science (particularly the theories of physics) that they are completely interrelated and entwined. Two websites that support some of the science around Reiki are www.reiki.org and https://centerforreikiresearch.com/. And if you work in the scientific community, here are a few things you may wish to try:

- If you are a researcher, try applying Reiki to one set of data and not to another and measure what happens.
- Presenting our research or data can be challenging. Every audience engages with different language and explanations. Reiki your voice box and ask for help discerning the wording and explanation that will work for each audience.
- If you are writing, Reiki can assist with discernment here too. Activate your sacral chakra and voice box with Reiki, asking for assistance and insight; then begin writing. If you are like me, you will read what you wrote and say, "Wow, I wrote that?" Reiki helps words flow.
- Send Reiki ahead to projects and experiments and use it in their planning.
- Send Reiki to funding opportunities.
- Clear your space regularly and send Reiki to colleagues, managers, supervisors, etc.
- Send Reiki to your organization for its improved or continued health.
- If you are working on a theory or principle and it's on the edge of your brain, ask Reiki to help. It can allow a smooth integration. And it can open us to possibilities we may not have considered.
- Reiki can shift your perspective. If you are working on something that is not flowing, ask Reiki to help with perspective. You may find a completely different way of looking at the problem.
- Send Reiki to attract teachers, colleagues, and research that will help you continue to learn and grow and assist you in pursuing your scientific achievements.

Reiki, Accounting, and Finance

I know, I know–but seriously, these do go together. And quite well too. Some people are drawn to this work. And Reiki is compatible with the financial industry. If you work in these areas, here are a few things you can do:

- Use Reiki to help with any new computing software you need to learn to use.
- Send Reiki to your spreadsheets before you begin to work. You will find that they balance easier and flow better.
- Clear your space and yourself regularly.
- Send Reiki to your clients and customers so that they can present their data to you efficiently and effectively.
- If you need to attract clients, create a Reiki grid and send Reiki ahead to them.
- Write down your goals, add them to your Reiki grid, and regularly charge your grid.
- Activate Reiki on your way to work and send it ahead to your day.
- Use Reiki with challenging situations or clients.

Reiki and Computers/Technology

It may seem odd, but Reiki is completely compatible with computers and technology. You can even "charge" an electronic device somewhat with Reiki if you need to. One of my students decided to try this and managed to keep an iPod with 1% battery going for over an hour to make it through a dead radio zone as she drove. Here are a few ways you can use it:

- Clear your space, equipment, devices, and programs regularly.
- Use Reiki to plan your projects.
- Activate Reiki at the beginning of your day to help your

day go smoother and remind you to take breaks and do regular self-care when you get involved in your work.
- Send Reiki to your colleagues. It tends to facilitate working relationships and bring everyone into the same wavelength.
- If a device or program is acting "buggy" for no real reason, you can reset it with a Reiki attunement.
- Are you making decisions about software? Hardware? Programming? Ask Reiki to help.

Reiki in the Retail and Service Industry

I think it's important for everyone to work in the service industry at some point in their lives to gain an appreciation for the people there. I have a friend who says, "If the garbage collectors ever went on strike, we might all realize how important the people in the service industry are." It's a visual image of what people in the service industry do for all of us. And yet, this can sometimes be the most under-appreciated and even abused sector of society. While this is unfortunate if you are one of the selfless individuals called to the retail or service industry, Reiki can help. Here are a few things you can try:

- Clear your space and yourself regularly.
- Activate Reiki in the space you work in. Ask it to replenish all who enter the area, releasing their worries or cares.
- Activate Reiki and send it ahead to your day.
- Imagine creating "beaded" curtains at the opening or doors of the business with "beads" of the power symbol or any other symbol you choose. These will sweep away any superfluous energies and baggage from your potential customer and allow a clearer, smoother transaction.
- Place your Reiki symbols under a mat at the entrance that

people step over to walk through. It will ground them and cause them to leave anger or baggage at the door.
- When encountering a problematic customer, remember, it is not the pure, beautiful soul of your customer reacting; you are speaking to an injury or trauma within that person. Surround them with Reiki and ask Reiki to ease their burden. And repeat to yourself, "Just for today, I will not anger, I will not worry, I will be devoted to my work, I will be kind to all others, and I will be filled with gratitude."
- If you are involved with staffing, ask Reiki to help you work out schedules. You will be amazed at how much more smoothly it all goes.
- If you have goals for sales, your business, financial success, etc., create a Reiki grid and regularly send Reiki to your goals.
- Be kind to others in the service industry–in your industry and others. And let them know you appreciate their work.

Reiki, Music, and Sound Healing

All sound has the potential to heal. All sound is music. It is said that churches used to be built over energy lines so that the sound healing from the songs in the church would be broadcast over the community. You have probably noticed that certain songs instantly lift your mood or move you into nostalgia. Others are calming. You may not be aware that specific frequencies create a particular brain wavelength while other frequencies moderate the heartbeat or create physiological changes in the body. So Reiki, music, and sound healing go beautifully together. Here are a few things you can do.

- Attune or imbue your instruments with Reiki so that the sound they make is automatically imbued with Reiki.

Check out Colleen Benelli's article "How to Imbue Objects with Reiki."[1]

- If you are playing music for an audience, clear the space with Reiki, place Reiki symbols around the room, and send Reiki ahead to the event or gig with the distance symbol.
- Use the distance symbol and send Reiki ahead to the audience. Ask Reiki to attract the people whom your music will touch.
- Music is an expression of the soul. If you feel vulnerable or are intimidated to use your voice, present a new composition, or present to a particular audience, ask Reiki to assist you and release the blocks and barriers that are in the way.
- Clear yourself regularly with Reiki.
- If you are working on a project or composition, activate Reiki and ask it to work with your creativity. You may be amazed at what flows.
- If you find yourself creatively blocked, use Reiki to clear the block.
- If you are in charge of marketing or advertising campaigns, activate Reiki before you do. And ask Reiki to assist you in creating the campaign and attracting exactly the right audience to do so.
- If you struggle to make a living at what you love to do, ask Reiki to help you release any blocks to financial abundance and assist you to be comfortable as you pursue your passion.
- Many artists subscribe to the "starving artist" theory. If this is you, ask Reiki to shift you into a different perspective so you can thrive.

Reiki, Religion, and Spirituality
Reiki is compatible with every religion and spiritual practice.

There are people within some religions or spiritual belief systems who believe it is not compatible, but that is only because they do not understand the nature of Reiki. Reiki is spiritually guided life force energy. It is impossible to make a case for excluding it from anything. For the followers of any religion, it deepens the experience. And when used alongside any spiritual practice, it facilitates the practice. There are many ways you can use Reiki alongside Religion and Spirituality. Here are a few:

- Activate Reiki energy before reading religious or spiritual texts. It will deepen your experience and give you a more rounded understanding of the meaning.
- Activate Reiki before you pray or meditate. You will know your heart and mind more intimately. And the prayers and meditations will be more meaningful.
- Before conducting rituals or spiritual practices, activate and include Reiki, and they will touch you more deeply.
- If you are speaking to an audience, activate your voice box and ask for the discernment and language that is most appropriate for that audience to flow from you.
- Activate Reiki before services, sessions, conferences, or meetings. They will have a better feel and flow.
- If you are working on any projects or plans, activate Reiki and ask that your ego and personal energy step aside and remain aligned with the purpose and principles of the work you are doing.
- Activate Reiki before conducting any act of service and ask that it work in the best interest of everyone involved.
- Ask Reiki to help you be the best you can be within the religion or practice you are in.
- Invite Reiki to assist you with opportunities for continual growth and learning.
- If you struggle to understand or accept a perspective outside of your own, ask Reiki for assistance. Everyone

wins when we stop bracing against each other and move into a place of understanding and acceptance.

ProTip
Julie Russell, LRMT California, USA
Orange County Whole Family Wellness[2]
When I train therapists at my hospital job, I tell them, "You're not going to create anything unless you can imagine it." So imagine what you want to create and then add Reiki to it. It's like supercharging it. It's another excellent way to use the Reiki tools you've been given. I call them the keys to the universe because we can supercharge anything with love, light, and compassion.

When developing a business of any sort, there can be thousands of options. When you start envisioning it, that's the construct of creation. And it's bringing form to the formless, which William Rand said when Holy Fire Reiki came in.

I'm going to buy this book myself. I had had a book like that, especially in the beginning. Reiki was a big jump for me because I didn't even know what metaphysics was. I was a very linear, left-brained, scientific, research-oriented person, jumping off a bridge of really? There are other ways to be? To create? To work? It changes your operating system. If you think of yourself like a computer, it changes your operating system so that you see things from different perspectives. You have a wider lens.

I credit Reiki with all I have accomplished because when Reiki guided me to do different things like, take a class but I don't have the money, I ask Reiki to help. If you do that, you will have the money. I always say if this is supposed to be, then show me the way.

I've been a Registered Nurse for over 40 years, and my specialty is mental health. I am a corporate director for nine outpatient mental health programs in four hospitals. I do a lot of different things in my job like performance improvement, forms and policies, procedures, and education manuals. I do research if we want to bring in new processes. I write the education pieces and conduct some of the education myself. If we have litigation cases, I determine our options. If we don't get paid, I contact insurance companies and take them to court if necessary. For the last 18 years, we have gotten paid on almost every client, which is pretty unheard of. It's never dull. And I like that. But how do you weave Reiki into all of those things?

I start my morning by Sending Reiki to all our programs and then clear the spaces so the staff has a better place to work because we have anywhere from 30 to 50 clients with severe mental illness come through every day. Patients are severely depressed, psychotic, suicidal, aggressive, et cetera. There's a lot of energy dropped off. So once I clear those spaces, I fill them with Reiki so it's available for those who want it.

IF I CHAIR A MEETING, if I'm doing a project, I use Reiki for every single thing. I Reiki myself before the meeting and clear the space. I set intentions for the meeting. I activate my Reiki grid. I use Reiki to ensure that people feel heard and accepted. I ask it to help me to be the best leader possible. I may not sits and do 20 minutes of self Reiki in one sitting each day. I may get Reiki as I sit at a stoplight for two minutes or waiting for a meeting for three minutes. Instead of scrolling on my phone, I do Reiki. Reiki never leaves me. I talk to Reiki like it's my best friend all day long. At first, Reiki is something unfamiliar, and you need to get to know it. But it will become your best friend.

I'm constantly opening up my higher states of awareness so I can be innovative, creative, and compassionate. And hopefully, I hold space for my colleagues to be inspired to create in their programs.

But even when I'm creating projects or paperwork, Reiki guides me to make the forms or the projects.

I also think it works very effectively for communication in the workplace. I work with different departments, and sometimes people don't get along. But I have Reiki as a tool, so I will often work on the situation energetically to try to have the situation de-escalate so that people can come to a place of understanding. Everyone feels like a winner when you're done.

I have become more like a consultant. I have work I have to get done, but when I do it and how I do it is totally up to me. There are several days when I have a lot of flexibility. So I see Reiki clients three afternoons a week from about three o'clock and until seven or eight pm. As you give a session, you get a session, so it's my healing time just as much as it is for anyone who comes to see me.

My sessions are anywhere from 90 minutes to two hours long. They are a combination of the variety of modalities that I practice. I never really know what the mix will be until the person gets there. I generally do a Holy Fire® healing experience; then, hands-on Reiki. Then I may combine that with sound healing, crystal healing, guided imagery, hypnosis, and/or my bio-mat. I also have a phototherapy machine which pulsates color and light into the chakras and do intuitive life coaching and angel therapy. Reiki guides me the whole time.

Reiki weaves into everything that I do, making it easier and more effortless. I trust that if something's supposed to be, it will be. And if it isn't, then it won't be.

I occasionally overbook myself, and Reiki says, "You need to slow down." So I look at my calendar to see what can be stretched out because I love everything I do. Reiki has seen to it that 99% of everything I do, I love to do. The only thing I don't love doing is taxes, so my husband does them for me.

Sometimes, you forget that not everybody is like that, and you can be pretty annoying. But most of the time, I see everything as an opportunity. And I love that I can discern when something upsets me that there is some step I need to take or if it's time to let it go.

We live in duality and people are here to have experiences. That's why souls come here. Don't get in their way. Through these experiences, there's incredible soul growth. And I don't think the soul growth ends when we do Reiki; it just becomes effortless and joyful.

When I read the Reiki ideals of do not worry, do not anger. It's not that I never worry or get angry, but it doesn't stick anymore. I might have a bad hour, a bad five minutes, and even a bad couple of days, but it won't stick.

I've had students from all kinds of professions who use Reiki in what they do. I have students who own a restaurant. We discussed what it would be like if you attuned all your interested employees so they can activate Reiki while they're making the food in your restaurant? There's a name for it. It's called intentional kitchens where the food is blessed as it is prepared.

I tell my students who like to cook, you can bless your food with Reiki. The Institute of Noetic science has scientific research showing that when food is made with an open heart and with love, people always pick the food blessed with love over the same food that has not been blessed.

Reiki yourself while getting ready in the morning and notice if people say, "Wow, you look great today."

I encourage school teachers to clear themselves during their day to bring the best version of themselves to their classroom and to clear their classroom using Reiki. I like to put Reiki on the floor and the ceiling with the understanding that whatever children or people in the classroom would like to receive Reiki, it's there and available to them.

I have a lot of nurses that come to my classes, and we talk about doing self Reiki, clearing themselves between clients, and clearing the space because all of that fear goes somewhere; it's often stuck in the space.

I saw in your book that there was one person who said they didn't use the word Reiki; they used another word. And that's also what I teach my students: you don't always have to use the word Reiki. Sometimes I say, you want me just to hold your hand and give you some good vibes. And if the person says yes, I give them the best vibes I have–Reiki. And if it's not for the highest good or they don't want it, it won't work.

I've had some judges, lawyers, and physicians who use Reiki in their work. That's why in my classes, I always ask people, I'd like to know what your profession is so that we can talk about how you can weave this into your professional life because Reiki is so much more than just giving it to yourself Reiki or putting someone on a table or chair for treatment. If you're a mom, it helps with parenting skills. You can give Reiki to your children. You can clear the space. You can clear yourself when you're having a bad day. You can send Reiki to your kids when they're starting to get too wild and crazy.

The ways you can use Reiki are unlimited. You can't use it only if someone doesn't want it, or it's not the right time, the right place, or you're not the right person. But you can weave this energy into every action you take.

And if you become a Reiki practitioner, even if you never do one bit of Reiki on anyone, you've changed your energetic blueprint. You are emanating a light that most do not emanate unless we're attuned to Reiki. And so, just your being in a space brings light which overcomes darkness every time. No exception.

If you're a Reiki master-teacher, remember that not everyone wants to be a practitioner. I have several doulas that do a wellness series for pregnant women or going through IVF. They teach an abbreviated Reiki one and two class, where they instruct their clients how to do self Reiki and Reiki for their infants with the understanding that if they want to learn more, they come back and take a Reiki practitioner course. I've also taught shortened "Reiki for children" and "Reiki for families" classes. Sometimes I have a whole family that comes to learn Reiki.

Sometimes I get people who have service animals who think their animal might want to become a Reiki practitioner. So I have them send me a picture of their animal. Connect to the animal, and I ask it, would this be for their highest good, and do they want this? And then if I get a yes, I do a Reiki one attunement with that animal, and I give them a little certificate that says I've been attuned to Reiki, and it has little animal paw prints around it with their name and the date that they've been attuned to Reiki.

I've given Reiki attunements to people whose family members are dying, and they were able to provide support to themselves, the dying person, and the family as a whole. There are so many different ways, depending on your gifts and talents of how you might want to spread the use of Reiki. It's only limited by our imagination.

My biggest obstacle, in the beginning, was impatience. I'm very action-oriented, and sometimes it doesn't go as fast as I'd like. Starting out, I was like, okay, where are my students? Where are my clients? And in the beginning, I thought, "This is going too slow," but looking back, it was all in divine time, not my time. So enjoy the journey. Those were beautiful memories of growing and learning and stretching myself to do things I usually wouldn't do.

Sometimes, I have a week or a month where there are no phone calls or emails. I've learned Reiki has turned off the spigot because you need to slow down for a little while. And when it's time, the faucet will get turned back on. Just keep coming from an inspired place. When I look back, I realize I needed that slow month because I was doing too much. I'm still trying to work on balance.

If you want to blend Reiki with other modalities, follow your inspiration, turn on Reiki and ask Reiki to guide you. And if it feels good, if you feel excited, that's Reiki telling you to go ahead and try it. Stretch yourself. Reiki has helped me bring back that inner child. The more I develop my business with playfulness, the more I enjoy my business and the better the results.

My path comes from inspiration. I took classes from different lineages of Reiki. I think it was great and would be all excited then I'd come home, and never used it. Reiki would say, oh, that's just for you to have so that you can see the contrast. Now you can see different things about different types of Reiki, energy, and how they're different, but that's not going to be your flavor.

You're this flavor right now. And could your flavor change? Yep. The more you let go and allow the energy to guide you, things will come in that you will say, if somebody told me I was going to do this, I would have never imagined it.

So that's my advice; make it playful and fun.

When I took my first Reiki class, I got permanently polarized sunglasses. So get attuned to Reiki and put on your polarized sunglasses because that's what Reiki did for me. Everything had more color, more substance, more texture, and more vitality. Then let Reiki be your guide to have a broader perception, a larger lens for life.

Check out our podcast on this chapter.[3]

AUTHOR'S NOTE: Thank you for being the beautiful light that you are, for coming with me on this journey, and for having the courage and willingness to spread the light of Reiki.

May you be blessed with peace, joy, happiness, and success as you venture out into the world with Reiki. You've got this.

I'm so proud of you.
And I know Reiki is too!
Thank you.

---

1. https://reikilifestyle.com/imbue-your-sacred-objects-with-reiki/
2. https://www.ocwholefamilywellness.com/
3. https://www.buzzsprout.com/1364386/10490651

ACKNOWLEDGMENTS

I want to thank my editor, Karen Caig, for her tireless work and for being an all-around amazing person. I'm lucky to know you.

And the ICRT and my Reiki mentors and teachers: Ellen, Pam, William, Carolyn, and Colleen. You are all inspirations. Reiki changed my life. I have you to thank for that. Thank you.

Thank you to my ICRT colleagues. When I asked for assistance presenting the book to the world, you were right there! I am so blessed to be part of such a warm and supportive community.

I also need to thank my husband for his support and for telling me to go to England, instead of putting that chunk of money toward our debt! And my children for all of the years they had to be quiet after school when mommy was still teaching Reiki. I couldn't imagine a more supportive, loving family. Thank you.

Thank you to my horses for pushing me in the direction of Reiki all those years ago when I was but a skeptic. I love and appreciate you and the beauty and grace you have brought to my life.

I want to thank the teachers who have come before us, bringing us these ways since ancient times. Usui Sensei, Dr. Hayashi, Mrs. Takata, and all of the wonderful teachers from every lineage who are diligently spreading the light and love of Reiki in the world today. Thank you.

And finally, thank you, the reader and the listener of our podcast. Thank you for being you with your big beautiful heart. Thank you for having the courage to say "yes" when you were "nudged" to spread Reiki to others. May you be blessed with joy, purpose, wonder, and prosperity along the way. May your path be clear and unencumbered. I am excited on behalf of the people who will be touched by Reiki because of you.

We are blessed to be of a lineage of light-bringers creating wellness on the Earth today.
   Thank you.
   Namaste.

ABOUT THE AUTHOR

Pam Allen-LeBlanc is a scientist, a businesswoman, and an internationally renowned speaker. Pam is a Licensed Reiki Master Teacher (LRMT) with the International Center for Reiki Training (ICRT), the co-author of the ICRT Animal Reiki course, and the author of several popular articles in the Reiki News Magazine.

Pam teaches Reiki, Animal Reiki, and Animal Communication online and around the world. She has a weekly newsletter[1] and podcast [2](Reiki from the Farm™), hosts a monthly online Reiki share,[3] and boasts a dedicated community of Reiki Masters, practitioners, and Animal Reiki students.

In 2020, in Heathrow airport, Pam received strong Reiki guidance to "teach the teachers" so Reiki Masters and Practitioners could discover the unique Reiki career that lights them up and allows them to share Reiki in the world.

This led to the creation of "The Reiki Master Mentor" course, which was so popular and successful that it needed to become a book in an attempt to share it with more people.

Connect with Pam at pam@reikifromthefarm.com or through www.reikifromthefarm.com

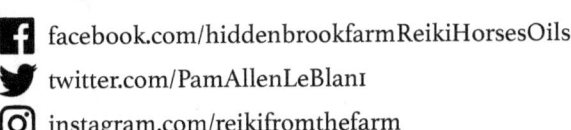

facebook.com/hiddenbrookfarmReikiHorsesOils
twitter.com/PamAllenLeBlanI
instagram.com/reikifromthefarm

1. http://eepurl.com/dFm-19
2. https://reikifromthefarm.buzzsprout.com/
3. http://eepurl.com/hWruP5

www.ingramcontent.com/pod-product-compliance
Lightning Source LLC
Chambersburg PA
CBHW072045110526
44590CB00018B/3046